Cultural Treasures
of the Internet

Michael Clark

For book and bookstore information

http://www.prenhall.com

Prentice Hall P T R
Upper Saddle River, New Jersey 07458

Library of Congress Cataloging-in-Publication Data

Clark, Michael
    Cultural treasures of the Internet / Michael Clark : with an
    introduction by Bill Washburn.
       p. cm,
    Includes bibliographical references and index.
    ISBN 0-13-209669-2
    1. Computer network resources. 2. Internet (Computer network)-\
    -Directories. 3. Humanities--Databases. 4. Humanities--Research-
    Data processing. I. Title
  QA76.55.C58 1995   95-3379
  025.04--dc20   CIP

Editorial/production supervision
  and formatting: *Harriet Tellem*
Interior design: *Gail Cocker-Bogusz*
Technical advisor: *Ann Sullivan*
Cover design: *Jeannette Jacobs Design*
Cover photo and part opening photo: *Vittore Carpaccio: St. Augustine in His Study. (Assumed to be a portrait of Cardinal Bessarion.) S. Giorgio degli Schiavoni, Venice, Italy. Art Resource, New York.*
Manufacturing manager: *Alexis R. Heydt*
Acquisitions editor: *Mark L. Taub*
Editorial assistant: *Dori Steinhauff*

©1995 by Prentice Hall P T R
Prentice-Hall, Inc.
A Simon & Schuster Company
Upper Saddle River, New Jersey 07458

The publisher offers discounts on this book when ordered in bulk quantities. For more information, contact:

Corporate Sales Department
Prentice Hall P T R
One Lake Street
Upper Saddle River, NJ 07458

Phone: 800-382-34119, FAX: 201-236-7141, E-mail: corpsales@prenhall.com

Printed in the United States of America

10 9 8 7 6 5 4 3 2 1

ISBN 0-13-209669-2

Prentice-Hall International (UK) Limited, *London*
Prentice-Hall of Australia Pty. Limited, *Sydney*
Prentice-Hall Canada Inc., *Toronto*
Prentice-Hall Hispanoamericana, S.A., *Mexico*
Prentice-Hall of India Private Limited, *New Delhi*
Prentice-Hall of Japan, Inc., *Tokyo*
Simon & Schuster Asia Pte. Ltd., *Singapore*
Editora Prentice-Hall do Brasil, Ltda., *Rio de Janeiro*

*For
Andrew
and
Emily*

Contents

Part 4 *Appendices* *269*

Introduction

The Internet and the Humanistic Tradition

How familiar are you with the Internet? What do your colleagues appreciate most about the Internet? Are you already utterly excited about the unexpected utility and friendliness of the World Wide Web? Are you already endowed with a clear sense of the power, depth, and ease of use of this fiber matrix? Do you have friends and colleagues who work among the seemingly chosen few who routinely make use of the vast electronic resources on the global net every day of the week? Perhaps you would like to survey and search rarefied databases in Europe? You are standing on the brink of some unprecedented opportunities and surprises.

Maybe you already communicate hourly with colleagues working in other time zones or countries. If you'd like to study, explore, or revisit special libraries in distant locations and you don't use the Internet yet, you have some wonderful surprises in store for you. I know the Internet may still appear to be unfriendly for some, but it also offers a rich and rapidly expanding storehouse of sources and information resources that can provide great advantages to you now. If you love conversation, you can hardly avoid the telephone, and if you love words and language, philosophy, religion, debate, diversity, or detective work, you can't ignore the Internet any longer.

Just as we have already learned that computers are not simply calculators on steroids or typewriters with an attitude, it is also important to know that the Internet is not just for teams of computer scientists and engineers. The World Wide Web/Internet is especially, and most of all, a boon to authors, humanists, historians, biographers, and social scientists. Writers and researchers, for example, who work entirely alone, can enjoy all of the benefits of instantaneous access to colleagues, friends, families, editors, and an immense selection of public resources without ever leaving their desks, however isolated. Of course, a few things are essential before you can make use of the Internet: a computer, a modem, a (dedicated) telephone line, an account with an Internet service provider, a good introductory book or two, and Professor Clark's *Cultural Treasures of the Internet*. There is no better guide to the rich treasures of the Internet available today.

The Internet and the Information Revolution

The "Information Revolution" is the oldest, most profound, and probably the least appreciated of human developments. The advancement of communication, knowledge, and wisdom is really about the unprecedented development of language. Long before agriculture and the earliest civilizations appeared, we invented the most important human tool—lingual communication. Our primordial ancestors started with perhaps the biggest single step we have ever taken: abstract speech, signals, and signs. Petroglyphs, cave drawings from the Stone Age, appear to be the earliest extant efforts to record human communication. (If you would like to take a peek at one, see the entry for the WWW site Cave Arce in the Art History section of the directory in this book.) Today the most fashionable of new concepts, the idea of cyberspace, has really existed since the first petroglyphs. Seeing a petroglyph stimulates us to imagine something of which we have no direct or personal experience. This is the same sort of thing as electronic or digital cyberspace. Homer's stories, religious scriptures, Shakespeare's plays, novels, radio—like the earliest cave pictures—all came into existence because of our ability to create and to participate in what Susanne Langer, the prominent writer on aesthetics, many years ago termed "virtual space." But cyberspace is not merely another example of this phenomenon; it is the most profound manifestation of it.

Writing—recorded speech—demarcates prehistoric from historic cultures and societies. Writing "technology" is so basic in our modern world it is no longer even seen as technology. Before the Gutenberg press, however, literacy was rather different, being quite limited. Historically, the elite of any given culture have sought to control literacy and thus access to written texts. This would seem to be so because information, learning, knowledge, and expertise constitute a distinctly unique and important source of power. It was the first humanists of the Middle Ages who tapped the enlightening powers of literacy and thus began the ineluctable process to make all information and knowledge accessible, in principle, to every human being. It was the humanists of the last few centuries who recognized the importance of collecting, preserving, and disseminating knowledge. Like the unobtrusive children of Prometheus, they took information out of the control of the elite and set humanity on the path toward moral enlightenment, social debate, and concrete individual political rights.

The ability and proclivity of human beings to preserve and utilize prior knowledge and expertise is the foundation on which the contemporary world stands. It was the dedicated, far-flung community of humanists throughout the Western World emerging out of the high Middle Ages and the Renaissance that honed, refined, and disseminated this core expertise into mainstream, everyday society. Indeed, one of the least recognized but more profound promises of today's blossoming global web of inexpensive telecommunications is that we can teach and utilize the critical tools of the humanists everywhere on the planet, not just in urban centers and the elite institutions of higher learning.

In an important sense, the profound ease of storing and communicating essential information is the core value of the Internet to scientists and humanists alike. The freedom to share and disseminate, to preserve and reproduce knowledge very inexpensively, and on a global scale to boot, transforms teaching, learning, research, and cultural transmission. The global matrix of computer-to-computer telecommunications is ubiquitous, inexpensive, and accessible so that writers, historians, philosophers, and linguists will soon choose the Internet as their preferred mode of communication. And above all, the humanists will create the greatest value and the most challenging ideas for the Internet. Now is the time to invite greater participation in the deepening and broadening of our knowledge of human beings and their ideas and creativity.

Tomorrow we will likely see the cost of computers and communications—all forms of telecommunications—decrease by an order of magnitude. The literacy rate on our planet will jump to unimaginable levels in country after country as the efficiencies of the Internet become irresistible. Education and cultural transmission of knowledge are the sources of great wealth and social benefit to individuals. There is much fear that computer and networking technology will contribute to the development of further impoverishment of people through the division of the information "haves" and "have-nots." This need not be the case. In fact, basic Internet services are now available that cost considerably less than what most people pay for monthly cable TV connections, while the hardware needed is no more expensive than a high-quality television itself. (And of course, in the years to come, the cost of hardware is expected to keep falling.) Moreover, the future will, no doubt, bring greater opportunities of public access (such as in public libraries and perhaps even in government service areas such as post offices). But there is no need to wait. The knowledge, the learning, and the ideas of the writers and historians of this planet are available to you now —the natural culmination of the original Gutenberg revolution, which first unleashed the power of the book. This is the great human promise of the Internet. Experience its cultural treasures, and see for yourself.

Bill H. Washburn

How Do People Use the Internet?

When I was completing this manuscript for publication, it occurred to me to ask again the question that I had posed implicitly in beginning the undertaking: How do humanists use the Internet? Since computers have long been characterized as antagonistic to humanistic endeavor, arriving at a clear and unequivocal answer might have seemed a daunting task. But since I had used the Internet for some time and since I knew of other people of a similar background who did too and since I also knew that there were many cultural resources available on the net, I was sure that the answers would be not only helpful to others but also essential to their personal and professional lives.

I knew from personal experience, for example, that 538 people from all walks of life, from various professions, meet daily in Cyberspace to discuss something very close to their hearts, classical music: styles, influences, comparative evaluations, anecdotes, and broccoli (well, lists must be kept "on-topic," so the subject became something like how to prepare broccoli to best complement a meal served to the accompaniment of Beethoven's early string quartets!). I had also used File Transfer Protocol (FTP) to acquire files of texts, sound, and pictures. And I had traced down quotations from Shakespeare and from the Bible. In anticipation of traveling, I had also once checked to see what the weather would be like in San Francisco the following day. Most striking of all, though, is that in writing and rewriting the various chapters, I daily sent drafts by e-mail to colleagues, friends, and editors (some of whom lived in other countries), who were able to give me valuable feedback (often in a shorter time span than I could have sent the chapters by way of first class mail!).

I could have looked about and identified many other uses of the Internet, many of which are obvious from even a superficial contact with the "information superhighway." Instead, I thought I would inquire directly of users, ask them of their experiences. In the old days–say 4 or 5 years ago—I would have typed up a questionnaire, developed a mailing list, and addressed envelopes (making sure to include a s.a.s.e.). After a few weeks, the responses would have finished dribbling in. But in 1994 I could do something very different: I sent an e-mail query to a number of lists that I subscribed to, soliciting comments on how people used the Internet and why it was important to them. The results were staggering. Within a few hours, my computer mailbox was jammed with replies, and many more arrived and continued to arrive over the next few days. The responses are instructive.

But before I begin, a *caveat* is in order: the Internet is no nirvana, no Garden of Eden, no golden underground, no isle melodious. Like any other aspect of life, traffic on the Internet can be mundane, boring, uncivil, offensive, trite, and truly inessential. The Internet, in short, is just like life itself, and that means, of course, that the judicious person can not only avoid its pitfalls, but also benefit greatly from its virtues. How?

Here are some examples contributed by people who responded to my query:

➤ Paul Brassey (brassey@fas.harvard.edu), a graduate student at the Harvard Divinity School, uses a gopher connection to check the job openings as advertised on line by the *Chronicle of Higher Education*. He is able to do this from his desk at home, saving a trip to the library.

➤ James McShane (jamesmc@queens.lib.ny.us), who works at the Queens Borough Public Library, compiles in-depth bibliographies. He uses telnet to connect to libraries (such as the Library of Congress) to discover new sources and to check bibliographic citations. Not only does the Internet give him access to all the information that he needs, but it also saves him money and travel time. His previous bibliography took 5 years to complete, whereas, by using the Internet, he finished his most recent project in under 5months.

➤ Beverly Smith (bsmith@sun.cis.smu.edu), a graduate student at Southern Methodist University, was doing dissertation research in Kenyan medical anthropology. She discovered that photocopies of the documents she needed were at Syracuse University in the United States. At home in Texas, she telneted to First Search and found several libraries near her that had copies of the guide to the Syracuse collection. Knowing that, she was able to do valuable preliminary work at home before she traveled to New York for the actual research.

> ➤ Fred Flaxman (teleflax@aol.com), an award-winning columnist, radio and television producer, writes a monthly article about compact discs for a public radio magazine which is circulated in rural southern Oregon and northern California. He used a classical music list to track down a rare copy of Faure's Barcarolle no. 1 in A Minor, performed by Faure himself in 1913. When Flaxman placed a query on the list, he had a response within 24 hours from someone willing to send him a tape recording of the record. Flaxman also uses the Internet list to extend the readership for his CD columns throughout the country and abroad.

> ➤ Betty Guthrie (eguthrie@benfranklin.hnet.uci.edu), who is a language program coordinator, created a mailing list for foreign language supervisors and coordinators and discovered that it has been of inestimable value in communicating with her peers. The process, she says, not only allowed her to make extensive contacts in her field, but it also gave renewed vigor to her professional life.

> ➤ Similarly, Kathleen Therrien (kmt@strauss.udel.edu), a graduate student in English at the University of Delaware, writes of the increased opportunities for academic discourse offered by the Internet.

> ➤ Lorena Russell, a graduate student in English at the University of North Carolina-Chapel Hill, writes that her participation in lists **qstudy** and **wmst-l** have given her an opportunity to engage in dialogues not readily available to her otherwise.

> ➤ Lois Feuer (lfeuer@dhvx20.csudh.edu), a professor of English at California State University, Dominguez Hills, writes that e-mail has permitted her to communicate effectively with her colleagues even though they are separated by great distances. Not only does much of the work get done more efficiently than it had in the past, she notes, but electronic mail also increases the sense of immediacy and the closeness of the collaboration.

> ➤ Steve Palmquist (stevepq@ctsc.hkbc.hk), the founder of Philopsychy Press, used the Internet to market several publications, including his edition of four of Immanuel Kant's neglected essays. The results, he reports, were much better than his previous method of using bulk mail advertising.

> ➤ Laura Fillmore (laura@editorial.com), president of the Online BookStore (OBS), not only advertises her company's books on the Net, but she actually publishes them there. The most recent title was a hypertext project, published on the Mosaic platform.

> ➤ Paul Brians (brians@wsuvm1.csc.wsu.edu), a professor of English at Wash-

ington State University, also found lists to be an invaluable resource. In searching for the copyright holder of a translation of a Japanese book of mythology, which was published in Tokyo in 1926, he sent a query to a Japanese language list; the response led him to the person who could resolve the problem.

➤ Gail Guntermann (atgcg@asuvm.inre.asu.edu) found that e-mail was a boon to her professional activities. While editing a book, she used e-mail to communicate with the authors, and she found that the revision process, as well as the meeting of deadlines, was facilitated immensely by e-mail. For those authors who had to rely only on the telephone, Guntermann felt that they—and she—were at a distinct disadvantage in the project; revisions came harder and deadlines were more difficult to meet.

➤ Don Mabry (djm1@ra.msstate.edu), the associate dean of the College of Arts and Sciences at Mississippi State University, teaches a Mexican history course via e-mail and manages The Historical Text Archive (see the Resources — HISTORY). He also tells of how the common interest of a history list led to both his and his wife's establishing not only professional acquaintances but also lasting personal friendships in England.

➤ Laura Kimoto (kimotol@uhunix.uhcc.hawaii.edu) maintains that far from being an alienating factor in her life, her computer puts her "in touch with the world" by way of her Internet connection. Like many people, she feels that the Internet increases her ability to communicate effectively with others. The increased ability to communicate is not only professional, but also personal.

➤ Steve Schwartz (sschwa@nomvs.lsumc.edu), who works as a computer analyst, writes that through the use of such software as X.500, Netfind, Gopher phone books, and finger, he has managed to reestablish friendships with people who would have otherwise disappeared from his life.

➤ Arthur Chandler (arthurc@mercury.sfsu.edu), who is a professor of humanities at San Francisco State University, reported that he used a list for his class in a course entitled "Cyberspace/Humanities." His major objective was to get the students (especially those who are quiet in class) to participate in the exchange of ideas. In fact, the goal was achieved, but the major result of the class list was something unforeseen: the formation of a genuine civic ideal. As Chandler notes, "The people (no longer 'students') who revealed themselves to each other, and who moved from class discussion to personal revelation and then to perspectives on the human condition and its transformation on the net—such people must TRUST those to whom they make such intimations. The class turned into a community."

As this last example suggests, in addition to the many practical uses that people had discovered for the Internet, another thread ran through the responses. It was persistent, sometimes explicitly stated, sometimes running only as a murmur under the anecdotes that people sent. It had to do with a sense of community that the Internet fostered. I do not mean a community only in the sense of a group of engineers discussing the latest developments in TCP/IP protocol (which is also one community that exists), but rather a community in the sense of people with shared values communicating ideas in a public forum, the kind of experience that is a throwback to the town meeting or perhaps even the nonritualized sense of religious communion. Indeed, several respondents invoked religious language to describe the experience of being on the Net. Ann Travers described herself as feeling like an "Internet evangelist." And Ron Smallwood wrote, "E-mail lists are a gift from God. (And I am very religious, so I don't say that lightly.)" I do not mistake what these people are saying. They do not mean that computers have become our god. They do not mean that technology is the new Baal. Instead, these are people who feel comfortable in using the new technology—who for all practical purposes do not necessarily see the technology and who are not concerned about it but who are nevertheless benefiting from it in a profound way. In short, the Internet allows people to fulfill the most basic and important of human needs: allowing people with shared ideals and values to communicate. If indeed, as David Riesman said, modern culture has made us a "lonely crowd," the Internet seems to many to be a source of alleviation of our anomie.

Over and over, the single most prominent reaction—whether explicitly or implicitly stated—to my informal poll was that the Internet increased the sense of community that people felt.

This Book

This book is intended to provide an overview of Internet resources that are most useful to humanists. I interpret the term humanist here broadly, to include anyone interested in humanistic endeavor: teachers, librarians, students, artists, writers, music aficionados, and book lovers, among others.

Part I of the book deals with practical information. How does one discover basic Internet resources? What are gopher, World-Wide Web, and FTP? Though an understanding of FTP (to use one example) may seem daunting to the Internet novice, it and other such tools play an essential role in the full utilization of the Net. But not everyone will need or want to utilize all Internet applications. Most Internet users start with basics, such as e-mail, and with experience, add higher-level skills as needed.

In this section of the book, I give examples and provide summaries of the essential commands for using the particular process or application. I also include a brief overview of the subject matter to allow for a general understanding of the task so that the user may transfer the skills learned in the example to other similar tasks. This section, however, does not attempt to treat exhaustively all of the technical aspects of accessing the Internet. Such an effort here would only duplicate the work of the many excellent guides that have already been published.

Part II of this book consists of two very important chapters. The section entitled "Resources" contains an alphabetical catalogue of information available on the Internet. This section is as exhaustive and as up-to-date as possible in the quickly changing world of the net. It provides a unique and essential "map" to the humanist's territory. This long catalogue of resources, along with the appendix of lists (electronic discussion groups) relevant to humanists, should allow you to find useful and interesting resources quickly and to take advantage of these valuable tools with a minimum of effort.

The fact that the Internet is exploding at a phenomenal rate makes it difficult for any individual to stay abreast of the developments. Moreover, it is commonplace to say that no book can truly capture the protean nature of the Internet. Immediately upon publication, a hard copy book will be outdated before it can be shelved in a bookstore or library. However, the second chapter of Part II— "Keeping Current"—addresses this very concern. This chapter contains meta-resources—from "**alt.services.internet**" to "Yanoff's Internet Services List"—lists, newsletters, Usenet groups, and other resources that are devoted to late-breaking information and special resources. These will allow you to maintain a constant awareness of new information, and not just information about humanities areas. In short, for keeping current, this book is the last resource book that you will have to buy. Of course, any one person probably will not utilize every one of these sources. But some investigation will show which sources deliver the information that you want to find out about on a daily basis. *In toto*, the sources listed in this section will give you the ability to create a "virtual source book" of the Internet—one that is updated daily and that is never out of date.

The prominent twentieth century philosopher Pierre Teilhard de Chardin once predicted that modern culture was evolving into a new condition. He called this the "noosphere." In *The Future of Man*, Teilhard asks, "Why should we not simply define Life as the specific property of Matter, the Stuff of the Universe, carried by evolution into the zone of highest complexity?" (New York: Harper & Row, 1964, p. 91). For him, science and technology are not antagonistic to our spiritual lives. Rather, they allow for its fulfillment. The machine, he says, plays a "constructive part in the creation of a truly collective consciousness" (p. 173). Rather than being an enemy, technology aids humans not only by relieving us of the grueling physical and mental labor, but also by allowing for a tremendous increase in our consciousness: by the "miraculous enhancing of our sense, through its powers of enlargement, penetration and exact measurement, it constantly increases the scope and clarity of our perceptions. It fulfills the dream of all living creatures by satisfying our instinctive craving for the *maximum of consciousness* with a minimum of effort!" (pp. 238–39).

I feel certain that Teilhard would see the Internet as human consciousness raised to a higher level. Whether the activity is searching for an old friend through a "whois" program, following a hypertext link on the Web, collaborating closely through e-mail with colleagues, retrieving a treasured piece of literature from an FTP site, gophering through cyberspace to find a job, or following the latest scholarly commentary on a new development in Shakespearean studies, the net is a vast neuronic network that is rapidly evolving, and by intensifying our perceptions, it is maximizing our consciousness itself. I hope you will find this book to be a useful gateway to this higher level of consciousness.

Acknowledgments

In one way or another, writing a book is always a collaborative project. This book was not the exception. Many people helped me—answering queries or providing unsolicited suggestions. If I tried to name everyone whom I pestered, I would surely appear to be ungrateful by unconsciously forgetting to mention a few.

I would like to thank especially the many people at Widener University who provided assistance, encouragement, and resources, thus making this project possible: Jan Alexander, Teresa Cartularo, Steve Foxman, Debra Holl, Ray Jefferis, Ilene Lieberman, John Neary, Bob Neveln, Barbara Norton, Larry Panek, Norene Shay, Linda Taylor, and Terri Walklett. Special thanks go to President Robert Bruce, Provost Lawrence Buck, Vice President David Eckard, and Dean Kenneth Skinner, for their continued encouragement and support of my research interests and in particular for the sabbatical which gave me the time to complete this manuscript.

Julie Still of Trenton State College read the manuscript and gave me many invaluable suggestions.

Mark Taub, my editor at Prentice Hall, provided many suggestions and much-appreciated encouragement for this project.

Should there be faults yet in this book—despite the assistance of these good people—I claim them as my own.

The Basics

Getting On Line

Where Is the Internet?

The Internet is an anarchic system (to use an oxymoron) of public and private computer networks that span the globe. These networks have grown at a geometric progression, from about 100 in 1985, to 200 in 1987, 500 in 1989, 2,200 in 1990, and well over 10,000 today.

Because the media is spending more and more time covering the Internet, the name has a familiar ring to most readers. No doubt, though, the *presence* of the Internet is not so keenly felt. To most people, the Internet seems like an abstraction, a complex technological reality that is given the weight of the familiar only by the metaphor of the information superhighway. Yet, in some measure, this figure of speech does a disservice to the network, for a highway is, tangible, immediately recognizable, and obviously useful. But where are the on-ramps for the Internet? Perhaps located in that other, more familiar metaphoric topography, Silicon Valley? In fact, you will be happy to know that the on-ramps are practically next door—as close as a computing center for some, a local telephone call away for others.

Getting Connected Through the Workplace

If you are employed by a college, a university, or a corporation, contact the computer operations center and ask if an Internet connection is available through its local area network (LAN). Chances are improving daily that it is. If you are lucky enough to have access through the workplace, connecting to the Internet will probably be a breeze.

On-line Services

If your employer does not provide Internet access, there are a number of commercial on-line providers that you might sign on with: America Online (AoL), CompuServe, Delphi, GEnie, MCI Mail, and Prodigy. The services that these companies provide vary greatly. All have e-mail capabilities; other options may vary. To make an informed choice as to which provider to sign on with, ask yourself which services you will want (gopher, telnet, FTP, Archie, Usenet News, Chat).

Commercial Service Providers

America Online
8619 Westwood Center Drive
Vienna, VA 22182-9806
1 800 827 4595
E-mail: AOBStaff16@aol.com

CompuServe
P.O. Box 20212
5000 Arlington Centre Blvd.
Columbus, OH 43220
1 614 457 8600
Membership Sales: 1 800 848 8199
Customer Sales: 1 800 484 8990
E-mail: sales@cis.compuserve.com

Delphi
1030 Massachusetts Avenue
Cambridge, MA 02138
Support: 1 800 695 4005
Business: 1 617 491 3393
FAX: 1 617 441 4903
E-mail: info@delphi.com
Registration by modem: 1 800 695 4002 (Login: JOINDELPHI;
password: INTERNETSIG)

GEnie
P.O. Box 6403
Rockville, MD 20849
1 800 638 9636
E-mail: feedback@genie.geis.com

MCI Mail
1133 19th Street NW
Seventh Floor
Washington, DC 20036
Phone: 1 800 444 MAIL
FAX: 1 202 416 5858

Prodigy
445 Hamilton Avenue
White Plains, NY 10601
Phone: 1 800 776 3449

SLIP/PPP

If your organization's LAN does not provide Internet access and you choose not to go with one of the on-line commercial providers, you still have another option—an independent Internet service provider.

All Internet connections are made possible by communications software known as TCP/IP. The acronym stands for Transmission Control Protocol/ Internet Protocol, and this software allows the various types of computer systems on the Internet—and there are many different system architectures—to "talk" to one another. (If you are using Windows to connect to the Internet, you must also have Winsock software, such as Trumpet Winsock.) It is not important for the average user to know the finer points of TCP/IP; however, you must be aware that in order to access TCP/IP by a modem, you must have three things:

➢ either SLIP support or PPP support

➢ a fast modem, preferably a 14.4 kbps minimum

➢ an account with a service provider

Some Internet Providers

Note: The following list identifies Internet service providers across America—at least one from each telephone area code. It may prove useful for those people who do not yet have Internet access and thus cannot obtain one of the more extensive lists obtainable by e-mail, FTP, gopher, or World Wide Web. Please be aware that there are many other providers and that it is highly recommended that you comparison shop before you choose a service. For further information, see "ACCESS—Internet" in the RESOURCES Section.

Area Code Served	Telephone Number	Name
201	408 554 8649	Netcom
202	301 220 2020	Digital
203	718 392 3667	Dorsai
204	204 474 9727	MBnet
205	201 691 4704	Planet
206	206 281 5397	Cyberlink
207	207 780 6381	Maine.net
208	602 230 9330	Evergreen
209	707 586 3060	California Online
210	415 837 5300	CRL
212	212 240 9600	Maestro
212	212 741 4400	Panix
212	212 267 3636	The Pipeline
213	213 644 9500	Earthlink
214	817 332 5116	DFW Internet Services
215	215 960 0972	Net Access
216	216 261 4594	Exchange
218	612 342 2570	Minnesota Regional Network
301	301 220 2020	Digital

Area Code Served	Telephone Number	Name
302	302 378 1386	SSNet
303	602 230 9330	Evergreen
304	304 293 5192	WVNET
305	305 428 4283	CyberGate
310	415 903 2242	ViaNet
312	408 554 8649	NetCom
313	313 998 4562	MSEN
314	713 684 5969	NeoSoft
315	614 292 8100	NYSERNet
316	800 TYRELL1	Tyrell
317	317 259 5050	IQuest
319	800 546 6587	INS
401	800 IDS 1680	IDS
402	402 472 7600	MIDnet
403	800 947 4754	CICnet
404	404 410 9000	Internet Atlanta
406	800 DIAL WLN	WLN
407	305 428 4283	CyberGate
408	510 988 0680	CCnet
409	713 684 5969	NeoSoft
410	202 331 5771	CAPCON
412	412 268 4960	PSCNET
414	708 367 1870	World Wide
415	619 338 9000	ElectriCiti
416	416 363 8676	Internex Online
419	800 627 8101	OARNET
501	501 521 4660	Sibylline
502	800 436 IGLOU	IgLou
503	503 233 4774	Internetworks
504	800 TYRELL1	Tyrell
505	800 592 1240	Internet Express
506	800 561 4459	NBnet
507	612 342 2570	Minnesota Regional Network

Area Code Served	Telephone Number	Name
508	617 593 3110	North Shore
509	509 927 RAMP	Internet On-Ramp
510	707 586 3060	California Online
512	512 322 9200	Onramp
513	513 887 8877	Internet Access Online
514	514 626 8086	LOGiciel
515	800 546 6587	INS
516	516 626 2090	Savvy
517	313 998 4562	Msen
518	518 271 6005	Wizvax
519	519 747 4110	Hookup
602	602 870 1010	Primenet
603	603 635 3857	Destek
604	604 936 8649	Wimsey
606	800 436 IGLOU	Iglou
608	608 246 4239	FullFeed
609	609 896 2799	New Jersey Computer
610	610 337 9994	Fishnet
612	612 941 9177	StarNet
613	902 468 NSTN	NSTN
614	800 627 8101	OARNet
615	615 455 9915	Edge
616	313 764 9430	MichNet
617	617 593 3110	North Shore
619	619 287 5943	ESNET
701	701 232 2227	Red River
702	702 832 6911	Sierra
703	800 82PSI82	PSI
704	704 338 4670	FXnet
705	404 410 9000	Internet Atlanta
707	707 586 3060	California Online
708	800 967 1580	InterAccess

Area Code Served	Telephone Number	Name
712	800 546 6587	INS
713	713 527 4988	Sesquinet
714	310 214 3349	DHM
715	608 246 4239	FullFeed
718	212 989 1128	Interport
719	800 900 RMII	Rocky Mountain
801	801 539 0852	XMission
802	603 635 3857	Destek
803	803 762 4956	SIMS
804	804 924 0616	VERnet
805	805 730 7775	Datawave
808	808 956 3499	PACCOM
810	800 456 0094	Rabbit Network
812	812 246 8032	The Point
813	305 428 4283	CyberGate
814	412 481 3505	Telerama
815	708 367 1870	WorldWide
816	800 TYRELL1	Tyrell
817	817 332 5116	DFW
818	818 858 9261	Lightside
819	613 567 6925	Resudox Online Services
902	902 468 NSTN	NSTN
904	407 635 8888	Florida Online
906	313 764 9430	MichNet
908	201 691 4704	Planet
909	714 638 2139	KAIWAN
910	800 377 3282	VNET
912	404 410 9000	Internet Atlanta
913	800 TYRELL1	Tyrell
914	212 989 2418	Phantom
915	505 345 6555	New Mexico Technet
916	707 586 3060	California Online
917	718 776 6811	New York Net

Area Code Served	Telephone Number	Name
918	800 221 6478	South Coast
919	919 890 6305	Interpath
Nationwide		
	800 4uu net4	Alternet
	404 454 4638	Internet Connection
	800 592 1240	Internet Express
	800 221 3756	Internet Online Services
	800 433 6444	Portal Information Network
		UUNET (See Alternet)

What Services Are Essential for You?

To tell people what Internet services they will need is as presumptuous as telling people what they should order for a meal. But you can be sure that like a good meal, a connection with a broad spectrum of options is going to be very satisfying. E-mail is the essential starting point. Lists and Usenet news will connect you to the electronic community. Archie, Veronica, and Jughead will allow you to search for information. Gopher, telnet, and FTP will enable you to obtain that information. And since traveling on the Internet highway is hard work that builds big appetites, you really should treat yourself to a delicious and healthy dessert of the World Wide Web. So I would advise someone who is connecting for the first time to go for the full-course meal.

A Checklist for Selecting On-line Vendors

Comparison shop. Prices will vary considerably. However, do more than compare prices. Talk to the individuals and shop wisely to find the service that will offer you the type of connection that you want. Here is a checklist of things you might want to inquire about:

_____ Company name

_____ Contact person

_____ Phone

_____ FAX

_____ Dial-up Internet connection: local or toll call?

_____ Baud rate

_____ E-mail

_____ File Transfer Protocol (FTP)

_____ Telnet

_____ Gopher

_____ USENET news

_____ LAN Connection

_____ World Wide Web

_____ Chat

_____ Technical Support

_____ Basic fees: _____

_____ Other fees: _____

Suggestions for Further Reading

Kehoe, Brendan. *Zen and the Art of the Internet,* 3rd edition. Englewood Cliffs, NJ: Prentice Hall, 1994.

Krol, Ed. *The Whole Internet User's Guide and Catalog,* 2nd edition. Sebastopol, CA: O'Reilly & Associates, 1994.

Netiquette

• General Rules • E-mail • Usenet News
• Mailing Lists • FTP

It's not often that you can add a few years to your life by reading a chapter of a book. If you take a few moments to read this section, you will do just that, for by following a few simple rules, you can avoid a great deal of stress in the coming years.

It would be nice to say that the information superhighway is like a little, peaceful, rural New Hampshire back road, but it is really like the Los Angeles Freeway: a fast, busy, crowded route, with vehicles sometimes going in the wrong direction and with the greater topography sometimes susceptible to earth-shattering disruptions. And I haven't even mentioned yet the testy disposition of some of the drivers, some of them lost! This labyrinth, after all, is huge.

So before you take your computer out for a spin, do yourself a favor and read the owner's manual, obey all highway signs, and get yourself an official Internet highway driver's license, which is automatically granted to anyone who memorizes the following few simple rules.

General Rules

➤ Do not "flame." Ad hominem attacks are symptomatic of eroding manners. Common courtesy should prevail on the net—just as it should in life generally.

➤ DON'T TYPE IN ALL CAPITALS—IT LOOKS LIKE YOU ARE SHOUTING!

➤ Have great tolerance for neophytes. A private e-mail message rather than a public rebuke is often called for when a "newbie" missteps.

➤ Respect copyrights. If you are quoting copyrighted material, be sure to follow the "fair-use" standard as set by the copyright law.

➤ Do not use objectionable language. The Internet is a very public place, and civility should always prevail.

➤ Do not initiate or participate in "chain letters."

E-mail

➤ Keep e-mail messages short and to the point.

➤ In e-mail messages, type short lines. Some mail programs do not have the features that we have come to expect in a word processor, such as word-wrap. If the mail system you are using does not include word-wrap, be sure to hit the return key well before the end of each line. Your readers will appreciate it.

➤ In e-mail, use language that is appropriate for a public forum. It is never acceptable to use offensive language.

➤ In every e-mail message, be sure to give a clear, succinct, and telling subject line—the kind that will allow someone who is not interested in the topic to delete the message and that will allow those interested to be sure to read it.

➤ Create a signature file for yourself that is appropriate—neither too long nor too brief. Get the essentials in—your name and your e-mail address as a minimum. Generally, it is advisable to stay under five lines. Some mail programs automatically cut off the fourth and succeeding lines anyway. You may be proud of your ASCII artwork, and it may really belong in a cyber museum, but resist the temptation to send several thousand extra bytes with every message. Keep it short.

➤ When responding to an e-mail message or to a message on a list, do the following:

• identify the writer of the original message to which you are responding;

• if possible, include a portion of the message to which you are responding;

- include only the most significant part of the message; delete the material that has no bearing on your response, especially if the original message is long.

➤ Resist the temptation to hit the "send" key until after you have read over your message at least once. Remember that electronic communication is very different from person-to-person encounters, where subtle clues of intonation, facial expressions and gestures amplify the meaning of one's words. In electronic communication, on the other hand, irony and understatement can be easily misunderstood.

➤ Use discretion when forwarding a private message to another person or to a general list. Consider the writer's intention. Often, when a message is for general redistribution, the writer will clearly mark it as such (e.g., "Please feel free to post this message to other lists").

Usenet News

➤ In order to increase the chances that your contributions will be suitable to the usenet group, read a newsgroup for an extended period (at least several weeks) before you post to it.

➤ Don't mail to a newsgroup unless you are really adding something significant to the thread.

➤ Choose carefully the newsgroups and the geographical areas to which you mail items.

➤ It is considered a courtesy when responding to a post to delete all unnecessary lines of the original. Include only pertinent material.

➤ Before responding to an article, read the rest of the articles with the same subject lines. A query may have already been answered or a necessary rebuttal may have already been made.

Mailing Lists

➤ Save your original subscription confirmation to each list. Most systems have a folder option that will allow you to store important documents long term. The original message will be valuable to you when you want to unsubscribe from a list.

➤ If you plan on joining discussion lists, take a few moments to learn the essentials of subscribing and signing off. The process of getting on/getting off is not very complicated, though it is easy to make mistakes. Avoid sending the subscribe/signoff messages to the list itself. Certainly one of the most consistent sources of aggravation on the Net results from the common mistake of sending signoff messages to the membership of the list at large. In addition, if you are having difficulty signing off from the list, do not complain about it to the list membership. They can do nothing about it; it wastes their time and uses up their disk space. Instead, do the following (in this order): (1) read carefully the initial sign on message, which usually gives explicit directions for signing off the list; (2) read the "Lists" chapter in this book, which gives the commands for signing off of various kinds of listservers; (3) contact the list owner directly for help (unless you have a better address for the list owner, try <listname>-request@<hostname> or <listname>-owner@<hostname>).

➤ Find out if the list has a FAQ (Frequently Asked Questions). If it does, read it.

➤ Learn the landscape. After you join a list, for example, "lurk" for a decent period of time before you contribute to the ongoing discussions or initiate a new thread. You also might want to check the archives of a list to make sure that your "new" thread isn't something that has already been killed with a stake through its heart.

➤ Remember that each list has a single focus. Respect that by avoiding extraneous topics—you can be sure that a large portion of the list members will be bothered by frequent off-topic messages.

➤ After you execute the reply command, always double-check the addressee. Depending on your mail system, the reply function may send your message to the membership of a list at large, or it may send it only to the single individual. Be careful in selecting your audience. If a message is not of general interest, it should be sent to the individual. (Individuals will often summarize for the list the responses they receive.)

➤ If you are requesting information from the members of a list, ask that replies be sent to your e-mail address; then as a courtesy post a summary of the results to the list at large.

FTP

➤ Many FTP and telnet sites are maintained by businesses and educational organizations. They often request that guest activities be confined to off-peak hours. Be courteous in this respect. Excessive violations will ultimately cause restrictions.

➤ Be sure to log off of your computer when you are done—especially if you are using a publicly accessible machine. An abandoned login session has been the source of many a sorrowful consequence. (Imagine all the messages that you would not want someone to send out under your name!)

Suggestion for Further Reading

Shea, Virginia. *Netiquette*. San Francisco, CA: Albion Books, 1994.

What Is E-mail?

Electronic mail has changed the way we communicate and our perception of communication in general. It will probably never completely replace the more traditional means of communicating—such as letters and telephone calls—but it has already made serious inroads into both of those methods of transmitting news and information. Unlike telephone calls, which can be costly (at least the long-distance ones) or which can be intrusive if they come at inopportune times for the recipient, or which can fail because the receiving party is not home, an e-mail message is cheap and waits patiently in a person's electronic mailbox. It is also quick (usually). A message sent halfway around the world might arrive within a minute or two. Moreover, e-mail is usually a cost-effective means of communicating, and since e-mail messages can usually be printed in hard copy with a minimum of difficulty, they share some of the virtues of traditional correspondence. Another advantage of e-mail is that with a single message the user can communicate with a large number of people at once (by using a mail list or an alias file). This is one of the more pleasant surprises awaiting the novice Internet user—and an extremely important time-saving device.

There are many e-mail systems available, all with their own unique sets of commands. Your system administrator can provide documentation on using your particular system. For our purposes here, we will discuss the general features that are common to most systems. Your mail program will have most of these features—and perhaps some others as well.

Some General Considerations

When using the mail program, the user generally will find a screenful of messages—assuming that one has already received some mail. In some mail systems, the messages will remain in the mailbox indefinitely. In others, the messages will be automatically deleted after a certain period (say 2 weeks).

Information provided in the "header" of the message might include the following:

➤ Date of message

➤ E-mail address of the sender

➤ Subject

➤ Length (number of lines and/or number of characters)

Electronic Addresses

Upon first encountering them, electronic addresses may seem confusing, but they have an order that is inevitable, and once one becomes accustomed to them, they seem most natural.   Let's look at a hypothetical example:

president@whitehouse.gov

The parts of this address break down as follows:

president   This is the **local name**. Sometimes addresses have generic local names, like "president"; sometimes addresses have particular names, like "Clinton" or "10586."

@   This is the "**at**" sign, which separates the local name from the hostname.

Whitehouse	This is the **hostname.**
gov	This is the **domain**.

Domain Names

The end of the electronic address will contain either a domain name or a country code. The most common domains include the following:

com	Commercial organization
edu	Educational institution
gov	U. S. government office
mil	U. S. military site
net	Network
org	Non profit organization

The United States country code (US), which sometimes appears as the far right part of the address, is usually omitted, but you will sometimes encounter it. For example, the US extension is used with some California addresses to prevent confusion with the country code for Canada (CA). For example, a popular American site is The Well, which is located in San Francisco, California. Its address is:

info@well.sf.ca.us

Without the "us" extension, the Internet mail routers would try to send this message to Canada (CA), and it would eventually be returned as undeliverable.

Some Common Country Codes

You will eventually come across e-mail addresses from foreign countries. Some of the more common country codes include the following:

AU	Australia
CA	Canada
CH	Switzerland
DE	Germany
ES	Spain
FI	Finland
FR	France
HK	Hong Kong
IL	Israel
IT	Italy
JP	Japan
NO	Norway
NZ	New Zealand
PL	Poland
RU	Russian Federation
SE	Sweden
UK	United Kingdom
US	United States

Note: For a complete list of country codes—along with a chart of international e-mail accessibility—see Olivier M. J. Crepin-Leblond's FAQ: International E-mail Accessibility. This is posted to **comp.mail.misc, comp.mail.uucp, alt.internet.services**, and other Usenet groups. A listing (in the file rfc 1394.txt) is also available by anonymous FTP from nic.merit.edu in the subdirectory /documents/rfc.

Basic Features

> Note: Some of the following options may be available on your e-mail system under a different name.

Though your e-mail program will probably have many features, there are three basic elements that you will want to be familiar with to begin: writing, reading, and replying. These three features will be the only parts of mail that many users will ever care about. (But just in case you are interested in more, see the "Advanced Features" section below!)

•Writing

Follow these few suggestions:

1. Start the mail program. You will be prompted to type in the electronic address of the person to whom you wish to send a message.

> Note: Unlike the U.S. Postal Service, which occasionally delivers in spite of incorrect addresses, e-mail requires accuracy; it has no tolerance for incomplete or inexact information: no matter how slight the error—for example, writing the letter "o" instead of a zero or a comma instead of a period—the message will eventually find its way back to your mailbox as undeliverable.

2. Supply a succinct but accurate "subject."

3. Keep your message short and to the point.

4. In closing, supply your own e-mail address.

5. Hit the "send" key.

•Reading

1. Start the mail program.

2. Choose a message to read and select the "read" option.

> Note: It is important to be aware of the length of each posting. You may have to scroll down or hit "next screen" in order to read the entire message.

2. Exit back to the mail list.

•*Replying*

If you wish to respond to a message, your mail program will usually allow you to select a "reply" option while the original message is on the screen.

1. Select the "reply" option.

> Note: After selecting the reply option, always double-check to make sure that the "TO: field" reflects the address you want to send your message to. In some instances, you may want to respond directly to an individual; other times you will want your message to go to a group of people. For example, if you read a message from a "list" and want to respond, your reply function may automatically fill in the name of the list as the addressee. This will send a response to the list at large—this could be to several thousand people (so be careful!). In some instances, however, you will want to respond directly to the individual who wrote the message, not to the entire list. Just remember to alter the address field when necessary.

2. You may wish to include—and it is often advisable to do so—at least part of the original message in your reply (see the following topic: "Adding or Interpolating a Letter"). If so, be sure to edit the original and to delete extraneous material; include only enough material from the original to indicate clearly the nature of your reply.

3. Write your response.

> Note: Many mail programs do not have sophisticated editors (though sometimes you can invoke an editor such as "vi" from within the mail program). Thus, if you do not have such conveniences as "word-wrap," you should use the return key to keep the length of the lines manageable.

4. Select the "send" option.

Advanced Features

Each e-mail program is unique, but all of them will support some of the following features.

•Adding or Interpolating a Letter

When you are responding to a message, this feature will allow you to include the original message as part of your response. (The mail program will probably include ">" signs along the left margin to indicate the material that has been added to your own message.)

> Note: If the original message was lengthy, you will probably want to edit it down so that only the relevant passage is included.

•Alias

Most mail systems will allow for "alias"—that is, you may create a shortened form of someone's address. This could be particularly useful if you frequently send mail to an individual or to a group (see "Distribution List" section). For example, it is much easier to type "bill" in the "TO:" field rather than

president@whitehouse.gov

Once you establish the alias, all you need to type is the shortened form in all future messages to that individual (or group of individuals).

•Blind Carbon Copies

This feature will allow you to send copies of your e-mail message to someone without the original recipient being aware of it (see "Carbon Copies," which follows).

•Carbon Copies

This feature allows you to send a duplicate of the message to a third party. Usually, the message to your recipient will indicate that an additional message is sent to another e-mail address. (See also "Blind Carbon Copy" above.)

•Certifying E-mail

Some mail systems have a certified mail option. In some instances, it may be important to know if—and when—someone receives your message. Selecting this feature will enable you to receive a confirmation that the message has been delivered.

•Confirming Delivery

If your mail system has this option, a message will be returned to you when your original message is delivered to the proper address.

•Copy

(See "Save" entry.)

•Distribution Lists

Some mail systems allow for the creation of distribution lists. These are individually generated lists that make distributing information fast and efficient. For example, if you are a history teacher, you might make a "list" of all the members of your class in Western Civilization I. Announcements, assignments, items of interest, clarifications—all can be sent to the students on the list by simply invoking a single address (the name of the list). In addition, such lists can be "open" or "closed." If they are closed, only you can send messages to the list. If they are open, then any member of the list can contribute. Thus, they can become open forums for discussion of class-related material.

It should be obvious from the example above that the distribution list is a valuable tool that can be applied to numerous diverse situations, from establishing a forum for discussion of issues to the dissemination of information, to the mailing of an annual Christmas letter to friends and associates.

> Note: If your mail system does not support the creation of distribution lists, you can probably achieve the same effect by using the "alias" feature.

•Expiration Dates

Some mail programs automatically delete messages after a specified period of time. Sometimes, these expiration dates can be altered to extend or shorten the time the messages are retained in your mailbox.

• Folders

This option will allow you to save like messages in a "folder" for later retrieval (see also "Save"). You can create folders for various topics of interest to you. For example, if you subscribe to one or more lists, you can create a folder entitled Lists in which you can save the original subscription message for the various lists. This information will inevitably be valuable later, when you have questions about managing the list. (See the "Lists" chapter for more information.)

•Forwarding Mail

This option will allow you to forward to a third party a message you have received. You may, for example, receive a message on the Holocaust from a history list and feel that a colleague who specializes in that field may be interested. You can forward the message.

•Help

Most mail programs will have a help option that will give you on-line information about the various functions (such as sending mail, forwarding mail, folders, etc.).

•Importing or Attaching Files

There may be occasions when you have a file in your account that you want to send to someone. For example, if you have a large data file that you wish to send to someone by way of e-mail, you can import it into your e-mail message.

> Note: The import function will vary from system to system. In Unix, one may invoke the vi editor while in the mail program and use the ":r" command to add a file to the message. Other systems may have a function key or an icon devoted to this process.

•Save

This option will allow you to "copy" a message in your mailbox to a file in your computer account.

•Signature File

Most mail programs will allow you to create a signature file. This is usually a brief file that is appended to your e-mail messages. (Again, depending on your mail program, attaching the sig file to your letter may be automatic or it may have to be done manually.) At the minimum, the signature file should contain your name and e-mail address. Sometimes, people add other information as well, such as telephone numbers, fax numbers, addresses, institutional affiliations, and even personalized logos—ASCII art.

> Note: Don't overdo signature files, keep them short.

•Sort

If your e-mail program supports this option, you will be able to sort your mail by various criteria (for example, date, sender, etc.).

An E-mail Sampler: America OnLine

To illustrate the way that some of the previous generalities might find specific application, the e-mail program for America OnLine will be examined. America OnLine is one of the fastest growing commercial service providers.

Once you have logged onto AoL, you can enter the mail program in either of two ways: (1) by clicking on the word Mail at the menu bar at the top of the screen (and then choosing the Compose Mail option or the Read New Mail option) or (2) by clicking on either the Mailbox or the Compose Mail icon (on the left side of the icon bar).

If you have mail waiting when you log onto the program, the YOU HAVE MAIL screen will appear automatically, and it will look like the following illustration.

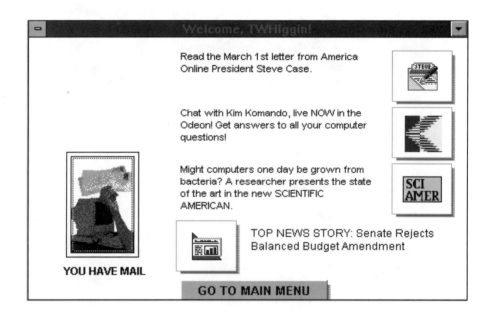

Reading Mail

To read your incoming mail, click on the YOU HAVE MAIL graphic with your mouse. Assuming you have mail, your next screen will look something like the following screen.

This screen shows three messages waiting, with the date, sender, and subject of each clearly marked.

The top message is usually highlighted with a colored bar. You can move the bar by clicking your mouse or by using arrow keys to select the message you would like to read. When the color bar is on the message of your choice, click on the Read button, and the program will take you to the next screen, which should look like the following:

The message will now be displayed on your screen. At the top of the message you will find four items of interest.

➢ Subj: This will indicate the subject provided by the sender of the message.

➢ Date: This will indicate the date and the time the message was sent.

➢ From: This will indicate the sender of the message.

➢ To: This will show your AoL screen name—the name you logged on with.

Below this information is the message itself.

At this point, there are four buttons on the screen, each indicating additional choices that you can make (proceeding clockwise from the lower right).

➢ Next   Will let you read the next message.

➢ Reply to All   Will let you send a message to all the recipients of the original message.

➢ Forward   Will let you forward the current letter to someone else with an e-mail address

➢ Reply   Will let you send a response to the writer of the original message

Replying to a Message _____

To answer the writer of this message, click on the Reply button. A screen similar to the following will appear.

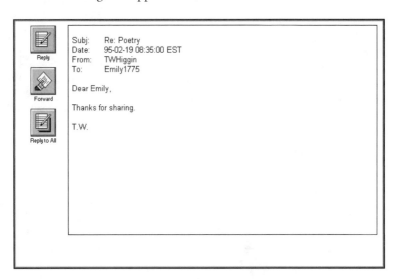

The "To:" address will automatically be entered by the mail program, as will the "Subject" line (preceded by a "Re:"). The CC: block is for sending copies of the reply to third parties. In addition to using the mouse to move the cursor to the body of the message and writing a response, you have several other choices:

➤ Attach   Will allow you to send files as attachments to your response.

➤ Address Book   Will allow you to select pre-established e-mail addresses, saving you the trouble of typing—and mistyping—long and often hard-to-remember addresses.

Writing Messages

When you write a message, the screen is very similar to the Reply screen (see the 3rd illustration in this chapter). Just select the "Write" icon from the menu bar, and you will be presented with the Compose Mail screen.

Summing Up

E-mail is one of the most useful—and powerful—features of Internet usage. It not only gives you the ability to communicate with millions of Internet addresses (the number grows daily), but it also can be used to process many of the traditional functions of the Internet (FTP, finger, etc.). If you have e-mail, but lack other forms of access, you might want to acquire the file "Accessing the Internet by E-Mail," which is available by e-mail from listserv@ubvm.cc.buffalo.edu (see Resources—"Mail" for details). See also Scott Yanoff's "Internet Services List," which is regularly distributed to **alt.internet.services**, **comp.misc.news.answers**, **comp.answers**, and **alt.answers** (among others), and which is also listed in the Resources section.

> Note: Before using e-mail, be sure to read the e-mail section of the Netiquette chapter.

Suggestions for Further Reading

Frey, Donnalyn and Rick Adams. *!%@:: A Directory of Electronic Mail Addressing and Networks*. Sebastopol, CA: O'Reilly & Associates, 1993.

Rose, Marshall. *The Internet Message: Closing the Book with Electronic Mail*. Englewood Cliffs, NJ: Prentice Hall, 1993.

Sachs, David and Henry Stair. *Hands-On Internet: A Beginning Guide for PC Users*. Englewood Cliffs, NJ: Prentice Hall, 1994.

Mailing Lists

• What Are Mailing Lists and Listservers? • Finding Lists
•Subscribing to a Listserv List • Participating in a Listserv
List • Retrieving a File of List Members • Searching a
List's Archives • Unsubscribing from a Listserv List • List
Commands. • Some Typical Listserver Functions.

What Are Mailing Lists and Listservers?

It is not an overstatement to say that participation in mailing lists can become a very rewarding part of your life. What is a list, you ask?

Lists are virtual communities of like-minded people who congregate at the various rest stops on the information superhighway, kind of like an information booth/espresso bar without the caffeine. Each list is organized around a specific topic, from Academic Advising (ACADV) to Zwriter Users Group (ZWSUG). Many of these lists have automated subscription, signoff, distribution, and archival processes, all made possible by a software program called a listserver.

> Note: In this chapter I will use the generic term "listserver" to refer to all five of the listserver software programs: **Listserv**, **ListProcessor**, **Mailbase**, **Mailserver**, and **Majordomo**. Since **Listserv** is the most common program you will encounter, the examples in this chapter will be from this type of server.

These are public forums where list members can ask questions, respond to queries, or just be "lurkers" (the name given to the list members who choose to read the posts, but not to contribute actively to the discussions—usually the majority of the list membership). Discussion "threads" develop. Sustained—and often lively—debate on a topic can last for several weeks

> Note: Since signing onto a list, receiving and participating in the daily postings, and unsubscribing from it are all performed by way of the e-mail function, it is imperative that the user be comfortable with the read, write, and reply functions of e-mail before joining a list.

The size and nature of these groups differ considerably. The smallest group will have only a handful of subscribers; the largest has somewhere in the neighborhood of 40,000. Similarly, the number of messages sent to any particular mailing list might range from a few per month to upwards of a hundred daily. Oftentimes, lists that are moderated have the virtue of staying focused and civilized, though often at the expense of creativity and spontaneity. Finally (though this can be a very subjective evaluation), the quality of the discussion on different lists varies greatly. Undoubtedly, you will have to experiment, sample here and there, in order to find the right forum for your tastes. However, because the many lists cover a very wide array of tastes and interests (Buddhism, horses, Mark Twain, etc.), you can be sure that you will find one worth joining.

Because mailing lists are very public forums, netiquette is an essential concern. For example, upon first joining a list, it is always a good idea to "lurk" for a while before contributing in order to get a feel for the tenor of the discussions. Also, before posting a query or initiating a discussion of a particular topic to a list at large, new subscribers might also search the list archives to see if a topic has previously been discussed. And "flaming" is always a bad idea. These and other fine points of list behavior should always be kept in mind. (See the chapter on Netiquette before subscribing to a list.)

The following details relate to activities involving a LISTSERV-based list, but they will give you a general idea as to how all five listservers operate. For some specific directions for dealing with all five types of listservers, see the section, "List Commands" later in this chapter.

Finding Lists

There are many sources of information on lists. See, for example, the "Lists" entry in the Resources section of this book for some of these. There are also published books dealing in whole or in part with the subject. Consult your local library or bookseller. Finally, see the appendix to this book for a list of lists that are of interest to humanists—though be aware that this appendix does not pretend to be exhaustive. There are thousands of lists catering to many different kinds of interests.

Subscribing to a Listserv List

For the purposes of illustration, we will subscribe to a list that is devoted to discussions of classical music: CLASSM-L. This list is maintained at the site at Brown University.

> Note: As a preliminary step, some definitions are in order. Note the difference between the following two items:
>
> **Listserv Address:**
> ```
> listserv@brownvm.brown.edu
> ```
> This is the address for all automated functions—such as subscribing, unsubscribing, setting no-mail, etc.
>
> **List Address**:
> ```
> classm-l@brownvm.brown.edu
> ```
> This is the address for communicating with the several hundred members of the list. A message sent here—even an accidentally misdirected "unsubscribe" message—will automatically be distributed to the readership at large.

Follow these three simple procedures:

1. Address your e-mail request to the listserver address (e.g., LISTSERV@brownvm.brown.edu), not to the list (e.g., classm-l@brownvm.brown.edu). In this instance, to subscribe, use the following e-mail address:

   ```
   listserv@brownvm.brown.edu
   ```

2. Leave the subject line of your message blank.

3. The body of your message should include only the following:

> SUB CLASSM-L <First Name> <Last Name>

Then send your message.

Notice that this message has three parts:

1. Identification of the activity, in this case: SUBscribe.

2. The name of the list to which you want to subscribe: classm-L1. (Be aware that the site "brownvm" has numerous lists; here you want to subscribe only to the one dealing with classical music.)

3. Your name. (I would emphasize the obvious here—only because I have often seen errors concerning this: type your own name. Do not type the words "First Name" or use the angle-brackets <>.) For example, if I were the one subscribing to this list, my message would appear as follows:

> SUB CLASSM-L Michael Clark

If you have followed the directions, you should receive a confirmation of your subscription—anywhere from a minute to several hours later.

> Note: The confirmation is an important notice and should be saved. Either print out a hard copy and file it away for future use or create a "folder" in your mail account for storing it electronically. In either case, you will want to refer to it when you have questions about your subscription. The confirmation can be particularly useful when you want to sign off the list.

As with the subscription command, all commands having to do with automated functions (e.g., setting digests, searching archives, unsubscribing, etc.) should be sent to the Listserver (LISTSERV) address, not the list itself (CLASSM-L).

Participating in a Listserv List

If you are a member of a list and wish to reply to a message that you have received, follow these steps:

1. Select the reply function. The addresses of most mailing lists are set up so that the return address will automatically appear in the "TO:" line of your message and the subject line will automatically insert the words "Reply to" before the subject line of the original message.

> Note: Take special care to be sure the address that your reply message is going to is correct. If, for example, you intend to reply only to the original sender of the message (and not to the list at large), you will undoubtedly have to change the reply to the specific individual. Always ask yourself who the appropriate audience is for your reply—is your reply of interest to the readership at large or only to the original sender? Be sure your reply is addressed appropriately.

2. Add the original message to your own message so that the reader(s) will be able to make sense of your response. (If the original message is long, edit it down to only the essential point to which you are responding.)

3. Compose your response.

4. Add your e-mail address (or your signature file).

5. Send the message.

Retrieving a File of List Members

Some mailing lists support the "review" function, which allows you to get a listing of all the people subscribed to that list.

1. Address an e-mail message to the host listserv. (For example, for classm-l, the address is:

    listserv@brownvm.brown.edu

2. Leave the subject line blank.

3. Include only the following message:

    review classm-l by name

(Adding the "by name" command will return an alphabetized file.)

Searching a List's Archives

Some listserver software allows for searching of the list's archives. In LISTSERV, for example, you will probably be able to find what you want by using the following template:

Send a message to the listserver (for example, `list-serv@brownvm.brown.edu`) with the following message:

```
// job echo=no
database search dd=rules
//rules dd *
search <text> in <listname>
index
/*
```

In the above, replace <text> with a keyword you are interested in searching for and replace <listname> with the name of the list (e.g., classm-l). For example, a search for references to Leopold (Wolfgang Amadeus Mozart's father) in the classm-l would look like this:

```
// job echo=no
database search dd=rules
//rules dd *
search Leopold in classm-l
index
/*
```

The results of your query will be returned from the listserver in something like the following format:

Item #	Date	Time	Recs Subject
000608	94/01/20	08:15 43	Humor in Music, etc.
001143	94/01/29	04:07 35	Re: Mark Feezell's...
002652	94/02/14	15:01 24	The Mozarts

[additional entries deleted]

The numerals in the left margin indicate the identification numbers for the various messages in which the name Leopold appeared. Any or all of those messages can be retrieved by sending the following instructions to the listserver, citing the number(s) of the messages that you wish to receive:

```
// job echo=no
database search dd=rules
//rules dd *
search Leopold in classm-l
print all of <item #>
/*
```

✳ Mailing Lists

In the line "print all of <item #>" replace the bracketed material with the number you wish to retrieve. In addition, this line may be replicated any number of times in a single e-mail message to retrieve several items at once. For example, you may replace the single line with the following:

```
// job echo=no
database search dd=rules
//rules dd *
search Leopold in classm-l
print all of 000608
print all of 001143
print all of 002652
/*
```

Note: If you would like to learn more about the extensive capabilities of the LISTSERV database searches (including Boolean searches), send the following command to a listserv:

```
Get listdb memo
```

Unsubscribing from a Listserv List

To unsubscribe from the list, do the following:

1. Address the message to the listserver address.

Note: Be sure to send your message to the listserver address (for example: listserv@brownvm.brown.edu), not to the list itself (classm-l@brownvm.brown.edu). Otherwise, (a) you will not get unsubscribed; (b) all the members of the list will get to read your message; and (c) you may become the object of flaming from the less-considerate members of the list—especially if you persist in sending the requests.

2. Leave the subject line blank.

3. Type only the following (again, we will continue using classm-l as the example):

```
UNSUBSCRIBE CLASSM-L
```

> Note: Messages to unsubscribe from a list must come from the same address as your original subscription request. Therefore, if you know that your e-mail address will be changing, unsubscribe from all lists and resubscribe after you have your new address. In the event that your address has already changed, contact the system administrator of the list so that he or she can manually unsubscribe you.

List Commands

The following five sections provide basic commands for each of the types of list-servers: Listserv, ListProcessor, Majordomo, Mailserve, and Mailbase. In each case, the "Help/info" requests will allow you to retrieve a file which will give you additional information concerning the listserver commands.

Listserv

Activity	Mail address [fill in the site name after the @]	Message
Subscribe	`LISTSERV@...`	`sub <listname> <first name> <last name>`
Unsubscribe	`LISTSERV@...`	`unsubscribe <listname>`

Help/info	`LISTSERV@...`	`get listserv refcard`
		`help`
		or
		`info`

ListProcessor

Activity	Mail address [fill in the site name after the @]	Message
Subscribe	`LISTPROC@...`	`subscribe <listname> <first name> <last name>`
Unsubscribe	`LISTPROC@...`	`unsubscribe <listname>`
Help/info	`LISTPROC@...`	`help`

Majordomo

Activity	Mail address [fill in the site name after the @]	Message
Subscribe	`MAJORDOMO@...`	`subscribe <listname>`
Unsubscribe	`MAJORDOMO@...`	`unsubscribe <listname>`
Help/info	`MAJORDOMO@...`	`help`

Mailserv

Activity	Mail address [fill in the site name after the @]	Message
Subscribe	`MAILSERV@...`	`sub <listname> <first name>` `<last name>`
Unsubscribe	`MAILSERV@...`	`unsubscribe <listname>`
Help/info	`MAILSERV@...`	`help`

Mailbase

Activity	Mail address [fill in the site name after the @]	Message
Subscribe	`MAILBASE@...`	`join <listname> <first name>` `<last name>`
Unsubscribe	`MAILBASE@...`	`leave <listname>`
Help/info	`MAILBASE-` `HELP@...`	`help`

Some Typical Listserver Functions

Finally, you should be aware that mailing lists provide many diverse and powerful commands to let you fully utilize such rich resources. The following are some of the commands that are possible on LISTSERV, the most popular of the five list-servers. Note that not all of the five types of listservers will support each of these commands. Consult the Help guide for each listserver to determine the commands available.

> Note: Special attention must be paid to the exact format used with each command. For example, the subscribe command would be sent by e-mail to the listserv address with only the following in the body of the message:
>
> SUB <listname> <first name> <last name>
>
> or
>
> Subscribe <listname> <first name> <last name>

➤ SUBscribe <listname>
Subscribes you to a list.

➤ UNSUBscribe <listname> or SIGNOFF <listname>
Unsubscribes you from a list.

➤ Conceal/Noconceal
Conceals your name when you are on a list. Other members of the list will not have access to your membership.

➤ SET acknowledgment/noack
Acknowledges that your posting to a list has been accomplished.

➤ SET mail/nomail
Turns off your mail. This is used instead of unsubscribing when you want a temporary interruption in your list activity.

➤ SET digests
This gives you the day's mail from the list in "digest" form—that is, you receive one composite mailing instead of receiving all the day's messages individually.

➤ SET Repro/norepro
You receive a copy of all of your messages to the list.

➤ REView list
This allows you to obtain a list of all members of a list.

➤ GET <filename>
Allows you to obtain a file from the listserver.

➤ Search <text>
Allows user to search the archives of a list to find information on a topic of interest.

> For more information on obtaining instructive files on listservers, see entry "Listservers" in the Resources section of this book.

Suggestions for Further Reading

Hardie, T.L. and Vivian Neou. *Internet Mailing Lists*. Englewood Cliffs, NJ: Prentice Hall, 1993.

King, Lisabeth and Diane Kovacs. *Directory of Electronic Journals, Newsletters and Academic Discussion Lists*, 4th edition. Washington, D.C.: Association of Research Libraries, 1994.

Sachs, David and Henry Stair. *Hands-On Internet: A Beginning Guide for PC Users*. Englewood Cliffs, NJ: Prentice Hall, 1994.

Usenet News

What Is Usenet News?

Newsgroups are very similar to lists. Both are organized by specific topics. Both newsgroups and lists are sometimes moderated. But as a general rule, newsgroups tend to be less formal and less given to rigorous academic debate, more oriented toward the leisure time and the technical. But in their own way, newsgroups also can be places for precision, insight, humor, information—and flaming.

There are thousands of Usenet newsgroups, sometimes referred to simply as "news." These are open forums for discussions on a broad range of topics. Groups are organized roughly into seven broad categories:

comp   Computer-related (computer science, software, hardware)

news   Issues regarding Usenet

rec	Arts, hobbies, and recreation (if it's fun, it's here)
sci	Science
soc	Social issues (culture, religion, politics, etc.)
talk	Just what it sounds like: anything worth debating
misc	The group for everything else

In addition, there are other popular categories that have evolved over the past few years:

alt	Alternative, an olio of topics, from abortion to 'zines
bit	Bitnet
biz	Business
clari	Clarinet news
k12	Education

(And you may occasionally see reference to a few other newsgroups that are highly specialized in nature: ddn, gnu, vms, etc.)

Newsreaders

The "newsreader" is the software that allows you to access (i.e., read and post messages to) the various newsgroups. The most popular readers are "rn," "nn," "tin," and "trn," and they are initiated by typing those letters at your system prompt (or by selecting the news icon on Windows systems). Though the basic commands of the various newsreaders differ somewhat, all of the newsreaders have the same basic features—the ability to subscribe to news, to read it, to reply to posts, and to send postings. The central part of this chapter will explain how to do these things with one of the most popular of the newsreaders, rn. Since newsreaders tend to have the same kinds of options, this discussion should prove beneficial regardless of the type of reader you have. The end of the chapter offers information on specific newsgroups.

If you are using a windows-type interface, your access to Usenet News will much simpler than the process outlined in this chapter, which describes accessing the News on a Unix-based system. For example, to read your news while on America OnLine, you simply click your mouse on "Internet Connection" (at the Main Menu), and then on successive screens, select the following items:

Newsgroups
    Read My News
        List Unread
            Read

The process is largely intuitive and will present few challenges. Nevertheless, since newsreaders like rn have many virtues—and many loyal users—it is not likely that they will be abandoned in the near future.

Using the rn Reader

The rn reader is one of the most popular, and it is not hard to master its basic commands. It operates at three levels:

★ the newsgroup selection level

★ the article selection level

★ the paging level

Note: Type "h" for help at any time, and depending on the level you are currently at (newsgroup selection level, article selection level, or pager level), you will get a list of appropriate commands.

The Newsgroup Selection Level

At this level, you are presented with the list of groups you are subscribed to. You can choose the ones you want to read. You are also notified when new groups become available and are given the option of adding them to your reading list (the .newsrc file).

To begin, type "rn" (or click on the news icon). As the program begins, rn searches the .newsrc file to see if there are any new groups, and if there are it prompts you, asking whether you would like to have the newsgroup added to your regular reading.

> Note: The .newsrc file contains a listing of all the newsgroups maintained by your site. It also keeps a record of the articles you have read. It is generated automatically the first time you invoke the newsreader

(Responding with the single keystroke "y" or "n" will either add that particular newsgroup to your .newsrc file or skip it. Don't worry if you decide to skip one: you can always add it later.)

When you complete the run of new newsgroups (or if there are no new newsgroups to add), the newsreader will present you with the list of your subscribed newsgroups with unread mail along with the number of unread items in each, allowing you the option to read all or part of the selection.

> Note: The following commands are particularly useful at this point:
>
> **L**   Will give you a list of all newsgroups supported at your site
>
> **g <newsgroup name>**   Will subscribe you to the newsgroup of your choice
>
> Note also that the commands indicated in this chapter are case-sensitive: an "1" is different from typing an "L" and the two commands will produce different results.

The menu will look something like this:

```
Unread news in alt.internet.services      5 articles

Unread news in philosophy.objectivism     1 article

Unread news in rec.arts.books             12 articles

*****    5 articles in alt.internet.services--read now?

[ynq]
```

The [ynq] prompt reflects your three possible choices:

y   Yes, read this newsgroup now.

n   No, skip this newsgroup for the time being (you can come back to it later).

q   Quit the newsreader.

> Note: When you are confronted with a selection of choices—such as [ynq]—the first element (in this case the "y") is the default value. In this case, hitting the space bar is the same as hitting the "y" key.

Though they are not offered by the screen prompt, there are many more commands that can be given at this level. Here are some of the more important ones:

=   This will select the newsgroup for reading but it will also list the subject lines before opening the individual messages.

n (lower case) Go to the next subscribed newsgroup with unread news.

N (upper case) Go to the next newsgroup.

p (lowercase) Go to the previous newsgroup with unread news.

P (upper case) Go to the previous newsgroup.

^   Go the first newsgroup with unread news.

g <newsgroup> Go to the specified newsgroup. If you are not subscribed to it already, you will be prompted as to whether you wish to do so.

l   Lists completely unsubscribed newsgroups.

L   List the newsgroup names as in the .newsrc file. This will include additional information on each newsgroup: (1) the number assigned to the newsgroup in the .newsrc file, (2) the states (subscribed or no unread articles), (3) the newsgroup name, and (4) the total number of articles posted.

c   Catch-up—marks all unread articles in this newsgroup as read.

> Note: For a complete list of commands at this level, see the manual pages for rn. (For example, type "man rn" at the Unix prompt.)

At this level, then, responding with a "y" or with a tap of the spacebar (if "y" is the default value) will allow you to read the first unread message—and it will also place you at the Article Selection Level.

The Article Selection Level

When you choose to read a newsgroup, rn automatically takes you into the first available article. If the article is a long one—more than one page long—hitting the spacebar will advance you to the next page.

> Note: Hitting the "n" key will skip you to the next article.

At the end of the article, you will be presented with a prompt, something like the following:

```
End of article 1543 (of 1548)--what next? [npq]
```

At this point, you are at the Article Selection Level. You again have many options; some of the more important ones are these:

[spacebar]	Go to the next article.
b	Go back one page.
n	Go to the next unread article.
^N (Control-N)	Go to the next article with the same subject line. This will make ^N (subject search) the default.
p	Go back to the previous unread article.
P	Go back to the previous article, whether read or unread.

> Note: Use this command to read old news articles. You can search previous articles at the article selection level by typing a significant keyword, using this format:
>
> ?<keyword>?r

^P   Go back to the previous article with the same subject.

j   "Junks" (i.e., marks as read) the current article.

k   Kills all the subsequent articles with the same subject line. (You can also create a "kill file" to mark as read automatically any article with the same subject line.)

m   Marks the current article as unread.

s   Hitting "s" will save the post to a file—either to "mbox" or to a file you specify (s <filename>).

u   Unsubscribe to this newsgroup.

c   Catch up in the newsgroup (mark all articles as read).

r   Reply to this message.

R   Reply to this message and add the current message to your reply.

q   Quit reading this newsgroup.

Once again, there are many additional commands. See the rn manual pages for details.

> Note: Some articles or parts of articles arrive encrypted in the "rot13" mode. (There are various reasons for this: to avoid revealing the surprise ending of a movie, to shield the reader from potentially offensive material, etc.) Rot13 is a simple encryption code that merely "rotates" each letter of the alphabet to a letter 13 steps forward (i.e., a=m, b=n, etc.). Use the command ^X to restart the article and to decrypt the message.

The Pager Level

The Pager Level is within the article. While you are reading messages, the following commands will prove useful:

[space bar]   If the post is more than a single screenful, hitting the spacebar will move you down a page. If the message is one page or less, hitting the spacebar will take you to the next message.

d   Display half a page more.

b   Go back one page.

q   Go to the end of the current article.

j   Junk the current article.

x   Display next page and decrypt as a rot13 message.

> Note: The command "h" will provide a complete listing of available commands.

Posting Articles to News

There are three ways to post articles to newsgroups: reply, follow-up, and Pnews.

> Note: When you post an article to a newsgroup, you want to take care to choose the geographic distribution that is appropriate for your article. For example, an announcement of a meeting of a local horticultural club does not merit worldwide distribution.

Reply

Use the reply mode when you are reading an article and you want to post a response to it. Two commands are available:

r   When you are in a news article, this command will send a response to the message you are reading.

R	This command is the same as "r"—except that it will include the text of the original message (which you should edit, deleting material that is extraneous to your response).

rn will automatically start your text editor (such as emacs or vi). Type your response. When you are finished, exit from the text editor (in vi, for example, type <ESC>:wq). At this point, rn will prompt you with the following message:

```
Send, abort, edit, or list?
```

Enter the first letter of the choice you would like, according to the following:

Send	This will send the message to the newsgroup.
abort	This will abandon the message session.
edit	This will allow you to make changes to the message.
list	This will allow you to see the message displayed on the screen.

Follow-up

Like the reply command, follow-up also has two similar commands:

f	Submits a follow-up article.
F	Submits a follow-up article and includes the old article.

Note: rn has an -F option that allows you to specify the left margin's prefixes to the quoted material (the default being >).

Choose one of the options and type your message. Again, your text editor will be called up.

Pnews

With rn, you can also post to newsgroups from your system prompt. At the prompt, type

```
Pnews <newsgroup name>
```

You will be prompted to provide the geographical distribution for your post.

> Note: If you would like additional help with rn, consult the on-line manual.

Other Newsreaders

There are many other newsreaders, the most popular of which are nn, tin, and trn.

nn

To start: type "nn" at the system prompt (or select the news icon in X Windows). For help, type

```
?

:help [for additional help]
```

tin

To start: type "tin" at the system prompt (or select the news icon in X Windows). For help, type "h"

trn

To start: type "trn" at the system prompt (or select the news icon in X Windows). For help, type "h"

Selected Newsgroups

The following newsgroups may be of interest to people in the humanities (but see also the RESOURCES section of this book: "USENET NEWS—Active Newsgroups"):

```
alt.answers
alt.art.com
alt.best.of.internet
alt.binaries.pictures.
    fine-art.digitized
alt.books.anne-rice
```

alt.books.reviews

alt.censorship

alt.comp.acad-freedom.news

alt.comp.acad-freedom.talk

alt.cult-movies

alt.etext

alt.fan.rumpole

alt.fan.woody-allen

alt.feminism

alt.gopher

alt.hypertext

alt.internet.services

alt.music.progressive

alt.mythology

alt.postmodern

alt.prose

alt.prose.d

alt.revisionism

alt.stagecraft

alt.usage.english

bit.listserv.allmusic

bit.listserv.cinema-l

bit.listserv.film-l

bit.listserv.gutnberg

bit.listserv.literary

clari.news.arts

clari.news.briefs

comp.ai

comp.ai.philosophy

comp.edu

comp.edu.composition

comp.infosystems.gopher

comp.infosystems.www.misc

comp.infosystems.www.providers

comp.infosystems.www.users

comp.internet.net-happenings

comp.os.ms-windows.announce

comp.os.ms-windows.apps

comp.os.ms-windows.misc

comp.os.msdos.misc

comp.text.sgml

misc.writing

news.announce.newsgroups

news.answers

rec.arts.books

rec.arts.cinema

rec.arts.dance

rec.arts.fine

rec.arts.int-fiction

rec.arts.misc

rec.arts.movies

rec.arts.movies.reviews

rec.arts.poems

rec.arts.prose

rec.arts.sf-lovers

rec.arts.sf.misc

rec.arts.sf-reviews

rec.arts.sf-announce

rec.arts.sf.fandom

rec.arts.sf.marketplace

rec.arts.sf.misc

rec.arts.sf.movies

rec.arts.sf.reviews

rec.arts.theatre

rec.arts.tv

rec.fine.arts

rec.food.cooking

rec.food.drink

rec.food.restaurants

rec.gardens

rec.music

rec.music.cd

rec.music.classical

rec.music.classical.guitar

rec.music.classical.performing

rec.music.folk

rec.music.misc

rec.music.reviews

rec.puzzles.crosswords

rec.running

rec.sport.baseball

rec.sport.basketball

rec.sport.football

rec.travel

sci.logic

sci.philosophy.meta

sci.philosophy.tech

soc.answers

soc.college.teaching-asst

soc.culture.african

soc.culture.british

soc.culture.celtic

soc.culture.french

soc.culture.german

soc.culture.greek

soc.culture.europe

soc.history

soc.culture.italian

soc.culture.mexico

soc.culture.soviet

soc.culture.spain

```
soc.feminism

soc.history

soc.women


talk.philosophy.misc
```

Getting a Complete List of Usenet Newsgroups

For a complete listing of newsgroups, anonymous FTP to ftp.uu.net.

Suggestions for Further Reading

Fristrup, Jenny A. *Usenet: Netnews for Everyone*. Englewood Cliffs, NJ: Prentice
Hall, 1994.

Todino, Grace and Dale Dougherty. *Using UUCP and Usenet*. Sebastopol, CA:
O'Reilly & Associates, 1991.

Veljkov, Mark and George Hartnell. *Using and Navigating Usenet*. Westport, CT:
Meckler, 1994.

Gopher

- Gopherspace • Connecting to Gopherspace
- The Gopher Menu • Maneuvering Within Gopherspace
- Moving Within a Menu Level • Moving Through the
Gopherspace Hierarchy • Gopher Mailservers
- Exploring Gopher

Gopherspace

If the Internet is a highway, gopher is a chauffeur. Give it simple directions, and it will take you where you want to go—even if you don't look out the car window on your journey. Upon arriving, you don't have to know where you are or how you got there. And your chauffeur won't bother telling you how you got there. The windows on this limousine are tinted on the inside as well—all you know is that you went on a journey. But the chauffeur is unusually reliable. Gopher will get you there and bring you back.

Gopher is a search tool for accessing hierarchically arranged data, and it operates by way of "links" to various sites. These links are transparent to the user, and the files may be on the local computer or at another computer halfway around the world. Select a menu item that seems useful, and the gopher software does the rest. (The software was created at the University of Minnesota and takes its name from the school's mascot—the Golden Gophers. It is a particularly apt name for software that "burrows" into the net, finding otherwise hidden resources for the user.)

Connecting to Gopherspace

If your computer system or service provides a gopher connection, you should be able to access simply by typing a command such as "gopher" at the system prompt or by selecting gopher as a menu item, or by clicking your mouse on the Gopher icon.

Most systems will also allow you to make direct gopher connections to foreign hosts. So, for example, you might type at the system prompt the following:

```
gopher infoslug.ucsc.edu
```

This should establish a direct connection to the gopher at the University of California, Santa Cruz.

If your system does not support gopher, you can still make a connection through a host computer in a telnet session. For example, at the system prompt, give the following command:

```
telnet consultant.micro.umn.edu
```

login: gopher

> Note: Although you will be able to make connections to other gopher sites through this address, this connection will provide you with only limited capabilities. For example, you will not be able to use the "m" function to mail a file back to your own computer.

> For some publicly accessible gopher sites, telnet to one of the following:
>
> ```
> consultant.micro.umn.edu
> ```
>
> login: `gopher`
>
> ```
> infoslug.ucsc.edu
> ```
>
> login: `infoslug`
>
> ```
> infopath.ucsd.edu
> ```
>
> login: `infopath`

The Gopher Menu

Here is a sample gopher screen, this one taken from the introductory gopher screen at the University of Illinois at Urbana-Champaign:

Internet Gopher Information Client v2.0.14
University of Illinois at Urbana-Champaign

1.	Welcome to the U. of Illinois at Urbana-Champaign Gopher
2.	Campus Announcements/
3.	What's New?/
4.	Information about Gopher/
5.	Keyword Search of UIUC Gopher Menus <?>
6.	Univ. of Illinois at Urbana-Champaign Campus Information/
7.	Champaign-Urbana & Regional Information/
8.	Computer Documentation, Software, and Information/
9.	Libraries and Reference Information/
10.	Publications (U of I Press,Newspapers, Newsletters, etc.)& Weath./
11.	Other Gopher and Information Servers/
12.	Phone Books (ph)/
13.	Internet File Server (ftp) Sites/

There are several important features of the gopher screen.

1. The top line will let you know that you are in the Gopher menu and will announce the version of the software client.

2. The second line will let you know the title of this gopher site, in this case the University of Illinois at Urbana-Champaign.

3. The menu proper here consists of 13 numbered items, any one of which you may select. The items may be further broken down into three parts:

   a. Along the left margin are the item numbers (here, 1–13):

   b. the descriptive titles; and

   c. the terminal marks.

Note: The terminal marks are important. They indicate the type of link for each item. Here is a thumbnail summary of the different types of marks you will encounter and explanations as to what they represent:

/	Choose an item with this mark, a slash, and you will be taken to a submenu.
.	Choose an item with a period and you will find a text file.
\<TEL>	Choosing an item marked with this will initiate a telnet session with a remote host. Usually, you will be able to terminate this session by using the "Ctrl-]" command.
\<?>	The question mark indicates a searchable database.
\<CSO>	This is a name server. Selecting this item will permit you to search for the name and e-mail address of an individual at this site.
\<Picture>	This indicates a binary file. Do not access this file unless your gopher client is configured with the appropriate viewer software. Also, be aware that these tend to be very large files, which will take a long time to download.

Maneuvering Within Gopherspace

If you are new to gopherspace, you might want to set aside some free time for exploring. If you are curious by nature, you will undoubtedly be gratified, for gophering is a serendipitous experience.

At the introductory—and each subsequent—menu screen, you can maneuver by using just the arrow keys.

Note: The following basic commands will assist you in your travels in gopherspace. Use the following arrow keys:

Up   Move up a line
Down   Move down a line
Right (or [return])   Select current item
Left (or [u])   Exit current item

Instead of using the arrow keys, you could also enter the number of the item you wish to select and hit the enter key. That will take you one item down into the menu hierarchy. Typing the letter "u" will take you back up.

One particularly useful command in the gopher system is bookmarks. If you happen to find a gopher site that is especially noteworthy, you can mark it with your own personal bookmark. By doing so you are saving a reference. In the same way that a literal bookmark will save a page in your favorite novel, the gopher bookmark will save to file a reference to a gopher site that you wish to revisit at some later time. The advantage of using the bookmark is that when you do want to go back to the site, you can do so directly, without having to negotiate through the hierarchical levels of the gopher menu system.

Useful Gopher Commands

Bookmark Commands:

a   Add current item to the bookmark list
A   Add current directory/search to bookmark list
v   View bookmark list
d   Delete a bookmark/directory entry

Other Commands:

s   Save current item to a file
m   Mail current file to your account
D   Download a file
q   Quit with prompt
Q   Quit without prompt
o   Open a new gopher server
O   Change options
/   Search for an item in the menu
n   Find next search item

Moving Within a Menu Level

If a menu selection takes up more than one screen, the number will appear on the lower right of the screen, such as 1/2 or 1/13, meaning the current screen is the first of two or the first of thirteen screens. You can move backwards and forwards among these various screens by using the spacebar (to move forward) or the "b" (to go back).

Moving Through the Gopherspace Hierarchy

To move down a hierarchy, select the item of the number you wish to investigate. You can do this either by using the arrow keys to move the cursor and then hitting the return key or by simply typing the item number you wish and then hitting the return key. The result will be the same: You will move down one level in the gopher hierarchy.

Gopher Mailservers

You can connect to the resources of gopher even without accessing a gopher menu or even without having Internet access (save e-mail). Just use a Gopher-Mail server. It works by mailing successive menus of Gopher screens, which you mark and return to the GopherMail server. When you mark an item, that menu screen is returned to you. By negotiating through Gopher menus in this fashion, you will eventually retrieve the information that you desire. Granted, it is not as convenient having direct Gopher access, but the program is a sophisticated search mechanism which has a number of useful options (such as splitting messages after a certain file size is reached). To get a guide to using GopherMail, send an e-mail message to one of the following (with a simple "help"—without quotation marks—as the message):

gophermail@calvin.edu

or

gopher@ucmp1.berkeley.edu

Exploring Gopher

The essential starting point for an investigation of gopherspace is the gopher-jewels site, which can be accessed by gophering to:

```
cwis.usc.edu 70
```

path: Other Gophers and Information Resources
Gophers by Subject
Gopher Jewels

Note: You will sometimes see the number "70" (or another number) after the gopher address. This is the particular "port" that gopher is run on. The number 70 is the default for gopher sites. It is not necessary to type that number. The connection should occur whether you use it in the address or not. For example, both of these addresses should work:

```
cwis.usc.edu 70
```

or

```
cwis.usc.edu
```

However, if another number is given in the gopher address such as in this hypothetical address:

```
cwis.usc.edu 3001
```

then you must include the number when making the connection.

Suggestions for Further Reading

Sachs, David and Henry Stair. *Hands-On Internet: A Beginning Guide for PC Users.* Englewood Cliffs, NJ: Prentice Hall, 1994.

World Wide Web

- What Is the World Wide Web? • Accessing the Web
- URLs • Using a Graphical Browser • Using Lynx
- Using Line Mode

What Is the World Wide Web?

As a convenient means of accessing the Internet, the Wide World Web (usually referred to as WWW or sometimes as W3) is quickly growing in popularity, and for good reason. Its hypertext format has significant advantages over other forms of access, including greater flexibility in the presentation of information. In brief, "hypertext" means that a document is not constrained by the traditional limits of a text—that is, where information is presented in linear fashion, starting at the beginning of a document and proceeding logically to a conclusion. Instead, in hypertext, information is presented on an "as needed" basis. If the user accesses a hypertext document and begins reading about Beethoven (Document A), and comes across a reference to the Fifth Symphony, he or she can pause at that point, open a second file (Document B) by clicking the mouse on the word "Fifth," and read about that subject. (The pre-established link has previously been made by the maintainer of the first document—the current user does not have to worry about where the new document is located.) Upon completing that reading, he or she can revert to the original file (Document A) to complete a reading of that file.

> Note: Depending on the software being used in the WWW connection (Line browser, Lynx, or Mosaic), the user will make the link to another document by typing an item number, using the return key, or clicking the mouse.

The links between Document A and Document B are transparent; that is, the user does not need to know that it is even a separate document. Moreover, it is not even necessary for Documents A and B to be at the same physical location. Document A could be located on a computer in Ann Arbor, Michigan; Document B could be in Switzerland. The software "links" that connect the two documents are pre-established. Not only are more WWW sites being added daily, but existing sites are constantly being revised to add more links, resulting in the growth of connections that eventually promises to be a virtual library of inexhaustible information in almost every field of interest.

But the WWW is more than a hypertext. It is also a hypermedia format. That is, it is not simply texts, but it also encompasses visual and auditory media. So, for example, to continue the example begun above, in coming across a reference to Beethoven's Fifth Symphony, the user may connect to a text file that tells more about that work, to an audio file which plays a sample of the opening bars, or to a visual image of the original score. Needless to say, the possibilities are staggering.

Accessing the Web

There are two ways to access the WWW, either through a Web browser or through line mode, which we will examine later in this chapter.

The Web browsers are, by far, the most popular forms of access, and they fall into two categories: (1) graphical interfaces (such as Mosaic and Netscape), and (2) character-based interfaces (such as Lynx). Browsers such as Mosaic and Netscape are far more popular than Lynx simply because of their stunning use of graphics. On the other hand, because Lynx does not transfer huge binary files (a necessary component of graphical interfaces), it is much faster and gets the job done quicker.

Before we discuss WWW in detail, it is important to define a very important element, URLs. WWW connections, like all remote connections (gopher, telnet, FTP), depend on a uniform method of designation. Uniform Resource Locators (URLs) fit the prescription. URLs are unique electronic addresses for various access modes and sites. Examples of URLs include the following:

WWW	http://sunsite.unc.edu
gopher	gopher//gopher.mit.edu
telnet	telnet://library.princeton.edu
FTP	ftp://ftp.etext.org

Often you will find these presented without the prefix. That is, the first example above might be listed simply as

sunsite.unc.edu

Sometimes this address is also given in its numerical form:

198.86.40.81

Anatomy of a URL

URLs have identifiable constituent parts.

Protocol:	Identifies whether the software is WWW, gopher, telnet, etc.
Separator:	://
Address:	The unique Internet address. This will have either a hostname or an IP Number.
Port number:	Different ports at a single address may be dedicated to a unique function. For example, Gopher is usually port 70 (though that number may be omitted; if the address is configured differently, the port number could be another number, in which case, it must be specified).
Path:	The subdirectory where the specific file is found.

Here is an illustration:

http://www.lysator.liu.se:7500/sf_archive/sf_main.html

This is the site for computer-interested students at Linkvping University in Sweden. Its WWW address breaks down like this:

Protocol	http (the designation for the www)
Separator	://
Address	lysator.liu.se
Port	:7500
Path	/sf_archive/sf_main.html

Using a Graphical Browser

One of the most popular graphical browsers available is Mosaic, which has significant advantages over browsers such as Lynx. It makes stunning use of graphics, and its handling of links is visually appealing and very intuitive. It also has a full range of options that allows the user maximum convenience and practicality (from creating personal annotations for links, to keeping a HotList of essential URLs, to keeping a record of all links).

At the system prompt, click on the Mosaic icon or at the system prompt type

```
Mosaic
```

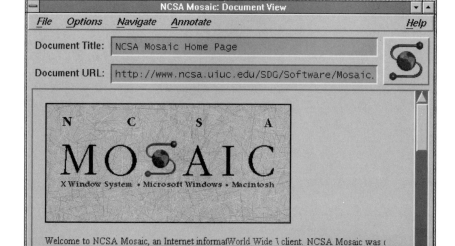

Across the top of the Mosaic screen, you will find the following menu items:

File   Options   Navigate   Annotate

Click your mouse on "File" and a drop-down menu with numerous items will appear.

New Window

Close Window

Open URL

Open Local

[others deleted]

The choices are in large measure intuitive, and with a little experimentation you will quickly discover the range of Mosaic's power. However, it is enough to know only a few of the options. The most important for our purposes now is the selection "Open URL." Point your cursor to that item and click the mouse. A box will open in the center of your screen. It will have tabs for the following four options: "open," "clear," "dismiss," and "help." It will also have a window for entering a WWW address. Using your mouse, place your cursor within the window that opens and type in a WWW address.

> Note: If you recall, URL is an acronym for Uniform Resource Locator. Every Web site has its own unique address, each beginning with "http:// . . ." At this point you might check the RESOURCES section and select one of the many web sites listed there. I would recommend the "roulette" site at the University of Kansas, which connects to a new WWW site at random.
>
> `http://kuhttp.cc.ukans.edu/cwis/organizations/`
> `kucia/uroulette/uroulette.html`
>
> Note also that you will not be able to type in the address unless the cursor is within the window. After you try the "roulette" site, try the home page of Prentice Hall at:
>
> http://www.prenhall.com

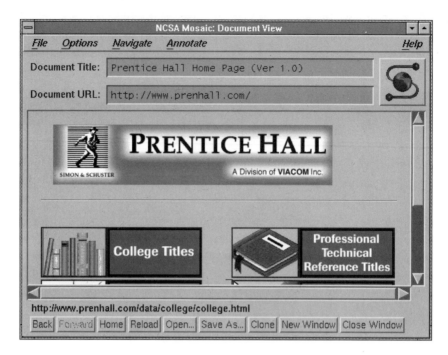

After you type in a complete address (remember to type carefully and to double-check the result), move your cursor to "Open," and click the mouse. The globe in the upper right corner of the screen will become active, indicating that a connection is in progress. Be patient. Since some web sites have considerable art and graphic images on their home pages, it may take some time for the appropriate files to transfer and for the screen to open.

> Note: If you believe that a link will have a lot of graphics, use the Delay Pictures option for a faster connection.

An activity bar on the lower part of your screen will indicate the progression of the files transferred. When the new home page appears on your screen, your connection has been established.

How to Interrupt a Transmission

Many of the files involved in the Mosaic connections are extremely large and may take some time. If the globe in the upper right-hand corner of the screen is spinning, a connection is in progress. To stop a transmission, simply place the cursor on the globe and click the mouse.

The Mosaic screen will present you with three important elements: the scroll bar, the menu bar, and the home page with highlighted links.

The Scroll Bar

Along the right side of the screen will be a thin scroll bar. If you place your cursor on the scroll box, depress the left button on your mouse and move the cursor downward, the text and images on the screen will "scroll" up, revealing more of the home page. (This, of course, assumes that the home page is longer than one page, and most of them are.) Even if you are a novice Windows user, this procedure will be very familiar to you.

The Menu Bar

Along the bottom of the screen will be a menu bar that will provide you with many choices:

Back Forward Home Reload Open Save As Close New Window Close Window

All of these commands can be invoked by clicking the mouse. These commands allow you to perform the following tasks:

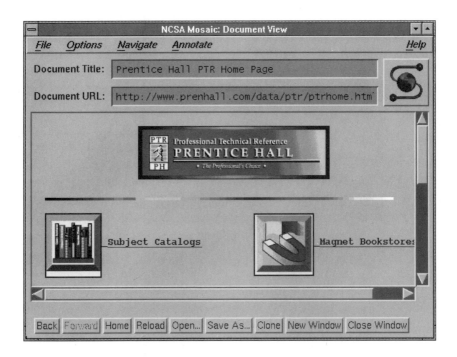

Back	This will allow you to navigate through the web hierarchy. At the home page, this function is disabled—because there is no "back." You are at the starting point.
Forward	This allows you to go forward into the web hierarchy.
Home	Will take you to the home page.
Reload	Refreshes the screen.
Open	Allows you to open a new web home page by prompting you for a new URL.
Save As	Allows you to save a document to your home directory on your own computer.
Close	Closes the home page.
New Window	Opens another Mosaic window.
Close Window	Closes the Mosaic window.

The Home Page and Highlighted Links

Within the home page, there will be some words or phrases that are highlighted by different-colored fonts. These are hypertext links that will take you to related documents. If you place your cursor on one of those elements and click the mouse, Mosaic will connect you to a new screen.

When you return from a link to the previous page, you will notice that the link is no longer highlighted by a different-colored font. This is to help you remember which links you have already made, which files you have already read.

> Note: If you are interested in creating your own home page, use the File-View Source option to view the source that creates a page that you particularly admire. The View Source option allows you to see the complex formatting that lies behind the finished image.

To exit from Mosaic, click your mouse on the Close Window option.

> Note: For information on obtaining browsers such as Lynx and Mosaic, see the RESOURCES—WWW section.

Using Lynx

If you do not have access to a graphical browser such as Mosaic, your system or provider may have Lynx browser software installed.

If your site does not have a Lynx browser, you can telnet to one of these publicly accessible Lynx sites:

ukanaix.cc.ukans.edu   [Kansas]
login: www

www.tky.hut.fi   [Finland]
login: lynx

sunsite.unc.edu   [North Carolina]
login: lynx

Lynx software is also available by anonymous FTP at

ukanaix.cc.ukans.edu
login: anonymous
password: <your e-mail address>
path: pub
    lynx

Though Lynx is not as popular (nor as sophisticated a browser) as Mosaic, it allows easy mobility on the World Wide Web. As with all telnet connections, always use the closest geographical location (see box above).

The Lynx site at the University of Kansas is an excellent place to begin experimenting with Lynx. This site has many resources, including many electronic texts on line. If you have an interest in such things, you may want to make special note of the following address and path, which we will be accessing in the example that follows:

ukanaix.cc.ukans.edu

path: Inter-Links

    Library Resources

        Poetry

           Beowulf

For the purposes of illustration, suppose the following problem arises. You have an interest in the Old English poem *Beowulf* and desire to know at what points in the Old English poem the name Grendel—Beowulf's formidable opponent—appears.

To begin, telnet to the site at the University of Kansas, using the following command:

```
telnet ukanaix.cc.ukans.edu
```

or you can use the numeric address for the same site:

```
telnet 129.237.33.1
```

At the login prompt, respond with

```
www
```

At the prompt for terminal type, choose

```
vt100
```

Note: In this case—and on many other occasions—the host machine will not only prompt you for a terminal type, but it will also present you with a default value. For example, the following will appear on your screen:

```
Your Terminal type is unknown!
Enter a terminal type: [vt100]
```

The bracketed response (vt100) is the standard terminal emulation for remote log-ins. Since the host already provides that as the default value (giving it to you in brackets), you simply have to hit the return key in order to establish that emulation.

The directions at the bottom of the screen indicate that you should hit the space bar to go to the second page of the opening menu. Do so, and the new screen will offer the following two choices:

```
* WWW Information By Type
```

```
*Inter-Links, Internet access made easy
```

The commands at the bottom of the screen indicate that the major means of navigating are by using the arrow keys.

Arrow key	Action
Up and Down	Takes you through a menu
Right	Links to the highlighted item
Left	Returns you to the previous menu

> Note: Type `help` at any point for more information.

Use the down arrow key until the cursor is on "`Inter-Links, Internet access made easy`." By hitting the return key, you will link to the following screen:

```
INTRODUCTION

*About Inter-Links
*New Features

FEATURES

*Internet Resources
*Fun and Games
*Guides and Tutorials
*News and Weather
*Library Resources
*Reference Shelf
*Miscellaneous
*Search Inter-Links
*Feedback
```

Then choose in succession the following menu items by using the up and down arrows to select and then hitting the return key:

```
Library Resources [return]
Poetry [return]
Beowulf [return]
```

With the final selection ("`Beowulf`"), you are in the text file of the poem, a 1910 translation by Francis B. Gummere. (This text was originally published as volume 49 of the *Harvard Classics* and is now in the public domain.)

> Note: Many of the commands available in Lynx are displayed across the bottom of the screen. For additional information, type "H" for help.

At this point, you can search for any text within the poem. To initiate the search, hit the "/" key. You will be prompted for text to search for. Type in

```
Grendel
```

and hit the return key. At this point, you will be at the first mention of the name Grendel in the poem. To find the next mention of the name, type

```
n
```

The on-screen commands for the Lynx program are self-explanatory; additional commands can be found in the help file, activated by hitting "H".

To go back through the various levels to the main menu, use the left arrow key. After you have sated your curiosity in exploring at this site, type "Q" to quit. You will be prompted with a "Y" to quit. Hit [enter] to do so.

Note: Here is a summary of the more useful Lynx commands:

up/down arrows	move between menu selections
right arrow	jump to highlighted topic
left arrow	return to previous topic
+ (or space)	scroll down next page
- (or b)	scroll up to previous page
?	help
d	download the current link
m	return to main screen
p	mail a file to you
q	Quit
Q	Quick quit
/	Search for a string in current doc
n	Go to the next search string
z	Cancel transfer in progress
CTRL-R	Reload current file/refresh screen
CTRL-U	Erase input line
CTRL-G	Cancel input or transfer

Using Line Mode

Obviously, some people will not have access to a browser, but they can still access the World Wide Web via a simple telnet connection. Line mode is the least sophisticated of the access methods. Though this method lacks the graphics capability that comes with a program such as Mosaic, it does allow one access to the text at WWW sites.

```
Some publicly accessible WWW sites:

telnet.w3.org
login: [none needed]

vms.huji.ac.il
login: WWW
(See also RESOURCES-—WWW)
```

When accessing WWW in line mode, you are confronted with a succession of text screens, all of which have bracketed numbered choices embedded
within them. To try this out, telnet to the following site:

```
telnet telnet.w3.org
```

The first screen that appears will have (among other things) the following:

```
A list of available W3 client programs[1]
Everything about the W3 project[2]
Places to start exploring[3]
The First International WWW Conference[4]

This telnet service is provided by the WWW team at the Eu-
ropean Particle Physics Laboratory known as CERN[5]
```

> Note: If you are curious as to where these links connect to,
> type "L" [return] for a list which gives the specific URL for
> each number.

The lower left portion at the bottom of the screen will contain the following:

```
1-5, Up, Quit, or Help:
```

The numbers 1–5 indicate that this web page has a total of five links.

The cursor will be sitting after the colon, awaiting a command. At this
point, you may choose any number (one through five), any of the commands
listed after the numbers ("U," "Q," or "H"), or any of the commands in the
Help menu.

Up   Takes you back one screen in the current menu.

Quit   Takes you out of the Web.

Help   Gives you a list of additional commands.

For example, type the number "3," "Places to start exploring," and a link will be established to that file. A new screen will appear that gives the user additional choices, each of them numbered. The best thing to do at this point is to start exploring. Each number selected will take the user deeper into the Web.

If you reach a page that has more options than can fit on a single screen, the command might look something like this:

```
1-111, Back, Up, <RETURN> for more, Quit, or Help:
```

In this case, there are 111 links, only a few of which are presented on the screen at one time. On this command line, there are two additional options:

Back   Takes you back to the previous menu.

<RETURN> for more   Takes you to the next screen of the current menu.

It is also possible to connect directly to other WWW sites by using the GO command. In order to use this, just type in a valid URL of another Web site. Though it is not displayed at the bottom of the screen, the "go" command can be typed just like any of the commands that are there (e.g., "**1-5**, **U**p, **Q**uit, or **H**elp"). For example, type

```
Go http://www.infi.net/vadiner/vadiner.html
```

and you will be connected to the home page of the Virginia Diner Restaurant in Wakefield, Virginia. You will be able to examine the menu, order a gift catalogue, and even find a new recipe.

To disconnect from the WWW at any point, type

```
Quit
```

Suggestion for Further Reading

Sachs, David and Henry Stair. *Hands-On Mosaic: A Tutorial for Windows Users.* Englewood Cliffs, NJ: Prentice Hall, 1995.

Telnet and FTP

Introduction

While Gopher and WWW allow you to make very elegant, seamless connections with other computers, telnet and FTP are a bit more obtrusive and demand a little more expertise. However, on the plus side, they give you more immediate control over what you are doing, and the satisfaction that obtains after the first successful FTP session can rank among the small pleasures of life. At any rate, with telnet and FTP, as with Gopher and WWW, users initiate commands that link them to computers at other locations.

This chapter approaches telnet and FTP from a Unix per-spective, which is still a widely used operating system. However, an ever-increasing number of Internet users ac-cess these tools in window-type environments. For exam-ple, to use FTP on America OnLine, the user simply points the mouse and clicks on "Internet Connection," then (on the next screen) on "FTP." Users of such systems can skip this chapter. However, users who do not have access to window-type interfaces as well as those who would like a better understanding of FTP and telnet, this chapter is es-sential reading.

Telnet

In many ways, telnet is the simpler of the two procedures. To "telnet" means to make a connection with a remote machine. This connection allows you to use the remote host. The software that permits this connection resides on the system where your computer account is held. One can, for example, telnet to databases and library catalogues at other sites and institutions. (And if you are away from home, you can telnet to your home computer system to read your e-mail.)

Making a Telnet Connection

Note: To make a telnet connection, you must either have an account on the host machine or the host must be a publicly accessible site.

To illustrate a telnet session, we will make a telnet connection to a publicly ac-cessible gopher site. (See the "Gopher" chapter for additional public sites.)

To begin a telnet session from your system prompt, type

```
telnet infoslug.ucsc.edu
```

After a short wait, a log-in prompt should appear. In response, type

```
gopher
```

In response to the TERM = (vt100) prompt, use the default value (vt100) by hitting only your return key. A policy statement will appear on your screen. Then instructions will appear that say you should

```
Press RETURN to continue
```

After that, a gopher screen will appear. You might explore this site if you are interested. When you want to exit from the site, hit

```
q
```

You will be prompted as to whether you really want to quit. Since the default value is "yes," you merely have to hit return to accomplish the task. This will probably leave you at your system prompt.

> Note: If upon ending a telnet session you find yourself at the TELNET> prompt, you can exit from that by first typing
>
> ```
> close
> ```
>
> to close the telnet connection. If after you do that the TELNET> prompt still remains, type
>
> ```
> quit
> ```
>
> If the "close" and "quit" commands do not allow you to exit from the telnet prompt, type help or ? at the prompt for a description of possible commands.

A Second Telnet Session: Some Variations

As a second example, we will telnet to another public gopher site, the Public Access Catalogue (PAC) at CARL. Telnet connections to any site can be made by using either the host name or the numeric address. At CARL, these addresses are "database.carl.org" and "192.54.81.76" respectively. At your system prompt, type

```
telnet
```

The Telnet> prompt should appear on your screen. Type the following:

```
open database.carl.org
```

Notice that this time, we did not have to type the word Telnet before the address because the TELNET> prompt was already on the screen.

> Note: If the telnet address also specifies a port number—
> though most often they do not—you will have to add that
> number after the internet address. For example, if the telnet
> address in the example above was port 3001 (and it is not—
> I am merely illustrating), your telnet command would have
> been:
>
> ```
> telnet database.carl.org 3001
> ```
>
> (with a space before the 3001).

Once the connection is established, you will be prompted to choose a terminal emulation. Usually, VT100 will suffice. Oftentimes, this terminal emulation is presented as the default value. For example, the prompt might read TERM= (vt100), in which case you merely have to hit [enter]. In this case, however, you are asked to choose a numbered selection. Type the number that corresponds to the emulation you desire and press enter. This puts you at the main menu. After you are done exploring at this site, you can terminate your session by typing

```
//exit
```

Essential Telnet Commands

telnet <address>	Used at your system prompt to initiate a telnet session.
open <address>	Used at your telnet prompt to initiate a telnet session.
close	Used to close a telnet session.
Control-]	This usually will break a telnet connection.
quit	Used at your **telnet prompt** to end a telnet session.
display	Display operating parameters.
send	Transmit special characters [type "send?" for a list].
set	Set operating parameters [type "set?" for a list of parameters].
status	Print status information.
toggle	Toggle operating parameters [type "toggle?" for a list of parameters].

| **z** | Suspend telnet session. |
| **?** | Used to get help. |

FTP

One of the most useful tools of the Internet is "anonymous FTP." FTP stands for File Transfer Protocol, but just think of it as meaning **F**etch **T**hose **P**ages (or **P**rograms). Simply put, it allows the user to transfer files from one computer to another. Many sites allow anonymous FTP connections; that is, the user does not need to have an account on the host machine. The user can connect, log in as "anonymous" (usually, one is expected to use his or her e-mail address as the password), and transfer files from any of the publicly accessible subdirectories.

Currently, there are thousands of literary and historical texts, indexes, songs, images, freeware, and software files residing in computers around the world. More are being added every day. These electronic files are, for the most part, available to anyone with a computer and an Internet connection. The software that allows you access to these files is FTP.

Supported by most computer systems, FTP allows you to establish a connection with another computer—the "host"—in order to examine the directories of the host computer and to obtain copies of the files on the host by transferring them back to your own computer. Oftentimes, INDEX or README will be the first file transferred, for files such as these allow you to read a summary of the files available. From the index you should be able to find the name and description of a particular file that you want.

Making an FTP Connection

Finding a File

There are several simple steps involved in executing an FTP.

> Note: Many FTP sites are computers whose time, space, equipment, and other personal resources are loaned against an otherwise very busy schedule of business and/or educational enterprises. Many of these sites request, therefore, that FTP activity take place at off-peak hours. Abuse of this courtesy will eventually result in the closing of the FTP sites. Therefore, every effort should be made to respect the parameters set up at the individual site, usually times other

> than normal business hours. (And remember: If the host
> computer is in another time zone, "normal business hours"
> must be determined by their clock, not yours.)
>
> To find local time of a host computer, try the following
> command:
>
> ```
> telnet <address> daytime
> ```
>
> This will usually produce the following information: day,
> date, time, and year.

1. The first step in the FTP process is to log on to your computer system and then at the command prompt type

```
ftp [ENTER]
```

After you hit enter, your prompt should change to

```
FTP>
```

2. Next you will open a connection with another computer. Let us assume that you want to establish a connection to the Gutenberg E-texts at the University of Illinois. After the FTP prompt (FTP>), type

```
open mrcnext.cso.uiuc.edu [ENTER]
```

This is a computer at the University of Illinois, Urbana–Champaign. The electronic texts we will be searching for reside in the following subdirectory: /pub/etext/etext93.

> Note: Just as one can use either the host name or the numer-
> ical address to establish telnet sessions, one can also use
> both types of address to establish FTP sessions. In this case,
> you could have given the following command:
>
> ```
> open 128.174.201.12
> ```

3. When a connection is established, a login request will appear on the screen:

```
Name (mrcnext.cso.uiuc.edu:clark):
```

Type

```
anonymous [ENTER]
```

4. Next, the following request appears:

Password:

Enter your e-mail address. For example, I would enter

clark@cs.widener.edu [ENTER]

On your screen, steps 1 – 4 above would look something like this:

```
% ftp
ftp> open mrcnext.cso.uiuc.edu
Connected to mrcnext.cso.uiuc.edu.
220 mrcnext.cso.uiuc.edu FTP server (Version 5.1 (NeXT
1.0) Tue Jul 21, 1993) ready.
Name (mrcnext.cso.uiuc.edu:clark): ftp
331 Guest login ok, send ident as password.
Password:
230 Guest login ok, access restrictions apply.
ftp>
```

At this point, the cursor will be sitting after the FTP prompt. It might appear as if nothing has changed, but you are connected to the host machine. You can check this by typing

ls   [ENTER]

After you do so, the screen will fill with a listing of the root directory's files and directories, something like this:

```
ftp> ls
200 PORT command successful.
150 Opening ASCII mode data connection for file list.
amiga
bin
wp
zip93
etc
etext
cache
```
[many directories and files deleted]
```
etext92
gutnberg.doc
lists
pcsig2
pub
226 Transfer complete.
186 bytes received in 0.081 seconds (2.2 Kbytes/s)
```

By typing the "ls" command in our previous example, we requested a great deal of information to be sent to our terminal, but it is useful to receive even more, which we can do by giving a command like the following:

```
dir
```

or

```
ls -l
```

Either of these will give the same file names as the "ls" command, but with much additional information, producing a screen similar to the following:

```
ftp> ls -l
200 PORT command successful.
150 Opening ASCII mode data connection for /bin/ls.
total 137
-rw-r--r--   1 187       1579 Jun  4  2000 README
-rw-r--r--   1 109       1798 Jan  4  2000 README.bak
drwxrwxr-x   2 root      1024 Oct  4  1999 amiga
dr-xr-xr-x   2 root      1024 Jul 14  2000 bin
lrwxrwxrwx   1 root         9 Aug 30  2000 cache ->
pub/cache
drwxr-xr-x   2 187       1024 Mar  8  2000 compucom
drwxr-xr-x   2 root      1024 Sep  6  1999 etc
lrwxrwxrwx   1 root         9 Aug 30  2000 etext ->
pub/etext
drwxr-xr-x   2 24        3072 Jul 22  2001 etext92
lrwxrwxrwx   1 root         5 Jun  4  2000 gutenberg->
etext
-rw-r--r--   1 24        4853 Jan 10  2001 gutnberg.doc
drwxr-xr-x   2 187       1024 May  9  2000 kites
drwxrwxr-x   2 root      1024 Jan 29 19:40 lists
drwxr-xr-x   3 root      1024 Jan 31 12:28 mac
drwxr-xr-x  11 187       2048 Jun 28  2001 nethack
-rw-r--r--   1 109      52064 May 23  2000 odipkt.zip
drwxrwxr-x   9 root      1024 Jul  3  2000 pc
drwxr-xr-x   2 root      1024 Mar  7  2001 pcsig10
drwxr-xr-x   2 187      50176 Oct 24 17:35 pcsig2
drwxrwxr-x   2 root      1024 Dec 19  1999 pspice
drwxrwxr-t   8 root      1024 Jul 16  2001 pub
drwxrwxr-x   2 root      6144 Jun 12  2000 simtel20
```

```
drwxrwxr-x  2 root         1024 Aug 12   2000 uiuc
drwxrwxr-x  2 root         1024 May 21   2000 unix
drwxr-xr-x  3 root         1024 Jun 20   2000 usr
drwxrwxr-x  2 root         1024 Dec 22 00:55 video
drwxr-x---  4 300          1024 Jul 31   2001 wp
drwxr-xr-x  2 24           1024 Jun 19   2001 zip93
226 Transfer complete.
remote: -1
1492 bytes received in 1.6 seconds (0.9 Kbytes/s)
```

The Difference Between Files and Directories

There is an essential piece of information that you need to be aware of: the difference between files and directories.

Files. In the above detailed listing of the directories and files, the single most critical piece of information has to do with the first character of each line in the first column. Note that each line begins either with a "d" or with a "-". The "d" denotes that line is a <u>directory</u>. The "-" indicates that the entry is a <u>file</u>. For example, the first line in the above directory is

```
-rw-r--r--  1 187        1579 Jun  4 2000 README
```

The hyphen in the initial position indicates that README is a *file*.

Directories. The third entry in this directory is the following:

```
drwxrwxr-x  2 root    1024 Oct  4 1999 amiga
```

Since the line begins with a "d," it is a directory. The name of this directory is at the far right: "amiga."

If you wished to do so, we could enter this subdirectory by typing "cd amiga" to find additional subdirectories and files. But at this point, we have not yet found the directory (or subdirectory) we want. We need to go down two additional levels. First type

<code>cd etext</code>

Then type

<code>cd etext93</code>

A message like this will appear:

<code>ftp> cd etext93</code>

<code>250 CWD command successful.</code>

Again, to clarify where we are, type "ls -l":

```
ftp> ls -l
200 PORT command successful.
150 Opening ASCII mode data connection for /bin/ls.
total 21642
-rw-r--r--  1 24       1166473 Sep  2 04:21 2sqrt10.txt
-rw-r--r--  1 24        552131 Sep  2 04:22 2sqrt10.zip
-rw-r--r--  1 24        247391 Dec 31 20:11 32pri10.txt
-rw-r--r--  1 24        124130 Dec 31 20:11 32pri10.zip
-rw-r--r--  1 24         38818 Oct  2 23:37 alad10.txt
-rw-r--r--  1 24         16197 Oct  2 23:03 alad10.zip
-rw-r--r--  1 24        275975 Jan  8 13:17 badge10.txt
-rw-r--r--  1 24        116147 Jan  8 13:17 badge10.zip
-rw-r--r--  1 24        494868 Dec  4 14:59 blexp10.txt
-rw-r--r--  1 24        197171 Dec  4 15:00 blexp10.zip
-rw-r--r--  1 24         61768 Jan  1 23:34 civil10.txt
-rw-r--r--  1 24         26407 Jan  1 23:35 civil10.zip
```

[many lines deleted]

Note: At first glance, the directory listing is mystifying. In addition to the initial "d" and "-" there are nine additional spaces that have either hyphens or the letters "r," "w," or "x." A brief explanation may be useful here.

Dante's tripartite division of hell is no more mysterious than this system; both seem arcane but explicable. The various codes pertain to the read (r), write (w), or execute (x) permissions for the three different classes of users: (a) the individual owner of the file, (b) a member of a group which has been given permission, and (c) all who have access to the directory.

Spaces	Permission
2–4	individual owner
5–7	specified group
8–10	all users

(Someone logging onto a host computer by anonymous FTP would fall into the last category.) It is not important to master every aspect of the directory system; you can FTP without doing so. Just beware that you will be FTP-ing a file—the line will begin with a "-" and the filename will be on the right. If the line begins with a "d," you cannot FTP it because it is a directory.

Just to get your feet on the ground, you might want to execute a PWD command. Type

> PWD [ENTER]

This last command tells the host to "print working directory." (If you are ever unsure as to where you are in a directory structure—whether in the root directory or one of the subdirectories—just type "pwd" for the answer.) The computer will respond with the following information:

> 257 "/pub/etext/etext93" is current directory.

At this point, type

> dir [ENTER]

A listing of the files in the subdirectory will cascade down your screen.

To summarize, the handful of commands that we have executed to arrive at the subdirectory was more than was actually needed. At the root directory, we could have simply typed

> cd etext/etext93 [ENTER]

It would have been more efficient, but you should also understand how to navigate from one level to another. There will be times that you will want to "browse" through the various subdirectories. Usually, you will be able to make do with only a handful of commands. (For a summary of the commands, see the end of this chapter.)

Transferring Files

Since we have arrived at our desired subdirectory, we are now ready to transfer the file back to our own computer. At times, you will be faced with a choice of files to transfer: ASCII or binary files.

Notice the following two files available from the etext93 subdirectory:

```
-rw-r--r--  1 24        275975 Jan  8 13:17 badge10.txt
-rw-r--r--  1 24        116147 Jan  8 13:17 badge10.zip
```

The first of these (with the .txt extension) is a plain ASCII text. This can be transferred without any special preparation and will arrive in your computer "ready to read" on your word processor.

The second file (with the .zip extension) is a compressed file. It is in binary format and cannot be transferred successfully without changing the transmission type to binary (unless you change the transmission type, the file you receive will be garbled—and unusable). Note that though these two files represent identical copies of the text of *The Red Badge of Courage*, they differ substantially in the total number of bytes, the compressed version (116,147 bytes) being less than half of the ASCII text (275,975 bytes). (You should be aware that on dialup connections, large files will take a long time to transfer.)

There are several advantages to the ZIP file. First, the amount of time that it takes to transfer the file over the Internet is substantially reduced, thus saving valuable network resources. Second, the file itself will be much smaller than the ASCII file and will take up much less room on your computer and on your floppy disk. This last consideration may be significant if your storage space is limited. Of course, one disadvantage to the ZIP file is that it has to be "unzipped" (uncompressed) before it can be used.

Transferring an ASCII File

We are ready to transfer the .txt file. Find any file in the directory with a .txt extension. For illustrative purposes, we will get badge10.txt.
Type

```
GET
```

The host computer will respond with the following prompt:

```
(remote file)
```

Type in the name of the text file you want to transfer (e.g., badge10.txt) and hit enter.

> Note: Since UNIX is case sensitive, you must be sure to type the name of the file you want in precisely the manner it appears in the directory. Thus "News.txt" would be a different file than "news.txt".

The host will respond with

```
(local-file)
```

Enter the name that you want the file to be called when it is transferred to your own computer (it could be the same or different from the file's original name). Hit enter.

The host will respond with something like the following:

```
200 PORT command successful
150 opening ASCII mode data connection for badge10.txt
(xxxxxxbytes)
226 transfer complete
```

After you hit ENTER, the cursor will seem to freeze for a little while—the transfer is taking place. It is completed when the `ftp>` prompt reappears.

> Note: In this last example, it is possible to stack the commands into a single line. For example, it is actually easier to type the command in the following pattern: <command> <file name on host> <new file name>. Thus, it would look like this:
>
> `GET badge10.txt badge`
>
> Thus, after it was transferred, the original filebadge10.txt would reside in your own directory with the new name badge.

At that point (unless you want to transfer another file), type "`close`." That breaks the connection to the foreign host. You will still have the `ftp>` prompt, but it is at your own machine. Type "`quit`" to return to your system prompt.

The file you transferred is now on your own computer system.

Transferring a Binary File

Receiving the File

To transfer a binary file, the procedure is very similar—except that a preliminary step must be taken. Before you issue the GET command, you must inform the host computer that you will be transferring a binary file. To do this, type

`binary [ENTER]`

The host computer should confirm that the FTP is set to binary mode with something like the following:

`200 Type set to I`

> Note: On some computers, the binary command may be enabled by a different command. If typing `binary` does not change the transmission mode, type `help` at the FTP prompt to see a listing of possible commands that are supported.

Now type the GET command and follow the directions as outlined in the previous section (transferring an ASCII file). If you were transferring the file named "sawyr10.zip," your session should look something like this:

```
ftp> binary
200 Type set to I.

ftp> get
(remote-file) sawyr10.zip
(local-file) sawyr10.zip
200 PORT command successful.
150 Opening BINARY mode data connection for sawyr10.zip
(176667 bytes).
226 Transfer complete.
local: sawyr10.zip remote: sawyr10.zip
176667 bytes received in 33 seconds (5.2 Kbytes/s)

ftp> close
221 Goodbye.

ftp> quit
```

Uncompression

Your ZIP file will have to be uncompressed before you can use it. You can use PKUNZIP to do this.
Follow these steps:

1. Use Archie (see the chapter on Archie) to find a copy of PKUNZIP.

2. FTP it to you computer.

3. Type PKUNZIP to uncompress the PKUNZIP file.

4. Print out the PKUNZIP manual on your printer and follow the directions for unzipping.

Some Useful FTP Sites

There are numerous FTP sites that will prove useful to you. Here are a few that are essential starting points for your exploration of the Internet.

Project Gutenberg

Project Gutenberg's self-proclaimed goal is "to give away one trillion etexts by December 31, 2001." It may succeed. Each year it doubles its monthly additions of text.

Current or soon-to-be-available works include Sophocles' *Oedipus Trilogy, The Scarlet Letter, Dr. Jekyll and Mr. Hyde, Paradise Lost*, the complete Shakespeare, *Aesop's Fables, Moby Dick*, the Declaration of Independence, the Bill of Rights, the U.S. Constitution, and many others.

These are available by anonymous FTP from

```
open mrcnext.cso.uiuc.edu
```

For a complete list of texts available, type

GET INDEX

If you have difficulty accessing this address, many other sites also have the Gutenberg etexts on file. Some of these are

quake.think.com

oak.oakland.edu

wuarchive.wustl.edu

The Oxford Text Archive (OTA)

Maintained at Oxford University, England, the OTA is a vast repository of literary texts in Greek, Latin, English, and many other languages, from early Arabic epistles to Joyce's *Finnegans Wake*.

These are available by anonymous FTP from

ota.ox.ac.uk

Get the file TEXTARCHIVE.INFO in the /ota directory for details of registering and securing etexts. For a listing of the files available, get the file textarchive.list.

cica.indiana.edu

For an extensive array of freeware and shareware programs for Windows, available by anonymous FTP from

ftp.cica.indiana.edu

Get INDEX for a description of files for desktop applications, screens, printer drivers, videos, fonts, programming, sound files, utilities, and many others.

Additional FTP sites are noted throughout the RESOURCES section of this book.

SUMMARY OF ESSENTIAL FTP COMMANDS

The following commands will serve most of your purposes for navigating through the subdirectories and for getting files:

ftp	At the Unix prompt, enables file transfer protocol
cd [subdirectory name]	Changes subdirectory
binary	Changes the transmission mode to binary
ASCII	Changes the transmission mode to ASCII
help	Help
PWD	Prints working directory
ls	Brief listing of the contents of a directory
ls -l	Full listing of the contents of the directory
dir	Same as **ls -l**
get	The command to fetch a file
cdup	Takes you up one level in the directory
cd ..	Takes you up one level in the directory
close	Closes the FTP connection
quit	Quits the FTP prompt

Suggestions for Further Reading

Sachs, David and Henry Stair. *Hands-On Internet: A Beginning Guide for PC Users.* Englewood Cliffs, NJ: Prentice Hall, 1994.

Veljkov, Mark and George Hartnell. *Transferring Files with File Transfer Protocol (FTP).* Westport, CT: Mecklermedia, 1994.

Archie, Veronica, and Jughead

Three Essential Search Tools

> • The Need for Search Tools • Archie • Veronica
> • Jughead •Veronica Searches of Files, Veronica Searches
> of Directories, and Jughead Searches

The Need for Search Tools

The Internet has many valuable resources, and they seem to be multiplying exponentially—in spite of the fact that sometimes sites close down or that sometimes files are no longer maintained on a particular machine. No single directory could ever keep pace with the changes. This quickly became apparent to users of the net, and within the last several years several search tools were developed to address this problem. Archie, Veronica, and Jughead all serve specific needs in this regard.

Archie

Archie is a search engine that allows the user to find specific files and directories at numerous anonymous FTP sites on the Internet. The Archie index is usually updated once a month, so the results of any particular Archie search will usually prove useful. The files in question could be software (freeware or shareware) or text.

Using Archie

To access an Archie site, telnet to one of the addresses listed below. Log in as 'archie.'

Archie Sites
United States
    archie.ans.net
    archie.rutgers.edu
    archie.sura.net
    archie.unl.edu
Canada
    archie.mcgill.ca
Finland:
    archie.funet.fi
Germany
    archie.th-darmstadt.de
United Kingdom
    archie.doc.ic.ac.uk
Note: As with any remote connection, always use the closest geographic site.

After you connect to the Archie server, the command prompt will look like this:

```
archie>
```

To search for a specific file, type the following:

```
prog <search string>
```

For example, to search for the compression/uncompression program PKUNZIP, you would type the following after the Archie> prompt:

```
prog PKUNZIP
```

The results of the Archie search will be displayed on your screen, something like the following:

Host gundel.zdv.uni-mainz.de (134.93.178.132)

Last updated 01:52 16 Nov 1994

Location: /pub/batch/etc/wpdb/100

FILE -rw-r--r-- 29378 bytes 08:40 1 Sep 1994 pkunzip.exe

with many other sites listed as well. This contains all the information you need to retrieve the file: host name (zdv.uni-mainz.de), subdirectory (/pub/batch/ etc/wpdb/100), and full file name (pkunzip.exe). You can now retrieve this by anonymous FTP.

Some Useful Archie Commands	
help	Returns a list of Archie commands
set <variable>	Important variables are:
	mail to <address>
	This will mail the results of a search to you.
	pager
	Setting this variable will prevent the search results from scrolling off the screen.
mail	Mails the results of the previous search to you.
quit	Exits Archie.

Using Veronica

Since the Internet has become such a diverse and vast terrain, it was inevitable that a search engine would be developed to find topical references on Gopher servers. At last count, the Veronica index held well in excess of 10 million items. Veronica searches the titles of files—not full-text searches of the files themselves. Since the naming of files is an inexact science, many files that may be useful to you will not be returned by this search. Nevertheless, Veronica is an invaluable tool.

You will find Veronica links on gopher menus. Most often they are on the main menu; sometimes they are down a level or two under headings such as

"Other Gophers" or "Other Resources." If your gopher menu does not have a Veronica link, you can gopher to

gopher.micro.umn.edu70

path: Other Gopher and Information Servers

Search Titles in Gopherspace Using Veronica

Or you can gopher directly to a public server at veronica.scs.unr.edu 70.

Composing a Veronica Search

Just choose the menu item for a Veronica search, and you will be prompted for a "search string."

> Note:
> - Only letters, digits, and underlines can be searched.
> - Search words must be two letters or longer.
> - A space or a "." is interpreted as an "and." For example, "Hamlet and Lear" is the same as "Hamlet Lear."
> - Asterisks may not be the first item in a search.
> - Upper and lower cases are treated the same.
> - Control-G will cancel your request.
> - Control-U will erase the previous request and allow you to type in a new one.

The search string may consist of key words that you are searching for as well as options that define the scope of your search. For example, the normal default value of a Veronica search is a return of up to 200 items (which are presented one per line), but this number can be changed. At that point, the user can connect to any one (or to all, each in succession) of the returned items to read the entire document.

Here are some guidelines, using Shakespeare's *Hamlet* as the specific example of the search:

Hamlet	This will return titles that include the name Hamlet (some of which will concern Shakespeare's character, though obviously some others may not).
Hamlet and Shakespeare	This will return items that have both Shakespeare and Hamlet in the title.
Hamlet Shakespeare	This will produce the same results as the previous search. (A space is equivalent to an "and.")

| Hamlet and Elizab★ | Use of the wildcard (★) will return items that have both Hamlet and Elizabeth or Elizabethan. Note that the wildcard character cannot be the initial element in the search. |

Other Commands

Number of Lines: You can change the default (200) by including an -m# option, where you replace "#" with the number of lines you wish. For example:

Hamlet -m250

will return 250 lines.

Titles: Use the -t# option, where you replace "#" with one or more of the following numbers:
 0 [to search for gopher text files only]
 1 [to search for gopher directories only]
 7 [to search for gopher indexes only]
 8 [to search for telnet links only]
 9 [to search for binary files only]

Domains: You can limit the domains to be searched by including the following option:

-d.<domain>

For example, "-d.edu" would search only education domains.

Wildcards: Use an asterisk [★] for wildcards.

Jughead _____

Or if you want, you can call it Jonzy's Universal Gopher Hierarchy Excavation and Display. It does what a Veronica search does—searches the titles only, not the full text—but the range of the search is much smaller, usually limited to the site of one gopher server. The advantage, though, is that it is much faster and does not use as much bandwidth as Veronica searches.

Note: Jughead software (jughead.1.0.4.tar.Z and jughead.
ReadMe) for local site installation can be retrieved by anonymous FTP from

ftp.cc.utah.edu

    path: pub

        gopher

            GopherTools

                jughead

Using Jughead

Like Veronica, Jughead can be found as a menu item on many gophers.

Special Commands for Jughead	
?help	Returns a help file.
?all <search string>	Returns all hits on the search string.
?limit=n <search string>	Returns the first 'n' items of the search string.
?version	Identifies version of Jughead.

Note: Only one command is allowed per query.

Veronica Searches of Files, Veronica Searches of Directories, and Jughead Searches

To illustrate the differences between Veronica searches of files, Veronica searches of directories, and Jughead searches, I used the keyword "Hamlet" and performed a search with all three. The number of "hits" (positive identification of a source) which were returned were as follows:

Number	Type of Search
9	Jughead
24	Veronica Search of Directories
247	Veronica Search of Files

Suggestions for Further Reading

Krol, Ed. *The Whole Internet User's Guide and Catalog*, 2nd edition. Sebastopol, CA: O'Reilly and Associates, 1994.

PART 2

Resources

> Note: In this directory, long addresses, paths, and messages are carried over to successive lines. However, these should be read as single-line entities and commands.

ACCESS—Internet

The following Internet resources are useful for locating service providers in your geographical area:

FAQ

For an Internet access provider FAQ, anonymous FTP to

    ftp.einet.net/pub/
        INET-MARKETING/
        inet-access.faq

Forgotten Sites List

This list is intended to supplement the PDIAL and NIXPUB service provider's lists. Available by anonymous FTP from

    login.qc.ca
    path: pub
           fslist

InterNIC Internet Service Providers List (U.S.)

InterNIC Information Services maintains a list of United States-based Internet access providers. This can be accessed by either anonymous FTP or by WWW. All providers listed offer at least interactive TCP connections (e.g., telnet, FTP). Commercial providers (e.g., CompuServe, America On-Line, Prodigy, etc.) are

not listed. Indexed by telephone area code.

Send an e-mail message to
mailserv@is.internic.net
subject: [blank]
message:
    begin
    help
    index
    send about-infoguide/about-
      infoguide
    end

gopher to
gopher.internic.net

telnet to
gopher.internic.net
login: gopher

anonymous FTP to
is.internic.net
path: infoguide
      getting-connected
      united-states

WWW to
http://www.internic.net/internic/
    refdesk.html

Network USA WWW

Network-USA has a WWW server that catalogs Internet access providers around the world. It is indexed by area code/country code.

WWW to
http://www.netusa.net/ISP/

NIXPUB List

The NixPub List contains public/open access UNIX sites (fee and nonfee). The list is published regularly on **alt.bbs**, c**omp.bbs.misc**, and **comp.misc**. In addition, it can be retrieved by e-mail by sending the following to

mail-server@bts.com
message: get PUB nixpub.long

PDIAL

Peter Kaminski maintains PDIAL, a list of Internet full-service providers offering public access (U.S. and international) dial-in Internet access (ftp, telnet, mail, Usenet, etc.). This is quite a useful list, having an area code index, an alphabetical listing, and a bibliography of essential Internet books. To obtain the latest copy of the PDIAL list, send an e-mail message to

info-deli-server@
  Kaminski,vip.best.com
message: Send PDIAL

If you would like to be placed on a mailing list for future, updated versions of this list, send an e-mail message to the same address with the following message:
  subscribe PDIAL

anonymous FTP to
ftp.best.com
path: pub
  Kaminski
  pdial-archive

See also the **Getting On Line** chapter.

ACCESS SOFTWARE

Point-to-Point Protocol (PPP) Software

Point-to-Point Protocol (PPP) for PCs is available by anonymous FTP from

ftp.merit.edu
path: internet.tools
  pp
  dos

Trumpet Winsock

For using Windows with a TCP/IP stack, you will need a copy of software such as Trumpet Winsock. To get a copy of this (twsk10a.zip), anonymous FTP to

ftp.halcyon.com
path: local
  campionf
  www

For WWW software, see **RESOURCES—World Wide Web**.

ADDRESSES

Electronic

Since there are millions of people currently connected to the Internet–with millions more being added each year, others disconnecting, and still others changing from one connection to another–it would be impossible to maintain an up-to-date single "telephone book" of Internet addresses. Yet it is often possible to track people down.

> Note: The last resort—and often the best first policy—is to contact the person by telephone and ask for the e-mail address.

Colleges and Universities

A file giving detailed information on naming conventions of e-mail addresses at U.S. colleges can be obtained by anonymous FTP from

ftp.qucis.queensu.ca
path: pub/
     dalamb
     college-email

The files are named faq1.text, faq2.text, and faq3.text.

By e-mail, you can obtain these files by sending a message to

archive-server@qucis.queensu.ca
subject: send dalamb/college-email

Converting Bitnet/Internet Addresses

If you need to convert bitnet addresses to Internet addresses (or vice versa), you can receive the latest conversion list from bitnic.educom.edu.

Send an e-mail message to

listserv@bitnic.educom.edu

Leave the Subject line blank, and in the body of your message type only

SEND INTERNET LISTING

This list is updated monthly.

See also **ADDRESSES–Gateways**.

European

For help in finding e-mail addresses for people in Europe, telnet to

paradise.ulcc.ac.uk
login: dua

Gateways

If you have Internet access but not bitnet access and want to send an e-mail to a bitnet address, you can either find the Internet equivalent of the mailing address or you can send mail to the bitnet address through an Internet gateway. For example, to send a message to listserv@utoronto.bitnet, use the following format:

listserv%utoronto.bitnet@<gateway address>

Use the gateway that is geographically closest to you. Here are a few (though your system administrator should be able to tell you the address of the one nearest to you):

cunyvm.cuny.edu
pucc.princeton.edu
vm1.nodak.edu

For example, if you are sending your message through the Princeton gateway, you should address it as follows:

listserv%utoronto.bitnet@pucc.princeton.edu

> Note: The original "@" in the address is replaced with a "%."

Gopher

The easiest search for an e-mail address involves people who have an address at an institution or company that supports a gopher site with a directory of addresses. Simply gopher to that installation, search for a menu item like "Phone Directory," and you should be able to track down the person you are looking for.

Guide

A useful general guide to finding Internet e-mail addresses is available by anonymous FTP from

    rtfm.mit.edu
    path: pub
        usenet
        news.answers
        finding-addresses

International

A FAQ on International e-mail accessibility and country codes can be obtained by anonymous FTP from

    rtfm.mit.edu
    path: pub
        usenet
        news.answers
        mail

Inter-Network Mail Guide

Information about sending mail between networks (e.g., Prodigy, CompuServe, etc.) can be obtained by anonymous FTP from

    csd4.csd.uwm.edu
    path: pub

It is also available by WWW at

    http://alpha.acast.nova.edu/cgi-bin/
        inmgq.pl

InterNIC Directory and Database Mail Server

For a user's guide to the InterNIC Directory and Database Services, including instructions for looking up addresses for individuals, send the following e-mail request to

    mailserv@ds.internic.net
    message: help

The NIC Locator database can be accessed by way of

    gopher: gopher.internic.net/1/pub/
        niclocator

    ftp: ftp.internic.net/pub/niclocator

It may also be accessed by way of rwhois by telnet at

    rs.internic.net

At the command prompt, enter an rwhois command in the following format:

    rwhois nic <search string>

Knowbot Information Service

This is a meta-service that searches white pages information from the NIC WHOIS service, the CSNET WHOIS service, the PSI White Pages, and MCI Mail, among others.

    telnet to
    info.cnri.reston.va.us 185

or

    regulus.cs.bucknell.edu 185

Netfind

Netfind offers a convenient way to locate people who have organizational or institutional affiliations.

For Netfind, telnet to one of the following installations; type "Netfind" in response to the log-in prompt (and when necessary to the password prompt as well):

archie.au
bruno.cs.colorado.edu
cobber.cord.edu
dino.conicit.ve
ds.internic.net
lincoln.technet.sg
monolith.cc.ic.ac.uk
mudhoney.micro.umn.edu
netfind.if.usp.br
netfind.ee.mcgill.ca
netfind.lut.ac.uk
netfind.oc.com
netfind.vslib.cz
nic.nm.kr
nic.uakom.sk
pascal.sjsu.edu
redmont.cis.uab.edu

PSI White Pages

Performance Systems International, Inc. (PSI) maintains a White Pages lookup service that maintains a database of personnel information from member organizations.

telnet to
wp.psi.com
login: fred

For a list of the organizations participating in the project, type "whois -org ★".

For more information, send an e-mail message to

wp-info@psi.com

Resolver

To find an IP address for a host name, send an e-mail message to

resolve@cs.widener.edu
message: site <address>

WHOIS

To search the WHOIS database at the DNN NIC host, telnet to

nic.ddn.mil

ARCHIE

Guide

For a comprehensive look at Archie and the many useful options it supports, see Chapter 3 of the EARN *Guide to Network Resource Tools*, which is available by sending an e-mail message to

listserv@earncc.earn.net
message: get nettools.txt

(or "get nettools.ps" for the PostScript version).

ARCHIVES AND LIBRARY RESOURCES

Bowdoin College Archives

Highlights: Bowdoin College Archives and Special Collections Manuscript Registers (in progress).

 gopher to
gopher.polar.bowdoin.edu

 for e-mail information:
gcolati@polar.bowdoin.edu
(Greg Colati)

The British Library

News, manuscripts, archives, browseable index and more are available on line.

 telnet to
portico.bl.uk
login: gopher
password: [return]
terminal type: [vt100]

Cambridge University

Cambridge University Library
West Road
Cambridge
CB3 9DR UK
Phone: +44 223 333000
FAX: +44 223 333160

 e-mail: library@ula.cam.ac.uk

The Center for Research Libraries

The Center for Research Libraries
6050 South Kenwood Avenue
Chicago, IL 60637-2804
Phone: 312 955 4545

This database contains over 385,000 records and can be searched by author, title, words in the title, OCLC bibliographic record number, CRL call number, ISSN, ISBN, or subject.

 telnet to
crlcatalog.uchicago.edu
login: guest
password: guest

College of William and Mary

College of William and Mary
Earl Gregg Swem Library
P. O. Box 8794
Williamsburg, VA 23187-8794
Phone: 804 221 3091
FAX: 804 221 3088

The manuscript collection focuses on early and recent Virginia history with a number of collections having national import. The rare books collection covers many areas of Western thought from history to science to literature with volumes dating from the 15th to the 20th centuries. The University Archives collects material documenting the history and activities of the College of William and Mary and its people from its founding in 1693 to the present.

 e-mail to
kjdomi@mail.swem.wm.edu
or
mccook@mail.swem.wm.edu

Cornell University

Curator of Manuscripts
Division of Rare and Manuscript
      Collections
2B Kroch Library
Cornell University
Ithaca, NY 14853

 WWW to
http://rmc-www.library.
     cornell.edu/

Duke University

Special Collections Library
Duke University
Box 90185
Durham, NC 27708-0185
Phone: 919 660 5820
FAX: 919 684 2855

The library's collection includes history and culture of the American South; history of Great Britain and the British Empire; romantic literature; eighteenth-century literature; Methodism; modern American literature; women's studies; history of economics.

 gopher to
iliad.lib.duke.edu

 telnet to
library.duke.edu

Harvard University

Houghton Library
Harvard University
Cambridge, MA 02138

Houghton Library is the central repository for manuscripts and rare books for the Harvard College Library. The collections number approximately 450,000 rare books and millions of manuscripts (not including the holdings of the Harvard Theatre Collection).

The Manuscript Collections include papyri; early and illuminated manuscripts; literary manuscripts of all periods and many countries, with particular concentration on American, English, and Continental authors; some political and missionary collections; Hebrew, Indic, Turkish, Arabic, Persian, and Syriac manuscripts.

Printed books include about 2600 incunabula, extensive collections of 16th and 17th century European books in many fields; major collections in English culture of all periods; extensive holdings in French, Italian, and German literature, and principal American holdings of Russian literature, Portuguese books, and modern Greek books.

 e-mail contacts:
Leslie Morris, Curator of Manuscripts
    houmss@harvarda.harvard.edu

Anne Anniger, Curator of Printing
   and Graphic Arts
   anne_anninger@harvard.edu

Indiana University

Lilly Library
Indiana University
Bloomington, IN 47405
Phone: 812 855 2452
FAX: 812 855 3143

The Lilly Library is the rare book, manuscript, and special collections library of the Indiana University—Bloomington libraries. Holdings of rare books include incunables, the New Testament volume of the Gutenberg Bible, the Shakespeare first folios, and the elephant folio edition of Audubon''s *Birds of America*. Manuscripts include such individual items as Robert Burns's "Auld Lang Syne," and J. M. Barrie's *Peter Pan,* as well as a collection of Medieval and Renaissance manuscripts, the papers of Upton Sinclair, and the papers of Nobel Prize winner Nadine Gordimer. The collections are particularly strong in British, American, and French literature; the voyages of exploration and the colonial empires of the Spanish, Dutch, and Portuguese; the history of science and medicine; music; early printing; and historical children's books.

Finding Aids On Line: Collection-level descriptions of all manuscript collections; an index to the more than 2000 chapbooks; detailed guides to selected collections.

 telnet to
iuis.ucs.indiana.edu
login: guest

 gopher to
lib-gopher.lib.indiana.edu
path: Special Collections
    The Lilly Library

 e-mail: liblilly@indiana.edu

Johns Hopkins University

Archives & Manuscript Collection
Johns Hopkins University
Baltimore, MD
Phone: 410 516 8348
FAX: 410 516 8596

In addition to the archives of Johns Hopkins University, many manuscript registers are on-line. Some highlights are medieval and Renaissance manuscript books, James Truslow Adams, John Quincy Adams, Association of American Universities, Sherwood Anderson, John Barth, British Illustrators Scrapbook, Calcutta Photograph Collection, Clyde Fitch, William Gass, Daniel Coit Gilman, Elisabeth Gilman, Johns Hopkins Family Collection, Iron and Steel Union Constitution, Rudyard Kipling Scrapbook, William Bennett Kouwenhoven, Lieselotte E. Kurth-Voight, Sidney Lanier, Antonio Magliabechi, Mary McCarthy, John Stuart Mill, On the Justice and Policy of Repealing the Laws, Notes on Sir Thomas Overbury, Edgar Allan Poe, Saul Collection of Theater Programs, Seventeenth Century, Maryland Collection, Robert Southey, Tudor and Stuart Club Collection, Alfred North Whitehead, and Angus Wilson. In addition, the Lester S. Levy Sheet Music Collection is available.

 e-mail to
Cynthia Requardt, Department Head:
cynthia.requardt@jhu.edu

 gopher to
musicbox.mse.jhu.edu
path: Eisenhower Library
    Special   Collections   and
    Archives

Library of Congress

Library of Congress
Washington, DC 20540
202 707 5205

For Library of Congress Information System
(LOCIS)

 telnet to
locis.loc.gov

For MARVEL

 telnet or gopher to
marvel.loc.gov
login: marvel

 WWW to
http://lcweb.loc.gov/homepage/
lchp.html

Louisiana Tech University

Manuscripts and Archives
Prescott Memorial Library
Louisiana Tech University
Ruston, LA 71272-0046

The collection includes books dealing with
the history of Louisiana Tech University,
the history, literature, and culture of Louisiana and the South.

Finding Aids On Line: Accessible via the
Louisiana Tech University gopher at

 vm.cc.latech.edu
path: Library Systems and Archives
Special Collections, Manuscripts

Printed Guide: Available at no charge.

For further information, contact

 Dr. Bobs M. Tusa, Head, Special
Collections, at
tusa@vm.cc.latech.edu

MELVYL

MELVYL is the on-line library catalog of
the University of California system, providing the user with access to over 8 million titles (books, journals, videos, etc.).

 telnet to
melvyl.ucop.edu

In response to the prompt for a terminal emulation, type

vt100

Then hit the enter key. You will get the following screen:
At the arrow prompt (-->), type

CAT

To end a session, type

End

> Note: The results of a library
> catalogue database search can be
> e-mailed back to you.

Michigan State University

Special Collections Division
Michigan State University Libraries
East Lansing, MI 48824-1048
Phone: 517 355 3770
FAX: 517 432 3532

The Special Collections Division houses over 250,000 rare books and one million manuscripts. Its most important collections are the Russel B. Nye Popular Culture Collection (Science Fiction, Westerns, Mysteries, Juvenile, and Comic Art); French Monarchy Collection; early British agriculture and gardening; cookery; Italian Risorgimento; early German criminology; Ray Stannard Baker Apiculture collection; and American Radicalism.

It is particularly strong in Comic Art (100,000 items), Charles and Ruth Schmitter Fencing Collection, Communist Party of the U.S.A., Veterinary Medicine Historical Collection, and University Writers Collection, including Jim Harrison, Thomas McGuane, Dan Gerber, and Richard Ford. Manuscript collections include those of Thomas McGuane, Dan Gerber, and Richard Ford.

Available through the gopher to Michigan State University.
For more information, contact Peter Berg, Head of Special Collections, at

 20676pib@msu.edu

National Archives and Records Administration (NARA)

Descriptive information about various records in the custody of and programs administered by the National Archives. Included on the gopher is a section with information about the records in the custody of the Center for Electronic Records at the U.S. National Archives. This section includes reports on topics such as World War II electronic records, the 1970 Census summary statistic files, electronic records relevant to research on the former Soviet Union, and casualty records from the Korean and Vietnam conflicts. Also available are descriptions of the Center for Electronic Records program, a description of the fee-based reference services, and the Preliminary and Partial Title List of Holdings—the primary finding aid to electronic records in the National Archives.

For access, gopher to the National Archives gopher server at

 gopher.nara.gov

 WWW to
http://www.nara.gov/

For a file containing the Center's Title List: A Preliminary and Partial Listing of the Data Files in the National Archives & Records Administration (TITLE.LIST.JUL2994), anonymous FTP to

ftp.nara.gov
path: pub
electronic

gopher to
gopher.nara.gov
path: Information About NARA
Holdings
Inform. About Records Ret.
by Wash. DC Area Repos.
Electronic Records
Title List

For information about electronic records, contact Theodore J. Hull at

cer@nara.gov

The Newberry Library

The Newberry Library
60 West Walton Street
Chicago, IL 60610
Phone: 312 943 9090

The Newberry Library holds more than 1.5 million volumes, 5 million manuscript pages, and 75,000 maps on Western Europe and the Americas from the Middle Ages to around 1920, focusing on history and the humanities. Special strengths include Italian Renaissance; Luso-Brazilian and Mexican history; history and theory of music; history of cartography; history of printing; local and family history and genealogy; American Indian history; American literature (especially midwestern); history of the American West; English Renaissance literature; early philology; American history; calligraphy; bibliography; and railroad history.

Part of the collection is accessible on Illinet.

telnet (using vt100) to
illinet.aiss.uiuc.edu

New York University

Elmer Holmes Bobst Library
New York University
New York, NY 10012-1019

gopher to
gopher.nyu.edu
path: Library Facilities and Catalogs
Bobst Library
NYU Library Resources
Special Collections

Oregon State University

Special Collections
Kerr Library 422
Oregon State University
Corvallis, OR 97331
Phone: 503 737 2075
FAX: 503 737 3453

Oregon State University Archives
Administrative Services B094
Corvallis, OR 97331-2103
Phone: 503 737 2165
FAX: 503 737 2400

e-mail: archive@ccmail.orst.edu

The Oregon State University Archives' collections provide information on the University's teaching, research, and outreach programs; faculty, administrators, and alumni; campus buildings and development; and student life. All major aspects of the Oregon economy—agriculture, forestry, engineering and technology, and marine resources—are represented. Guides to the Archives' holdings are available on the Oregon State University Archives Gopher. Collection-level descriptions and inventories for numerous record groups and manuscript collections are available.

The collection of the Ava Helen and Linus Pauling Papers includes all of the Paulings' personal and scientific papers, notebooks, and correspondence from 1916 to the present. There are over 250,000 items plus Dr. Pauling's books, medals, research models, and memorabilia.

gopher to
gopher.orst.edu 70
path: Libraries and Reference Services

For more information, contact Elizabeth Nielsen at

nielsene@ccmail.orst.edu

Pennsylvania State University

Penn State University
University Park, PA 16802

gopher to
gopher.psu.edu
path: Penn State Information
      Libraries, University
      Special Collections

telnet to
lias.psu.edu

Princeton University Special Collections

Library
Princeton University
Princeton, NJ 08544

gopher to
gopher.princeton.edu

telnet to
library.princeton.edu:
path: Princeton-specific Resources
      Princeton Manuscr., Arch. and
      Spec. Coll.

Research Libraries Group (RLG)

The Research Libraries Group
1200 Villa Street
Mountain View, CA 94041-1100
Phone: 415 965 0943
FAX: 415 964 0943

e-mail: bl.ric@rlg.stanford.edu

The Research Libraries Group, Inc. (RLG), is a not-for-profit membership corporation of university, archives, historical societies, museums, and other institutions devoted to improving access to information that supports research and learning. RLG develops and operates cooperative programs for its members. Both members and nonmembers can use RLG's databases and software.

The Research Libraries Information Network (RLIN®) holds more than 67 million bibliographic records and over 6 million authority headings, plus special databases for early printed books and art sales catalogs. It covers the entire range of information held by major universities, research libraries, and specialized archives: social sciences, sciences, and particularly the humanities.

RLG has established a WWW server that allows users to receive files (text, images, and digitized sound). It includes an on-line database of books from the 15th through the 18th century. WWW to

http://www.stanford.edu/welcome.html

Rockefeller Archive Center

Rockefeller Archive Center
15 Dayton Avenue
Pocantico Hills
North Tarrytown, NY 10591
Phone: 914 631 4505
FAX: 914 631 6017

The Rockefeller Archive Center, established in 1974, holds the papers of the Rockefeller family and their associates, the records of the Rockefeller Foundation, and of other philanthropic and educational institutions founded by the family, including The Rockefeller University and the Rockefeller Brothers Fund.

For information on archival and manuscript collections, research services, and special programs, WWW to

http://www.rockefeller.edu/arc_cent/arc_cent.html

For information, contact Valerie Komor, Archivist, at

komor@rockvax.rockefeller.edu

Royal Commission on Historical Manuscripts/National Register of Archives

Royal Commission on Historical Manuscripts/National Register of Archives
Quality House
Quality Court
Chancery Lane
London WC2A 1HP
Phone: 0171 242 1198
FAX: 0171 831 3550

e-mail: sargent@rs1-hr.sas.ac.uk

> Note: In this directory, long addresses, paths, and messages are carried over to successive lines. However, these should be read as single-line entities and commands.

Rutgers University Library

Special Collections and University Archives
169 College Avenue
New Brunswick, NJ 08903
Phone: 908 932 7006
FAX: 908 932 7637

The library has a 60,000-volume rare book collection, 15th century to the present; a 60,000-volume New Jersey Collection, 18th century to the present; a 2000-manuscript collection with over 5 million items relating to New Jersey and other fields, including the consumer movement in the United States, Latin American society and politics in the 20th century, and Westerners in Japan in the 19th century. The University Archives includes records, publications, artifacts, etc., from 1766 to the present.

On-line Access: Catalog is accessible through telnet to

iris.rutgers.edu.

e-mail:
becker@zodiac.rutgers.edu
Ronald Becker, Head of Special
    Collections

frusciano@zodiac.rutgers.edu
Thomas   Frusciano,   University
    Archivist

Address reference letters to Edward Skipworth at

skipworth@zodiac.rutgers.edu

Southern Methodist University

DeGolyer Library
P.O. Box 396
Dallas, TX 75275
Phone: 214 768 3231
FAX: 214 768 1565

The DeGolyer Library collections focus on the American West, especially the Southwest and the Spanish Borderlands, and on railroads around the world. The library also houses the SMU Archives and the Center for Notable Women.

e-mail: kbost@sun.cis.smu.edu

Stanford University

Department of Special Collections
Cecil H. Green library
Stanford University Libraries
Stanford, CA 94305-6004
Phone: 415 725 1022
FAX: 415 723 8690

The Department of Special Collections is the principal repository for Stanford's historical research collections in all formats including printed books, manuscripts, maps, photographs, and prints. The department's holdings comprise more than 200,000 books and 20 million manuscript pieces. Strengths of the department's collection are modern literature, the history and art of the book, the history of science, continental history and literature, classical literature and philology, children's literature, Mexican American history, and the history of the Stanford community. The department's resources fall primarily into three broad categories: printed books, manuscripts, and the Stanford University Archives. The printed book collections are maintained primarily as individual collections defined by subject scope, such as British and American literature, the book arts, or the history of science. Manuscripts and the archives are comprised of discrete collections and constitute over 20,000 linear feet of material. The scope of the collections is diverse in subject area and discipline.

e-mail contacts:

Linda Long, Public Services Librarian
cn.ljl@forsythe.stanford.edu

David Sullivan, Technical Services Librarian
cn.dss@forsythe.stanford.edu

Margaret Kimball, Head of Special Collections and University Archivist
cn.mjk@forsythe.stanford.edu

State Historical Society of Wisconsin

State Historical Society of Wisconsin Library
816 State Street
Madison, WI 53706
Phone: 608 264 6534

U.S. and Canadian history and prehistory; Wisconsin history; genealogy and local history; political, economic, and religious history; anthropology; archaeology; social reform and radical groups; left- and right-wing political and social movements; women and women's groups; immigrant groups and ethnic minorities; Wisconsin state and local publications.

Archives Division

gopher to
silo.adp.wisc.edu 70
path: UW-Madison Library Gopher
Wisconsin Library Catalogs
State Historical Society, Archives Div.

telnet to
silo.adp.wisc.edu 5034

Photography

gopher to
wiscinfo.wisc.edu 2070
path: Image
State Historical Society

SUNY Oswego

Special Collections
SUNY at Oswego
Penfield Library
Oswego, NY 13126
Phone: 315 341 3565

 e-mail: Nancy Seale Osborne,
Coordinator of Special Collections
osborne@oswego.edu

"The manuscript collection of SUNY Oswego mainly consists of post-eighteenth century documents relevant to the local history of Oswego County and its surrounding areas. The collection contains manuscripts, photographs, printed records and audio/video tapes produced or acquired by individuals, businesses and organizations pertaining to Oswego County history. Included in the collection are early town and city records, store ledgers and journals, personal and family papers, records of U.S. Customs House, and the Millard Fillmore Collection" [from the on-line file "Manuscripts Collection—Description"].

 gopher to
gopher.oswego.edu

University of California, Davis

John Skarstad
Acting Head of Special Collections
General Library
University of California, Davis
Davis, CA 95616
Phone: 916 752 1621
FAX: 916 752 3148

 e-mail: jlskarstad@ucdavis.edu

University of California, Los Angeles

William Andrews Clark Memorial Library
University of California, Los Angeles
2520 Cimarron Street
Los Angeles, CA 90018
Phone: 213 731 8529
FAX: 213 731 8617

The library is particularly strong in British culture of the 17th and 18th centuries, late 19th century British literature, and fine printing of the 19th and late 20th centuries.

 e-mail:
ecz5bid@mvs.oac.ucla.edu

University of California, San Diego

The Mandeville Department
of Special Collections
The University Library, 0175S
University of California, San Diego
La Jolla, CA 92093-0175
Phone: 619 534 2533
FAX 619 534 4970

 e-mail: rlindemann@ucsd.edu

 gopher to
infopath.ucsd.edu
path: The Library
Resources by Library Branch
Library Manuscripts
USCD Archives Finding Aids

University of Chicago

Special Collections
University of Chicago Library
1100 E. 57th Street
Chicago, IL 60637
Phone: 312 702 8705
FAX: 313 702 0853

The Department of Special Collections maintains the rare books, manuscripts, and archives of the University of Chicago. Collections include 250,000 books and 20,000 linear feet of manuscripts and archival collections. Manuscript and archival collections emphasize the history of the social sciences, physical sciences, social reform, modern poetry, Chicago medicine, and the careers of Stephen A. Douglas and Abraham Lincoln. Rare book holdings are particularly strong in English, American, and European history, literature, and drama; the history of philosophy, philology, and theology. Comprehensive history of science and medicine collections include 25,000 volumes in the John Crerar Collection of Rare Books in the History of Science and Medicine; the Ludwig Rosenberger Library of Judaica contains 18,000 volumes covering the social and cultural history of the Jewish people.

e-mail contacts for the Department of Special Collections:

Alice Schreyer, Curator:
ads8@midway.uchicago.edu

Daniel Meyer, Assoc. Curator and University Archivist:
arch@midway.uchicago.edu

Suzy Taraba, Public Services Librarian:
mstaraba@midway.uchicago.edu

University of Delaware

Special Collections
University of Delaware Library
Newark, DE 19717-5267
Phone: 302 831 2229
FAX 302 831 1046

Holdings of the Special Collections Department of the University of Delaware Library include books, manuscripts, maps, prints, photographs, broadsides, periodicals, pamphlets, ephemera, and realia from the fifteenth to the twentieth century. The collections complement the library's general collections with particular strengths in the subject areas of the arts; English, Irish, and American literature; history and Delawareana; and history of science and technology. [from the on-line file, "Collection Focus"].

Finding Aids: Available on line via the library gopher.

gopher to
gopher.udel.edu
path: Library Information
U. of D. Library Collections & Services
Special Collections

WWW to
http://www.lib.udel.edu

e-mail contacts:

Timothy Murray, Head, Special Collections
timothy.murray@mvs.udel.edu

Iris Snyder, Sr. Assistant Librarian
iris.snyder@mvs.udel.edu

L. Rebecca Johnson Melvin, Sr. Assistant Librarian
lrjm@brahms.udel.edu

Priscilla Thomas, Assistant Librarian
priscilla.thomas@mvs.udel.edu

University of Georgia

Richard B. Russell Memorial Library
The University of Georgia Libraries
Athens, GA 30602
Phone: 706 542 5788
FAX: 706 542 4144

 e-mail: sbvogt@uga.cc.uga.edu
mebrooks@uga.cc.uga.edu

Collections of William Tapley Bennett, Jr.,
D. W. Brooks, Howard H. Callaway, Rod-
ney M. Cook, John W. Davis. E. L. Forrest-
er, Roy V. Harris, William J. Harris, Dudley
Hughes, Sidney Marcus, Maston O'Neal, J.
L. Pilcher, Dean Rusk, George L. Smith, II,
Hoke Smith, Robert G. Stephens, Jr., Her-
man Talmadge, and S. Ernest Vandiver.

University of Iowa Libraries

Special Collections
University of Iowa Libraries
Iowa City, IA 52242-1420
Phone: 319 335 5921
FAX: 319 335 5900

The collections are particularly strong in the
areas of 19th and 20th century American and
English literature, 19th and 20th century
American history, children's literature, the
histories of printing, of hydraulics, and of
gastronomy.

 e-mail: robert-mccown@uiowa.edu

University of Louisville

University Archives and Records Center
University of Louisville
Louisville, KY 40292
Phone: 502 852 6674
FAX: 502 852 6673

For more information, contact

 archives@ulkyvm.louisville.edu

 gopher to
ulkyvm.louisville.edu

 WWW to
http://www.louisville.edu/

The University Archives is the official repository for the records of the University of
Louisville, one of the oldest municipal universities in the United States. It also acquires,
preserves, and makes available for research
primary historical materials relating to the
greater Louisville area. The Archives houses
9000 linear feet of research collections.
Available are minutes of trustee, faculty,
staff, and student meetings; publications; selected administrative files; photographs of
University people and places; building blue-
prints; and the personal papers of selected
faculty and administrators. The Urban History Collections include 19th and 20th century records of area businesses, cultural
organizations, social service agencies, and
churches; and personal papers of politicians,
scholars, members of the Jewish and African-American communities, women, and
other prominent and representative Louis-
villians. Its Oral History Center makes available more than 1100 interviews with
individuals of local, regional, and national
distinction. The Archives maintains collections of books, journals, and other reference
materials on local history and on the administration of archives, manuscripts, and oral
history.

University of Mississippi

Department of Archives and Special
    Collections
J.D. Williams Library
University of Mississippi
University, MS 38677
Phone: 601 232 7408
FAX: 601 232 5734

The holdings are particularly strong in
Faulkner books and manuscripts, including
the Rowan Oak papers and the Wynn collection of poetry. Another strength is Mississippi history broadly defined to include
political, cultural, and social works and selected theses and dissertations. The library
also has an extensive collection of works of
fiction written by Mississippians and individuals with Mississippi associations.

e-mail contacts:

Sharron Sarthou
    ulses@vm.cc.olemiss.edu

DebbieLee Landi
    ullandi@vm.cc.olemiss.edu

Lisa Speer
    ulspeer@vm.cc.olemiss.edu

University of Missouri, St. Louis

University of Missouri, St. Louis
St. Louis, MO 63121

Subjects: The Western Historical Manuscript
Collection (owned jointly by the State Historical Society and the University of Missouri).

gopher to
umslvma.umsl.edu
path: Library
    Western Historical Manuscripts

University of Nebraska—Lincoln

Library
University of Nebraska—Lincoln
Lincoln, NE 68588-0410
Phone: 402 472 2531
FAX 402 472 5131 (ILL)

Collection Highlights: UN-L Archives, Ber-
nice Slote Papers (Willa Cather material),
Mari Sandoz Papers, Benjamin Botkin Papers.

gopher to
cwis.unl.edu

e-mail:
michelef@unllib.unl.edu

University of New Mexico

Zimmerman Library
University of New Mexico
Albuquerque, NM 87131-1466
Phone: 505 277 6451
FAX: 505 277 6019

Focuses on New Mexico history and cultures, southwestern history and cultures, American Indian collections, travel narratives, Latin America, Mexican colonial history, Ibero-America, photo-archives, UNM archives, Oral History Program, Chaco Canyon archives, New Mexico Newspaper Project.

e-mail to
cswrref@unm.edu

oral@unm.edu
(Oral History Program)

University of North Carolina at Chapel Hill

Rare Book Collection
Academic Affairs Library
Wilson Library, CB# 3936
University of North Carolina at Chapel Hill
Chapel Hill, NC 27514-8890
Phone: 919 962 1143
FAX: 919 962 4452

The Rare Book Collection has over 100,000 printed volumes, 16,000 prints and broadsides, and 1170 manuscripts, dating from 2500 B.C. to the present and covering the full range of human knowledge. Materials are selected from the Collection based on date, fragility, value, and/or subject. The Collection has particularly strong holdings of incunabula, sixteenth-century imprints (most notably the Estienne family of scholar-printers), English literature, French history, and the history of the book. Special subject strengths include Samuel Johnson, Charles Dickens, George Cruikshank, George Bernard Shaw, crime and detective fiction, Sherlock Holmes, Spanish Cronistas, Southern history, Confederate imprints, nineteenth-century British and American publishing history, and Spanish plays, Seamus Heaney, Walker Percy, John Murray imprints, Smith Elder imprints, J. M. Dent imprints, Ticknor and Fields imprints, and Victorian Bindings.

telnet to
unclib.lib.unc.edu

e-mail to (for General information)
spcl@email.unc.edu

University of North Carolina at Charlotte

"American literature has been one of the main emphases of the Rare Book Collection since 1971 when [Harry L.] Dalton donated his copy of the first edition of Walt Whitman's *Leaves of Grass*. In those 20 years, the collection has grown to include works by such authors as Phillis Wheatley, James Fenimore Cooper, William Gilmore Simms, Ralph Waldo Emerson, Henry David Thoreau, Mark Twain, William Faulkner, and Ernest Hemingway. In November 1991, Mrs. Dalton donated a copy of the first edition of Herman Melville's *Moby Dick* as the library's 500,000th volume" [from the online file, "About Special Collections"].

Other Areas: Children's books, English drama of the 17th, 18th, and early 19th centuries, the history and literature of North Carolina.

For more information, contact:

Special Collections
Atkins Library
University of North Carolina at Charlotte
Charlotte, NC 28223
Phone: 704 547 2369
704 547 2449
FAX: 704 547 3050

speccoll@unccvm.uncc.edu

University of Oklahoma

Bizzell Memorial Library
University of Oklahoma
401 West Brooks Street
Norman, OK 73019
Phone: 405 325 2611

Western History Collections, history of science, Bass Business History and the Carl Albert Congressional Archives. The Western History Collection of manuscript and photographs can be accessed through the Oklahoma Library Information Network (OLIN).

 gopher to
gopher.uoknor.edu

University of Pennsylvania

Van Pelt-Dietrich Library
University of Pennsylvania
3420 Walnut Street
Philadelphia, PA 19104–6206
Phone: 215 898 7088
FAX: 215 898 0559

The Department holds over 9000 linear feet of manuscripts, including over 1500 codex manuscripts and several hundred manuscript collections. Codices include texts in Latin, Greek, English, French, Italian, Dutch, Flemish, German, and Spanish, covering the 12th through the 18th centuries. Modern manuscript collections comprise literary, historical, cultural, and scientific materials and include the personal papers of Marian Anderson, Robert Montgomery Bird, Theodore Dreiser, James T. Farrell, Edwin Forrest, Waldo Frank, Benjamin Franklin, Alma Mahler and Franz Werfel, John Mauchly, Lewis Mumford, George Seldes, May Sinclair, and Carl Zigrosser, among others. Institutional archives include the records of the American Musicological Society, Institute of Contemporary Art, Musical Fund Society of Philadelphia, Philadelphia Art Alliance, and Philadelphia Society for Promoting Agriculture.

Special collections include Aristotle and the Scholastic traditions; the transmission of the Classical Corpus; ecclesiastical history, institutions, and governance, in particular the Inquisition; Italian Renaissance literature; Spanish Golden Age literature; Shakespeare and Shakespeariana; 18th and early 19th century British literature, esp. Swift; history of chemistry; Benjamin Franklin; the French Revolution. Manuscript holdings for the 19th and 20th centuries focus on Philadelphia publishing; American literature and in particular Theodore Dreiser; and the tradition of socially and politically engaged literature; and the arts and culture in Philadelphia.

e-mail contacts:

Michael Ryan, Information
   ryan@pobox.upenn.edu

Nancy Shawcross, Manuscripts
   shawcros@pobox.upenn.edu

Daniel Traister, Books
   traister@pobox.upenn.edu

University of Southern California

Doheny Memorial Library
Department of Special Collections
University of Southern California
Los Angeles, CA 90089-0182
Phone: 213 740 5946 or 213 740 7173
FAX: 213 749 1221

The rare books and manuscripts collection includes the history of Philosophy, Darwin and evolution, British East India Company, R. L. Stevenson, Western History and Californiana. Printing arts: fine press and artist's books, Richard Hoffman Collection on the history of printing; American literature: especially Ambrose Bierce, William Dean Howells, Hamlin Garland, Jack London; Paul Bowles, Kenneth Rexroth, Charles Bukowski, Lawrence Lipton, Richard Wilbur. German Exile literature, especially the Lion Feuchtwanger archives (including Heinrich Mann and Hanns Eisler) and rare book collection; regional history, especially the Herald-Examiner, the Whittington, and the California Historical Society Collection of photographs; papers of Jerry Brown; papers of the Christopher Commission.

Finding Aids On line: In preparation.

gopher to
gopher.usc.edu
path: Library and Research
     Information
     Library Information
     USC Library Services,
       Collections & Hours
     The USC Libraries
     Department of Special
     Collections

e-mail contacts:

Victoria Steele:
   vsteele@calvin.usc.edu

John Ahouse:
   ahouse@calvin.usc.edu

Marje Schuetze-Coburn:
   schuetze@calvin.usc.edu

University of Tennessee at Knoxville

Special Collections
Hoskins Library
University of Tennessee-Knoxville
Knoxville, TN 37996-4000
Phone: 615 974 4480
FAX: 615 974 0560

About 300 mss. collection guides presently available, with 1700 shorter ones on line soon. Strengths include Tennessee, Southern Indians, Political History, and literature (especially James Agee, Alex Haley).

gopher to
gopher.lib.utk.edu 70
path: UTK Libraries Holdings
        Manuscripts

e-mail to
special@utklib.lib.utk.edu

University of Texas at Austin/HRHRC

Harry Ransom Humanities Research
        Center
The University of Texas at Austin
P.O. Drawer 7219
Austin, TX 78713-7219
Phone: 512 471 8944 (Administrative)
        512 571 9119 (Library Public
                Services)
FAX: 512 471 9646 (Administrative)
        512 471 2899 (Collections)

Collection highlights: Exploration and travel; Native Americans, history, American literature (Eugene Field, Edgar Allan Poe, Walt Whitman, Henry James, Ernest Hemingway, Henry Miller, Harlem Renaissance) and British literature (William Blake, Lord Byron, Samuel Taylor Coleridge, Percy Bysshe Shelley, William Wordsworth, Charles Lamb, and Robert Southey, Lewis Carroll, Charles Dickens, Gerard Manley Hopkins, Alfred Lord Tennyson, Dante Gabriel Rossetti, Joseph Conrad, Oscar Wilde, William Butler Yeats, George Bernard Shaw), photography, and theatre arts.

e-mail to
hmab103@utxvm.bitnet
Richard Oram, Librarian
        r.oram@utxvm.cc.utexas.edu

gopher to
gopherhost.lib.utexas.edu

Special Fields: Finding aids for mss. collections processed since 1990; collection analysis reports (books and manuscripts) for selected authors; WATCH (Writers and Their Copyright Holders) file containing current addresses and names for copyright holders of major authors.

telnet to
utcat.utexas.edu (OPAC only)

WWW to
http://www.lib.utexas.edu

University of Tulsa

Special Collections Department
McFarlin Library
2933 East 6th Street
Tulsa, OK 74104-2123
Phone: 918 631 2496
FAX: 918 631 3791

Tulsa collects in two areas: Historical Manuscripts (1200 feet) relate primarily to Indian Territory and northeastern Oklahoma. Documentation for the Cherokee, Creek, and Osage Nations is particularly extensive. Several collections document aspects of the petroleum industry. University records (1000 feet) are also part of Special Collections, and a 30,000-volume book collection supports the historical manuscripts.

Literary Manuscripts (1000 feet) relate to 20th century Anglo-Irish, British, and American writers and publishers. They include the personal papers of Cyril Connolly, Richard Ellmann, Anna Kavan, Richard Murphy, V. S. Naipaul, Jean Rhys, Paul Scott, Stevie Smith, and Rebecca West; the manuscripts of Muriel Spark and William Trevor; and the archives of Andre Deutsch, Ltd. 70,000 volumes in rare and special collections support these manuscript collections.

gopher to
tured.pa.utulsa.edu 70

For more information, contact

Sidney F. Huttner,
Curator of Special Collections:
sfh@vax2.utulsa.edu
Lori N. Curtis,
Associate Curator of Special
Collections
lnc@vax2.utulsa.edu

University of Virginia

Special Collections Department
Alderman Library
University of Virginia
Charlottesville, VA 22903-2498
Phone: 804 924 3025
FAX: 804 924 3143

"The Special Collections Department, located in Alderman Library, houses 10.1 million manuscripts, 2.4 million University archives, and over 228,000 rare books. Foremost among its special collections are the Tracy W. McGregor Library of American History, the Clifton Waller Barrett Library of American Literature, the William Faulkner Collection, the Douglas H. Gordon Collection of French Books of the sixteenth to nineteenth century, and the Virginiana collections, including papers and architectural drawings of Thomas Jefferson" [from the on-line guide, "About UVA Special Collections"].

Particularly strong in the following: William Faulkner, John Henry Ingram, Ellen Glasgow, James Branch Cabell, Mary Johnston, John Dos Passos, Jorge Luis Borges, Matthew Arnold, Richard Dodderidge Blackmore, Alfred Lord Tennyson, Thomas Jefferson.

Finding Aids On line: For over 200 manuscript collections:

gopher to
gopher.lib.virginia.edu
path: Special Collections

ftp to
ftp.lib.Virginia.edu
path: Pub
Special Collections

For more information, e-mail to

mssbks@virginia.edu

University of West Florida

Special Collections and West Florida
    Archives
University of West Florida
Pensacola, FL

e-mail to
ddebolt@uwf.bitnet

University of Wisconsin—Madison

Department of Special Collections
University of Wisconsin—Madison
Memorial Library
976 State Street
Madison, WI 53706-1494
Phone: 608 262 3243
FAX: 608 265 2754

English literature, American women authors,
little magazines, Mark Twain, 17th to 20th
century English grammars, alchemy, Swedish
dissertations, English political pamphlets,
Vichy/WWII pamphlets, papyri, Russian underground literature (1825–1905), Huguenot
material (Montauban, France), history of science.

Finding aids: In progress.

gopher to
silo.adp.wisc.edu 70

telnet to
nls.adp.wisc.edu (144.92.161.10)

WWW to
http://ww.library.wisc.edu

For archive information:

e-mail to
uwarchiv@doit.wisc.edu

For additional information, contact Jill Rosen-
shield, Associate Curator, Special Collections,
at

rosen@doit.wisc.edu

Washington University

Special Collections
Washington University
Campus Box 1061
One Brookings Drive
St. Louis, MO 63130
Phone: 314 935 5495
FAX: 314 935 4045

 e-mail:
spec@library.wustl.edu

The Americana collection includes core items on the early history of the St. Louis area and westward expansion. The Modern Literature Collection is devoted to the work of 115 British and American writers and includes first editions, variant prints, translations, a wealth of secondary materials and manuscripts, drafts, worksheets, and correspondence of a number of British and American writers of the 19th and 20th centuries. The Philip Mills Arnold Semeiology Collections document the history of signs and symbols, encompassing early printed books on memory, cryptography, decipherment of unknown languages, universal languages, stenography, and exploratory communications systems for blind and deaf persons. The University Archives houses a wide range of printed materials, university publications, historical visual and audio materials, administrative records and selected faculty papers documenting the life of Washington University. The Archives also collects materials relating to 20th century St. Louis political and social welfare history.

For access to Washington University, including information about the collections and services of the University Archives (including about 40 on-line collections guides)

 WWW to
http://library.wustl.edu/~spec/
homepage.html

 telnet to
library.wustl.edu
terminal type: vt100
user: [return]
password: [return]

Wheaton College

Wheaton College Archives and Special
Collections
Wheaton, IL 60187-5593
Phone: 708 752 5705
FAX: 708 752 5855

The Special Collections, part of Wheaton College's Buswell Library, contain over 65 collections. The Special Collections department has the papers of notable authors like Madeleine L'Engle and Frederick Buechner, poets like Robert Siegel and Luci Shaw, along with the corporate papers of such organizations as the American Scientific Affiliations and Open Doors with Brother Andrew International.

Particularly strong in the following: Malcolm Muggeridge, Harold "Red" Grange, Madeleine L'Engle, Frederick Buechner, Robert Siegel, Samuel Johnson, James Boswell, Charles Dickens, Southeast Asian studies, Mormonism, Keswick movement, Wesley G. Pippert, Coleman G. Luck, Jonathan Blanchard, David Aikman, and Jacques Ellul.

 e-mail:
wcarchiv@david.wheaton.edu

gopher to
gopher.wheaton.edu
path: libraries
    Wheaton College Manuscript
        Repositories
    Archives and Special Collections

telnet to
library.wheaton.edu
login: library

Other: The Billy Graham Center Archives collects material about North American Protestant nondenominational missions and evangelism. Contact

bgcarc@david.wheaton.edu

The Marion Wade Center includes the papers of Owen Barfield, G. K. Chesterton, C. S. Lewis, George MacDonald, Dorothy L. Sayers, J. R. R. Tolkien, and Charles Williams. Contact

wade@david.wheaton.edu

Yale University, Beinecke Library

Beinecke Rare Book and Manuscript
        Library
Yale University
Box 208240
New Haven, CT 06520-8240
Phone: 203 432 2977
FAX: 203 432 4047

For the e-mail addresses of particular staff members, see the Beinecke Library information listed in the Yale information gopher which follows.

Beinecke Manuscript Collections

"Beinecke Manuscripts include collections from the Yale Collection of Western Americana, the Yale Collection of American Literature, the Yale Collection of German Literature, the Osborn Collection (English literature and history), and the General Collection. Most of the collections contain material from the 18th - 20th centuries, although several British and European collections contain earlier material" [from the on-line file, "About the Collections and Searching"].

Enid Bagnold Papers, Benet Family Correspondence, Boswell collection, Cleanth Brooks papers, Rachel Carson papers, Ernst Cassirer papers, Hart Crane collection, Langston Hughes papers, James Joyce collection, Adele Gutman Nathan theatrical collection, Edmund Poley papers, Ezra Pound papers, Romanov correspondence, Maurice Sterne papers, and the Kurt Wolff archive.

Beinecke Papyrus Collection

Papyri.

Beinecke Pre–1600 Collections

Twelfth-century monastic libraries, scholastic/university literature of the 13th century, and the Italian Renaissance.

gopher to
gopher.cis.yale.edu
path: Research and Library Services
    Yale Libraries
    Beinecke Library
    Manuscript and Arch. Coll.

Yale University Divinity School Library

gopher to
gopher.cis.yale.edu
Yale Libraries
Divinity School Library

More Information

For an extensive description of library archives available on the Internet, gopher to the Clearinghouse Project at the University of Michigan and consult the "Guide to Archives on the Internet." Copies of this guide are available either through gopher-mail or through anonymous FTP

host: una.hh.lib.umich.edu
path: cd../inetdirsstacks
filename: archives:kaynthony

telnet to
una.hh.lib.umich.edu
login: gopher

See also **Libraries—Special Collections**.

AREA CODES

See **TELEPHONE SERVICES.**

ART AND ART HISTORY

Andy Warhol Museum
This web site includes a tour of the museum, samples of works by the artist as well as directions, times, admission fees, and other information.

WWW to
http://www.warhol.org/warhol

Art Crimes

Art Crimes is a graffiti art gallery featuring wall art from the United States and the Czech Republic.

WWW to
http://www.gatech.edu/desoto/
graf/Index.Art_Crimes.html

For more information, contact

sf15@prism.gatech.edu
or
winsome@mindspring.com

The Art Deadlines List

The *Art Deadlines List* is a newsletter that announces competitions and contests in all arts–related fields.

To subscribe, send an e-mail request to

rgardner@charon.mit.edu
message: subscribe deadlines
    <your full e-mail address>

@Art Gallery

@Art is a virtual Internet Gallery by the collaborative group ad319. It is committed to exhibiting the best in contemporary electronic art. Artists are showcased on a revolving basis, with each exhibition lasting six to eight weeks.

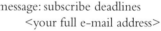
WWW to
http://gertrude.art.uiuc.edu/@art/
gallery.html

e-mail to
ad319@ux1.cso.uiuc.edu

School of Art & Design
408 E. Peabody Drive
University of Illinois
Champaign, IL 61820
Phone: 217 333 2977
FAX: 217 244 7688

Art on the Net

The Art on the Net site carries digital images, oil painting, photography.

WWW to
http://www.art.net

Art Serve

To see images of contemporary Hong Kong architecture, classical sites in Turkey, and the architecture of Islam, visit ArtServe at the Australian National University.

WWW to
http://rubens.anu.edu.au/

ArtsWire

Supported by the New York Foundation for the Arts, ArtsWire encompasses all aspects of the art world.

e-mail to
artswire@tmn.com

Combe d'Arc Cave Paintings

The French Ministry of Culture has added a web page for the recently discovered Combe d'Arc petroglyphs.

WWW to
http://ww.culture.fr/gvpda.htm

Dallas Museum of Art

gopher to
gopher.unt.edu
path: Denton, Dallas & Ft. Worth
    Information & Resources
    Dallas Museum of Art—
        Information and Images
    Museum Galleries

EXPO

The Expo connects the user to many collections of art and artifacts (Vatican exhibit, a Soviet archive exhibit, the 1492 exhibit, the Dead Sea Scrolls, the Paleontology exhibit, and the Spalato Exhibit).

WWW to
http://sunsite.unc.edu/expo/
    ticket_office.html

Note: Be sure also to stop by the EXPO Restaurant to enjoy the cuisine. You will find recipes for such dishes as Mousse au Chocolate aux Noisettes et au Whiskey.

FineArt Forum

One of the oldest network newsletters for the arts, *FineArt Forum* was founded seven years ago, edited by Ray Lausanna. Currently, its editor is Paul Brown.

gopher to
gopher.msstate.edu 70
path: Resources Maintained at
    Miss. St. Univ
    FineArt Forum Online

FTP to
ftp.msstate.edu
path: pub
    archives
    fineart_online

WWW to
http://www.msstate.edu/
    index-misc.html

To subscribe, send an e-mail message to

fineart_request@gu.edu.au
message: sub fineart <first-name>
    <last-name>

For items to be published in *FineArt Forum*, send information to

fineart@gu.edu.au

List of Lists

For a source of lists devoted to art,

WWW to
http://www.clark.net/pub/listserv/
    listserv.html

See also **APPENDIX—Lists.**

Museum Web

A home page for museums can be assessed by WWW at

http://www.primenet.com/art-
    rom/museumweb/

New York Art Line

This is a convenient source for art-related items on the Internet (information networks, e-zines, galleries, images, museums, etc.).

gopher to
gopher.panix.com 70
path: Arts Organizations
    NYC Artists

New York State Department of Education

This site holds an extensive array of items of interest to teachers.

gopher to
unix5.nysed.gov 70
path: k-12 Resources
    Arts and Humanities
    Gallery

Ohio State University Department of Art

This site maintains a extensive group of links with art resources (galleries, exhibitions, publications, etc.).

WWW to
http://www.cgrg.ohio-state.edu/
    COTA/Home.html
http://www.cgrg.ohio-state.edu/
    Newark/artsres.html

OTIS

Operative Term Is Stimulate (OTIS) is an on-line art gallery. It can be reached by

WWW at
http://sunsite.unc.edu/
otis.html

Russian Art

See **HISTORY: Russian and East European Studies**.

Texas A&M University

gopher to
gopher.tamu.edu

Texas Tech University

Among other resources, this site has an extremely useful menu item: "Picture and Images Searching in all of Gopher Space."

gopher to
cs4sun.cs.ttu.edu
path: Art & Images

University of Arizona

For an on-line exhibit of Mission Churches of the Sonoran Desert

WWW to
http://dizzy.library.arizona.edu/

University of California— Santa Barbara

For ASCII art, databases, graphics, and more

gopher to
ucsbuxa.ucsb.edu
path: UCSB Gopher Central
Infosurf
Gopher Central
The Subject Collection
The Arts Collection
Art and Architecture

University of Illinois—Chicago

For photography, ceramics, art-related links, and much more

gopher to
gopher.uic.edu
path: Researcher
Arts

University of Illinois— Urbana-Champaign WWW

Images from the National Gallery of Australia exhibit: Architecture of the Mediterranean Basin.

Sample WWW at
http://www.ncsa.uiuc.edu/SDG/
Experimental/anu-art-history/
home.html

University of Louisville

The gopher at the University of Louisville has links to Chicago museums, Dallas Museum of Art, Harvard Museums, and the Smithsonian Institution.

gopher to
ulkyvm.louisville.edu
path: University of Louisville Library
    Services
    Internet Resources by Title
    Gopher Jewels
    Education, Social Science, Arts
      and Humanities
    Arts & Humanities

University of Memphis Institute of Egyptian Art and Archaeology

WWW to
http://www.memst.edu/egypt/
    main.html

Virtual Museum of Digital and Telematic Art

For information, contact

vmodata@cc.newcastle.edu.au

WebLouvre

WebLouvre is a World Wide Web exhibit located in Paris, France, with over 1300 HTML pages and 800 pictures. The site is particularly strong in Impressionist painting.

WWW to
http://mistral.enst.fr/

The WELL

WWW to
http://www.well.sf.ca.us

AUDIO VISUAL

General

Purdue University maintains gopher links to a number of audio-visual rental catalogs (Indiana U., Purdue U., U. of Colorado, U. of Minnesota, U. of South Florida, U. of Texas at Dallas, U. of Utah, and U. of Wyoming).

gopher to
thorplus.lib.purdue.edu
path: Library Catalogs and Gophers
    Instruct. Media Centers
      (film & video)
    Rental Libraries

telnet to
thorplus.lib.purdue.edu
login: cwis
path: Purdue University Libraries
    Media Service Items
    Search Media Availability

Penn State Audio-Visual Services

One of the largest academic media collections in the United States may be searched on line.

gopher to
gopher.psu.edu
path: Information Servers at Penn
State University
PSU Libraries
at the LIAS prompt>>> type: sel media
For help at any LIAS prompt, type:
help medianet
For further information: e-mail to

psuavs@psulias.psu.edu

University Film & Video (UFV) at the University of Minnesota

gopher to
gopher.tc.umn.edu
path: Univ. of Minnesota Campus
Information
Dept. and College
Information
University Film & Video

See also **FILM.**

BANKING

First Union Corporation has established a Web site for the purpose of delivering Cyberbanking to its customers

WWW to
http://www.firstunion.com/

e-mail can be sent to
comments@firstunion.com

BOOKS

Antiquarian, Rare, Used Book Dealers

Many book dealers are currently on the Internet.

Acorn Books
Joel Chapman
740 Polk Street
San Francisco, CA 94109-7830
Phone: 415 563 1736

e-mail:
acornbks@netcom.com

Specialties: Art, California history, children's books, history, modern first editions, Americana, rare books, antique maps and prints, and the history of medicine.

Always Books
Jim McMillan
P.O. Box 378
Newman, IL 61942
Phone: 217 837 2610
FAX: 217 837 2553

e-mail:
to mcmillan@alexia.lis.uiuc.edu

Subjects: Antiquarian, out-of-print, and used religious books.

Other: Search service; mail order only; inventory listed on Interloc.

An Oasis Bookstore
James and Cheryl Davis
3911 3rd Avenue
San Diego, CA 92103
Phone: 619 299 8941

e-mail:
jamesd@cg57.esnet.com

Specialties: Science fiction, metaphysical, classics, children's.
Other: Walk-in store, open 7 days (11 A.M.–7 P.M.). Mail orders sent within two days of receipt of check or money order.

Argosy Book Store
Judith Lowry
116 E. 59th Street
New York, NY 10022
Phone: 212 753 4455
FAX: 212 5973 484

e-mail:
argosybook@aol.com

Bookmine: Old and Rare Books
Steve Mauer
1015 Second Street
Old Sacramento, CA 95814
Phone: 916 441 4609
FAX: 916 441 2019

e-mail:
bkmine@ns.net

Specialties: Western Americana, railroading, literature, Mark Twain, history of science and medicine, children's illustrated, maps, prints, art.
Other: Search service.

Boston Books Annex (used books)
Charles Vilnis and Helen Kelly
906 Beacon Street
Boston, MA
Phone: 617 266 1090

e-mail:
info@bostbook.com

Subjects: Used and out of print.

Boston Book Co. (rare books)
Charles Vilnis and Helen Kelly
705 Centre Street
Jamaica Plain, MA 02130
Phone: 617 522 2100
FAX: 617 522 9359

e-mail:
info@bostbook.com

Subjects: British and American literature, East Asia, Japan.

Meyer Boswell Books, Inc.
Jordan D. Luttrell
2141 Mission Street
San Francisco, CA 94110
Phone: 415 255 6400
FAX: 415 255 6499

e-mail:
meyerbos@netcom.com

Subjects: Legal history, constitutional law, international law, and trials.
Other: The entire inventory of antiquarian lawbooks (6000+ in stock) is searchable by anyone able to send Internet e-mail. To learn how to use the system, send a message with the word "help" (without quotation marks) in the body of the message to "rare-lawbooks@netcom.com" (again, without

quotation marks). Monthly lists and catalogues also available.

Larry Bowman Bookseller
458 Middle Turnpike
Storrs, CT 06268
Phone: 203 429 6542
FAX: 203 486 3347

e-mail:
bowman@uconnvm.uconn.edu

Subjects: Indian Ocean books.

Andrew Cahan, Bookseller, Ltd.
3000 Blueberry Lane
Chapel Hill, NC 27516
Phone/FAX: 919 968 0538

e-mail:
acahan@cybernetics.net

Specialties: Photography, Americana, fine and decorative arts, American literature, English literature.
Other: Hours by appointment; catalogues issued.

Barry Cassidy Rare Books
2005 T Street
Sacramento, CA 95814
Phone: 916 456 6307

e-mail:
misstacy@netcom.com

Subjects: Literature, American West, American Civil War,travel, voyages, antiquarian.

Collected Works
Andy Miller
223 Castro Street
Mountain View, CA 94041

Phone: 415 969 1990
FAX: 415 969 1978

e-mail:
JameZ1@aol.com

Subjects: Art, literature, literary criticism, children's, illustrated, western Americana, mystery, hunting and fishing, fine press, sci-fi/horror, juvenile, British and Irish studies.

G. Curwen Books
Jack Nessel and Ginger Curwen
1 West 67th Street, #710
New York, NY 10023
Phone: 212 595 5904

e-mail:
nessel@is.nyu.edu

Subjects: Modern first editions, detective fiction, science fiction, conjuring, culinary, and memoirs.

Dawson's Book Shop
Muir and Michael Dawson
535 N. Larchmont Blvd.
Los Angeles, CA 90004
Phone: 213 469 2186

e-mail:
dawsons@netcom.com

Subjects: Fine printing, photography, Western Americana, and miniature books.

Other: Founded in 1905 by Ernest Dawson; hours 9–5 Tuesday through Saturday. Internet inquiries should be directed to Nat Des Marais.

The Family Album

Ron Lieberman
RR1, Box 42
Glen Rock, PA 17327
Phone: 717 235 2134
FAX: 717 235 8042

e-mail:
ronbiblio@delphi.com

Subjects: American imprints pre-1800, European imprints pre-1700; German–Americana; bibles, bindings.
Other: Fine books in all fields bought, sold, and appraised; library and collection building consultants; 25 years in business.

Fireside Book Company

503 City Park Avenue
Columbus, OH 43215-5706
Phone: 614 621 1928

e-mail:
fireside@infinet.com

Rodger Friedman

Antiquarian Books
116 Pinehurst Avenue
New York, NY 10033
Phone: 212 923 7800 (ext. 2421)

e-mail:
rodgerf@delphi.com

Specialties: Nature, natural disasters, horticulture, exploration, urban civilization, the classical tradition, Neo-Latin literature, printed books 1500–1750.

Geiger's Books

Owner: Gary Decker
P.O. Box 66223
Scotts Valley, CA 95067
Phone: 408 335 5870

e-mail:
geigers@cruzio.com

Specialties: Western Americana, modern fiction, mystery fiction.
Other: Primarily mail order, book search service.

James & Devon Gray Booksellers

James Gray, Devon Gray
35 Charles Street
Winthrop, MA 02152
Phone: 617 846 0852
FAX: 617 846 2472

e-mail:
nous@delphi.com

Specialties: Early printed books. We sell only books printed before 1700.

Greyhavens Antiquarian Books

Richard Smith
P. O. Box 22513
Carmel, CA 93923
Phone/FAX: 408 624 3042

e-mail:
greyhave@ix.netcom.com

Specialties: Arts (decorative, graphic, performing), history (American, European, military, naval, and diplomatic), travel (foreign and description), fine printing, color illustrations.

Other: Inventory is on display at the Antique Arcade, 1823 El Camino Real, Redwood City, California.

Heldfond Book Gallery, Ltd.
Erik & Lane Heldfond
310 San Anselmo Avenue
San Anselmo, CA 94960
Phone: 415 456 8194
FAX: 415 383 3310

e-mail:
bkgallery@aol.com

Subjects: General antiquarian and illustrated books in all subject areas.
Other: Heldfond is an open bookstore, located in Marin County, just across the Golden Gate Bridge.

Jonathan A. Hill, Bookseller, Inc.
Jonathan A. Hill
325 West End Avenue
New York, NY 10023-8145
Phone: 212 496 7856
FAX: 212 496 9182

e-mail:
jonatha470@aol.com

Specialties: Science, medicine, natural history, bibliography, fine printing, wine.

Hill's Books
Ann and F. M. Hill
P.O. Box 1037
Kingsport, TN 37662
Phone: 615 247 8704
FAX: 615 247 8704

e-mail:
maynard@delphi.com

Subjects: The southern and border states, Civil War, Appalachia.

Horizon Books
Errol Porter
6 Brucedale Crescent
Willowdale, ONT M2K 2C7 Canada
Phone: 416 226 4282

e-mail:
errol@io.org

Subjects: Rare and out-of-print books on voyages, travel, exploration, natural history, plant hunting, and travels of naturalists.
Other: Closed shop—catalogue only.

David M. Lesser, Fine Antiquarian Books
One Bradley Road, Suite 302
Woodbridge, CT 06525
Phone: 203 389 8111
FAX: 203 389 7004

e-mail:
dmlesser@pcnet.com

Specialties: 18th and 19th century Americana, political and social issues through Reconstruction, the South, the settlement of the West, the development of cities, transportation, commerce, 18th century American imprints, political campaigns, constitutional and legal history, and maps.

Kate Lindemann Books
255 C North Plank Road
Newburgh, NY 12550

e-mail:
lindeman@whall2.msmc.edu

Specialties: Philosophy, illustrated, and travel.

Moe's Books

Moe Moskowitz
2476 Telegraph Avenue
Berkeley, CA 94704
Phone: 510 849 2087
FAX: 510 849 9938

 e-mail:
moe@moesbooks.com

 WWW to
http://moesbooks.com/moe.htm

 FTP to
moesbooks.com

Subjects: Over 175 catalogues available by e-mail, FTP, or through our WWW site, "Virtual Moe's." Antiquarian, new, out-of-print, and remaindered books on all subjects. *Other*: We do free book searches and accept want lists. E-mail us for more information.

Ogham Books

Michael Kelly
10, Lenaboy Gardens
Salthill
Galway, Ireland
Phone: 353 91 64343
FAX: 353 91 64343

 e-mail:
ogham@iol.ie

Specialties: Irish history and Irish music.

Other: Free book search.

Old England Bookshop

Judith M. and David J. Keyser
1916 Second Avenue North
Birmingham, AL 35210-1110
Phone: 205 956 4685
FAX: 205 956 4437

 e-mail:
75250.3475@compuserve.com

Specialties: Antiquarian books published in Britain from 1650–1899 in the areas of literature, history, travel, art, biography, theology, Bible, and religion.

Papyrus Books

Nancy Katsouras
34372 Dunhill Drive
Fremont, CA 94555
Phone: 510 790 1342
FAX: 510 790 2676

 e-mail:
papyrusb@ix.netcom.com

Specialties: New, out-of-print, rare, and scholarly books on ancient art, archaeology and ancient numismatics from Greece, Rome, Egypt, and the Near East.
Other: Free book searches in the above areas; catalogues upon request.

Parmer Books

7644 Forrestal Road
San Diego, CA 92120-2203
Phone: 619 287 0693
FAX: 619 287 6135

 e-mail:
parmerbook@aol.com

Subjects: New, out-of-print, antiquarian, and rare books on the Arctic, Antarctic, the

South Pacific, sea voyages, exploration, and discovery.

The Poisoned Pen, A Mystery Bookstore

Barbara G. Peters
7100 D East Main Street
Scottsdale, AZ 85251
Phone: 602 947 2974
Fax: 602 945 1023

 e-mail:
poisonpen1@aol.com

Subjects: New and used mystery. British imports. Signed first editions.
Other: Monthly newsletter.

Tony Power, Books

813 Sawcut Lane
Vancouver, B.C. Canada V5Z4A2
Phone: 604 877 1426
Fax: 604 731 0471

 e-mail:
power@freenet.vancouver.bc.ca

Subjects: Modern and hypermodern first editions (American, Canadian, and English).
Other: Closed shop; mail order only.

Quarto Books

Paul R. Sternberg
6623 Elwood NW
Albuquerque, NM 87107
Phone: 505 344 3540

 e-mail:
sternbrg@cs.unm.edu (temporary)

Subjects: Bibliography, books about books, art books.

Richard C. Ramer Old and Rare Books

Richard C. Ramer
225 E. 70th Street
New York, NY 10021
Phone: 212 737 0222
FAX: 212 288 4169

 e-mail:
5222386@mcimail.com

Subjects: Portugal, Spain, Brazil, Latin America.

B. & L. Rootenberg Rare Books

Barbara & Howard M. Rootenberg
P. O. Box 5049
Sherman Oaks, CA 91403
Phone: 818 788 7765
FAX: 818 788 8839

 e-mail:
blroot@class.org

Subjects: Rare books and manuscripts 15th to the 20th century in science, medicine, natural history, and early technology.

E. K. Schreiber Rare Books

Fred and Ellen Schreiber
285 Central Park West
New York, NY 10024
Phone: 212 873 3180
FAX: 212 873 3190

e-mail:
ekslibris@aol.com

Specialties: Early printed books, Incunabula, early editions of the Greek and Roman classics, Renaissance, Humanism, early illustrated books.
Other: By appointment only; appraisals; catalogues issued.

Schwartz Judaica
1934 Pentuckett Avenue
San Diego, CA 92104-5732
Phone: 619 232 5888
FAX: 619 233 5833

 e-mail:
schwartz@cts.com

Starosciak Art Books
117 Wilmot Place
San Francisco, CA 94115
Phone: 415 346 0650

 e-mail:
artbooks@netcom.com

Subjects: American art, modern European art, architecture, textile arts, and decorative arts.
Other: Member ABAA. Catalogues issued. Since 1972.

Tall Tales
Michael S. Kerstetter
16219 S. E. 137th Place
Renton, WA 98059
Phone: 206 228 2760

 e-mail:
msk@halcyon.com

 WWW to
http://www.halcyon.com/msk/
tlltales.htm

Specialties: Fine collectible science fiction, fantasy, and horror.
Other: Mail order only.

Taugher Books
Dennis Taugher
2550 Somerset Drive
Belmont, CA 94002-2926
Phone: 415 591 8366

 e-mail:
taugher@batnet.com

 WWW to
http://www.batnet.com/taugher/

Subjects: Modern first editions, including hypermodern literature, mystery/detective fiction, book collecting, black literature.
Other: By appointment; stocks the Ahern price guide; many signed books; mail order; twenty minutes south of the San Francisco airport; catalogues issued regularly; the entire stock is available for browsing through the WWW.

Tavistock Books
Box 5096
Alameda, CA 94501
Phone/FAX: 510 814 0480

 e-mail:
tavbooks@aol.com

Specialties: First editions, rare, collectibles, with special focus on Charles Dickens.
Other: Occasional subject catalogues; visits by appointment only.

Twice-Told Books

1578 Bardstown Road
Louisville, KY 40205-1154
Phone: 502 458 7420

e-mail:
twicetol
@iglou.com

Specialties: Modern first editions.

Wheldon & Wesley Ltd.

Att: Tony Swann
Lytton Lodge
Codicote
Hitchin Herts
SG4 8TE   UK
Phone: +44438820370
FAX: +44438821478

e-mail:
wheldwes@dircon.co.uk

Subjects: All natural history.

Wilsey Rare Books

Edward Ripley-Duggan
23 Mill Road
Olivebridge, NY 12461
Phone: 914 657 7057
FAX: 914 657 2366

e-mail:
ripleyduggan@delphi.com

WWW to
http://www.clark.net/pub/wilsey

Subjects: Fine printing, history of printing, illustration, the arts of book binding, calligraphy, paper making, typography, fine bindings, etc.

Other: Member ABAA, ILAB; hours by appointment only; three or four catalogues annually.

John Windle, Antiquarian Bookseller

1226 Johnson Street
Menlo Park, CA 94025
Phone: 415 327 4821
FAX: 415 327 4921

e-mail:
johnwindle@aol.com

Subjects: Incunabula, early and fine printing, illustrated and color plate books, bindings, press books, literature before 1900 (no modern firsts).

Other: Appraisals and evaluations. By appointment only.

Second Address:
49 Geary Street
San Francisco, CA 94108
Hours: Monday–Saturday, 9-6

Wonderland Books

Allan Friedman
7511 Fairmount
El Cerrito, CA 94530
Phone: 510 528 8475

e-mail:
alland@dnai.com

WWW to
http://www.dnai.com/~alland/
index.html

Specialties: Western Americana, modern firsts, illustrated, and antiquarian children's.
Other: Hours Tuesday through Sunday, 12 –5.

John T. Zubal, Inc.
2969 West 25th Street
Cleveland, OH 44113
Phone: 216 241 7640
FAX: 216 241 6966

e-mail:
johnz45897@aol.com

Subjects: Scholarly and antiquarian books, chiefly in the humanities and social sciences. *Other*: Auction department, which sells antiquarian and rare books, pamphlets, mss. 300,000 books in stock.

Bookstore List

To receive a file ("Catalogues") containing information about bookstores, book catalogues, and book clubs

anonymous FTP to
rtfm.mit.edu
path: pub
   usenet
   news.answers
   books

This file will provide information regarding book catalogues from such companies as Barnes & Noble, Boydell & Brewer, A Common Reader, Daedalus Books, Dover Publications, David Godine, Loompanics Unlimited, Oxford University Press, Reader's Catalog, SUNY Press, Texas A&M Press, and many others.

In addition, this list is regularly posted to the newsgroup

rec.arts.books

Clubs and Catalogues

For information regarding book clubs such as Conservative Book Club, Doubleday Book Club, Folio Society, History Book Club, Quality Paperback Book Club, The

Reader's Subscription, and other similar enterprises, see previous entry, "Bookstore List."

Out-of-Print Search Services

Bookbytes Out-of-Print Book Network
412 171st Place NE
Bellevue, WA 98008-4110
Phone: 800 827 6973 or 206 747 0511
FAX: 206 747 0635

e-mail:
bookbytes@aol.com

Other: Out-of-print books; connects people interested in exchanging books.

Glyn's Books
Glyn Watson
6 The Avenue
Lyneal, Ellesmere
Shropshire SY12 OQJ UK
Phone: 44 01948 720591
FAX: 44 01948 710591

e-mail:
glynbook@aladdin.co.uk
glynwatson@delphi.com
100447.1206@compuserve.com

Interloc: The Electronic Marketplace for Books

P.O. Box 5
Southworth, WA 98386
Phone: 1 206 871 3617
FAX: 1 206 871 5626

 e-mail:
Interloc@equinox.shaysnet.com
72411.2301@compuserve.com

Other: Interloc is an on-line database of books, photographs, maps, manuscripts, and recordings. On-line searches. Subscription is $10 per month. Additional connect time charges. No minimum on-line time required. No transaction charges.

See also **BOOKS—Antiquarian, Used, Rare**

Retail Stores and Other Book-Related Sites

B&R Samizdat Express

P.O. Box 161
West Roxbury, MA 02132
Phone: 617 469 2269
FAX: 617 469 4634

 e-mail:
samizdat@world.std.com

Public domain and freely available electronic texts (English, Latin, French) on IBM/Mac diskettes (most from the Internet). 312 disks today, adding 20–30 new ones each month. Mostly classic works of literature, government and UN information, and tools for teachers and librarians.

Book Stacks Unlimited, Inc.

200 Public Square
Suite 26-4600
Cleveland, OH 44114-2301
Phone: 216 861 0467
FAX: 216 861 0469

 e-mail:
info@books.com (information)

 telnet to
books.com

Services: Fast shipping, e-books, user-entered reviews, frequent buyer benefits, gift book service, electronic magazines, infobots (new releases), Biblio-Tech (on-line book discussion group).

BookZONE

A home page for BookZone, a collection of over 40 small and medium-sized presses, can be found at

 WWW to
http://ttx.com/bookzone

e-mail:
bookzone@ttx.com

> Note: In this directory, long addresses, paths, and messages are carried over to successive lines. However, these should be read as single line entities and commands.

Borders Books & Music

10720 Preston Road #1018
Dallas, TX 75230
Phone: 214 363 1977 (bookstore)
      214 363 3226 (music)
FAX: 214 363 7099
TDD: 214 363 0793

 e-mail:
books@borders.com

 gopher to
borders.com

 WWW to
http://borders.com

Internet Book Shop

 WWW to
http://www.bookshop.co.uk

J.F. Lehmanns Fachbuchhandlung

Berlin, Germany
Subject: German language.

 gopher to
gopher.germany.eu.net
path: Internet Shop

 WWW to
http://www.germany.eu.net/shop/
   jfl/jfl_kat.html

The Ohio State University

University Bookstore
Central Classroom Building
2009 Millikin Road
Columbus, OH 43210
Phone: 614 292 2991
Toll-free: 800 553 0094
FAX: 614 292 8983

 e-mail:
bookstore@osu.edu

Other: Accepts Visa, Master Card, and Discover.

OmniMedia

1312 Carlton Place
Livermore, CA 94550
Phone: 510 294 8153
FAX: 510 447 1771

 e-mail:
omnimdia@netcom.com

Subjects: Electronic books for Windows; reissues of public domain material.

Quantum Books

4 Cambridge Center
Cambridge, MA 02142
Phone 617 494 5042
FAX 617 577 7282

e-mail: quanbook@world.std.com
Mail List: quanlist@world.std.com

Subjects: Computer science, math, and physics.

Roswell Internet Computer Bookstore

1587 Brunswick Street
Halifax, Nova Scotia,
Canada B3J 2G1
Phone: 902 423 3161
FAX: 902 423 3161

e-mail:
roswell@fox.nstn.ca

Electronic bulletin board version of the actual specialty computer book store located in downtown Halifax, Nova Scotia, Canada. Carries over 6,000 titles in stock.

WWW to
http://www.nstn.ca/cybermall/
cybermall.html

gopher to
gopher.nstn.ca 70
path: cybermall
bookstores
Roswell Internet Computer
Bookstore

Seaside Book & Stamp

Jerry Tucker
5670 Spring Garden Road
Brenton Street Entrance
Halifax, Nova Scotia
Canada B3J 1H6
Phone: 902 423 8254
Toll-free: 800 37S TAMP

e-mail:
gtucker@fox.nstn.ns.ca

gopher to
gopher.nstn.ns.ca 70

WWW to
www.nstn.ns.ca/cybermall/
cybermall.html

Subject: Specializing in new and used science fiction, stamps, fantasy, and stamp collecting supplies.

Stanford University Bookstore

Stanford University
Stanford, CA 94305

telnet to
FORSYTHETN.STANFORD.
EDU
login: socrates
select: bookstore

Tattered Cover Book Store

2955 East First Avenue
Denver, CO 80206
Phone: 303 322 7727
Toll-free: 800 833 9327
FAX: 303 329 2279
TDD/V: 303 320 0536

e-mail:
books@tatteredcover.com [for individuals]
corporate@tatteredcover.com [for business accounts]

University of California-Irvine Bookstore

University of California
Irvine, CA 92717
Phone: 714 829 BOOK
FAX: 714 856 8545

e-mail:
books@uci.edu

gopher to
gopher.cwis.uci.edu
path: Departmental Informational
　　　Sources
　　　Bookstore

www to
http://bookweb.cwis.uci.edu:8042/

Specialties: Specialists in international orders for technical and trade books, computer books, humanistic studies (literary theory, philosophy), classical music and jazz on cd, Japanese animation on video and laser, medical books.

Other: Browseable database of nearly 100,000 currently stocked titles, rotating fine art and literary-themed exhibits in a hypertext environment, and special expertise in international shipping and payment options.

Wordsworth Books

30 Brattle Street
Cambridge, MA 02138
Phone: 800 899 2202
　　　617 354 1529
FAX: 617 354 4674

e-mail:
info@wordsworth.com

gopher to
gopher.wordsworth.com

WWW to
http://www.wordsworth.com

telnet to
wordsworth.com

Other: 100,000 titles in 95 subjects, trade books discounted.

BULLETIN BOARDS

For a list of BBSs accessible by telnet,

gopher to
gopher.tamu.edu:70/11/.dir/bbs.dir

CATALOGUES—COLLEGE AND UNIVERSITY

A comprehensive listing of catalogues available on the Internet would probably not be practicable. If you have an interest in getting information about a college or university, the simplest thing to do is to gopher there. The following catalogues are listed as examples:

Rutgers University

WWW to
http://www.rutgers.edu
path: Academics: Courses, Schedule
　　　School Catalogues

University of Chicago Graduate Catalog

WWW to
http://ap-homeboy.uchicago.edu/
AcaPubs/Default.html

CENSORSHIP

John Ockerbloom has created a home page featuring books that have been the object of censorship by legal authorities or by schools.

WWW to
http://www.cs.cmu.edu:8001/Web/
People/spok/banned-books.html

For more information, contact Ockerbloom at

spok@cs.cmu.edu

CLASSICAL STUDIES

ARIADNE, the Hellenic Civilization Database

This database contains information on Ancient Greek arts, sculpture, buildings, museums, and literature.

gopher to
ithaki.servicenet.ariadne-t.gr:70
path: HELLENIC_
CIVILIZATION

Yale University

gopher to
yaleinfo.cis.yale.edu

See also **HUMANITIES—Scholia.**

COMMUNICATIONS

Electronic Journal of Communication

A journal devoted to the study of communication policy, practice, research, and theory. To subscribe, send an e-mail message to

comserve@vm.its.rpi.edu
message: JOIN EJCREC

University of Iowa

gopher to
gopher.arcade.uiowa.edu 2270
path: Media and Mass
Communication

Vanderbilt University

This site maintains archives of TV news programs.

gopher to
vuinfo.vanderbilt.edu

COMPARATIVE LITERATURE

The American Comparative Literature Association can be reached at

acla@oregon.uoregon.edu

COMPUTER ABBREVIATIONS AND ACRONYMS

For a copy of "ABEL: A Glossary of Computer-Oriented Abbreviations and Acronyms,"

anonymous FTP to
ftp.temple.edu
path: cd /pub/info/help-net
    get babel95a.txt

gopher to
gopher.temple.edu
path: Computer Resources and
        Information
    Internet & Bitnet Information
        (Help-Net)
    Glossary (BABEL 95A.TXT)

e-mail:
listserv@vm.temple.edu
subject: [blank]
message: GET BABEL95A TXT
    HELP-NET

COPYRIGHT

Archive

gopher to
gopher.cni.org70
path: Coalition FTP Archives
    Coalition Electronic Forums/
    CNI-Copyright

Searches—LOC

To search Library of Congress records for copyrights,

telnet to
marvel.loc.gov
login: marvel

WATCH (Writers and Their Copyright Holders)

The Harry Ransom Humanities Research Center at the University of Texas at Austin and the University of Reading Library in Reading, England, have created an on-line database of authors and their copyright holders.

gopher to
gopherhost.lib.utexas.edu 70
path: Library Catalogs
        UT Austin Catalogs
        Harry Ransom Humanities
            Research Center
        WATCH

WWW to
http://gopherhost.lib.utexas.edu
path: 11
    Library Catalogs
    University of Texas at Austin
    Harry Ranson Humanities
        Research Center
    watch

Wiretap

For a collection of information on copyright

gopher to
wiretap.spies.com 70
path: Government Docs
        Copyright

DANCE

To access the Dancer's Archive (ballet, folk, flamenco, etc.)

gopher to
world.std.com

DISABILITIES

See **SPECIAL EDUCATION**.

DOCUMENTATION

Citation Formats

See **REFERENCE WORKS—Writer's Handbook**.

Electronic

Electronic sources are being quoted more and more frequently, and they can pose special problems when it comes to bibliographic citations. Two works that will prove useful are:

The Chicago Manual of Style, 14th ed. Chicago, IL: University of Chicago, 1993.

Li, Xia and Nancy B. Crane. *Electronic Style: A Guide to Citing Electronic Information*. Westport, CT: Meckler-Media, 1993.

DRAMA

See **THEATER**.

EDITING

Numerous documents on electronic editing and publishing are available by anonymous FTP from the University of Virginia.

FTP to
jefferson.village.virginia.edu

The same texts can be read on line via gopher at

jefferson.village.virginia.edu
path: Related Readings
     Electronic Publishing

WWW to
http://jefferson.village.virginia.edu/
   readings.html

EDUCATION

American Educational Research Association (AERA)

The AERA has established a home page which contains news for educational researchers, including information on AERA: membership, publications, annual meeting, and special interest groups.

WWW to
http://www.asu.edu/aff/aera/
   home.html

Arizona State University

Gene Glass of the College of Education, Arizona State University, Tempe, has compiled a gopher subject tree on education—including electronic journals (such as The Journal of Higher Education) and gopher connections (to EDUCOM, ERIC, IBM Kiosk, etc.).

gopher to
info.asu.edu
path: ASU-Campus-Wide
    Information
    College of Education at
     Arizona State
    Other Education Gophers
    Resources for K–12

ARTSEDGE

Supported by the John F. Kennedy Center, ARTSEDGE is a home page that features a newsletter about the arts in K–12 education, Goals 2000 information, links to art, and education-related resources.

 WWW to
http://k12.cnidr.org/

 gopher to
purple.tmn.com
path: Artsedge Information Gallery

AskERIC

For a database of lesson plans,

 gopher to
ericir.syr.edu
login: gopher

Association of International Educators (NAFSA)

To contact the Association of International Educators, send an e-mail message to

 inbox@nafsa.org

gopher to
gopher.colostate.edu

Bulletin Board

telnet to
nis.calstate.edu
login: intl

(U.S. Government Programs & Information; International Educational Grants and Resources; International Education Bibliography.)

CAUSE E-Bulletin

CAUSE, The Association for Managing and Using Information Resources in Higher Education, publishes Campus Watch, an electronic newsletter. To subscribe, send an e-mail message to

 mailserv@cause.colorado.edu
message: subscribe campuswatch

 WWW to
http://cause.www.colorado.edu

Classroom Connect

A new print publication, Classroom Connect deals with using the Internet and other on-line services in the classroom. For a free issue, send your snail-mail address to

 connect@wentworth.com

Daily Report Card

For a subscription to the Daily Report Card, a summary of news in K–12 education, send an e-mail message to

 listserv@gwuvm.gwu.edu
subject line: <blank>
message: subscribe Rptcrd
      <your name>

Education Central

This project at Central Michigan University provides resources for K–12 educators.

 gopher to
gopher.cmich.edu
path: Education Resources

 www to
http://www.ehhs.cmich.edu

Education Policy Digest

For a subscription to the Education Policy Digest, send an e-mail message to

 listproc@scholastic.com
subject line: <blank>
message: subscribe Edpol-D
    <your name>

EdWeb

The Corporation for Public Broadcasting has developed EdWeb, a WWW on-line educational resource guide. It focuses on the interconnection of education reform and information technology. It also offers a large collection of Internet and on-line resource information for educators.

 WWW to
http://edweb.cnidr.org:90

ERIC

See **U. S. GOVERNMENT—ERIC**.

FAQ

For FAQ for educators and school administrators who are considering adding an Internet connection in their schools

 WWW to
http://ds.internic.net/fyi/fyi22.txt

 gopher to
ericir.syr.edu
path: Internet Guides and
        Directories
        FYI on Questions and Answers

Goals 2000

For information on the U.S. Department of Education's Goals 2000, anonymous FTP to

 ftp.ed.gov
path: ED_wide
        initiatives
        goals

HotList of K–12 Internet School Sites

The HotList of K–12 Internet School Sites can be reached by WWW to

 http://toons.cc.ndsu.nodak.edu/
        ~sackmann/k12.html

IKE (IBM Kiosk for Education)

During the hours of 5 A.M. to 5 P.M. Pacific Time

 WWW to
ike.engr.washington.edu
        (128.95.32.61)
login: register

Indiana University

 gopher to
lib-gopher.lib.indiana.edu 70
path: Subject-approach
        Education Library Gopher

John and Janice's Research Page

This site includes statistics by state on the number of schools and districts with Internet connections.

 WWW to
http://k12.cnidr.org/janice_k12/
states/states.html

Jobs Corner

The Jobs Corner archives announcements of employment opportunities for educators.

 gopher to
info.asu.edu 70
path: ASU-CWIS
College of Education
Other Education Gopher
Jobs

KidLink Gopher

 telnet to
kids.ccit.duq.edu
login: gopher

Learning Link

 telnet to
sierra.fwl.edu
login: newuser
password: newuser

Linkway Archive

The International Archive for K–12 Public Domain Linkway Folders is maintained at the following anonymous FTP site:

 ftp.cic.net
path: pub
Software
pc
Linkway

List of Lists

For a source for lists devoted to education,

 WWW to
http://www.clark.net/pub/listserv/
listserv.html

Miscellaneous K–12

 gopher to
ids.cwis.uci.edu 7029
path: UC Berkeley Compendium

 WWW to
http://k12.cnidr.org

Mitch's Internet Resources

 e-mail:
mitch@mhs.mendocino.k12.ca.us

NASA K–12 Internet Project

A guide to Internet access options for K–12 teachers is available at this site.

 gopher to
quest.arc.nasa.gov
path: Teachers on the Internet
Getting US Teachers OnLine

 WWW to
http://quest.arc.nasa.gov

New York State Education Department

 gopher to
unix5.nysed.gov
path: K–12

Novae>> Group>>

The University of Idaho hosts the Novae>> Group>> listserver to provide timely news articles to classroom teachers. To subscribe, send an e-mail message to

majordomo@uidaho.edu
subject: [blank]
message: subscribe novae
    <your e-mail address>

The Online Educator

The Online Educator is published in both print and e-mail formats. A recent issue featured stories on using the Internet to teach geography and another on connecting to KIDLINK. For more information about subscription rates or to contribute news items, send an e-mail message to

ednetnews@aol.com

WWW to
http://www.cris.com/~felixg/
    OE/OEWELCOME.html

Scholastic Internet Center

The Scholastic Internet Center maintains a classroom-planning site which contains a wide assortment of lesson plans, activities, quick tips, interesting holidays, seasonal happenings, and calendar of historical events.

gopher to
scholastic.com 2003

WWW to
http://scholastic.com:2005/

United States Department of Education

A repository for many resources for American education run by the U.S. Department of Education, the Office of Educational Research and Improvement's (OERI) Internet site contains the National Standards for Arts Education, selected speeches by the Secretary of Education, statistical data sets, and many other files.

WWW to
http://www.ed.gov/

gopher to
gopher.ed.gov

anonymous FTP to
ftp.ed.gov

E-mail users can obtain a catalog and instructions by sending a message to

almanac@inet.ed.gov
message: send catalog

University of Illinois Urbana-Champaign

To visit the UIUC College of Education Learning Resource Server,

gopher to
gopher.edu.uiuc.edu 70

University of Massachusetts

To connect to the University of Massachusetts' site for K–12 educators,

 telnet to
k12.ucs.umass.edu
login: guest

Usenet Groups

k12.chat.elementary
k12.chat.junior
k12.chat.senior
k12.chat.teacher
k12.ed.art
k12.ed.business
k12.ed.comp.literacy
k12.ed.health-pe
k12.ed.life-skills
k12.ed.math
k12.ed.music
k12.ed.science
k12.ed.soc-studies
k12.ed.special
k12.ed.tag
k12.ed.tech
k12.lang.art
k12.lang.deutsche-eng
k12.lang.esp-eng
k12.lang.francais
k12.lang.russian
k12.library
k12.news
k12.sys.channel0
k12.sys.channel1
k12.sys.channel10
k12.sys.channel11
k12.sys.channel12
k12.sys.channel2
k12.sys.channel3
k12.sys.channel4
k12.sys.channel5
k12.sys.channel6
k12.sys.channel7
k12.sys.channel8
k12.sys.channel9
k12.sys.projects

Vocal Point

Vocal Point is published by the K–12 students of the Boulder Valley School District (Colorado). It features full-motion video, photos, and a hypertext layout.

 WWW to
http://bvsd.k12.co.us/cent/
CentennialHome.html

Web66

Web66, A K–12 World Wide Web Project, has been established to help educators learn how to set up their own WWW servers. Its goal is to provide educators and students access to the Internet and to allow them to find appropriate K–12 resources on the Web.

 WWW to
http://web66.coled.umn.edu

ELECTRONIC TEXTS

See **TEXTS—Electronic.**

ENGLISH

General

See **REFERENCE WORKS.**

American Literature Pedagogy

The Electronic Archives for Teaching the American Literatures has a home page containing syllabi, bibliographies, and electronic texts.

 WWW to
http://www.georgetown.edu/
tamlit/tamlit-home.html

Beat Generation

Literary Kicks is devoted to Jack Kerouac, Allen Ginsberg, and the Beat Generation.

WWW to
http://www.charm.net/~brooklyn/
LitKicks.html

Chaucer Bibliography:

The University of Texas-San Antonio maintains an on-line Chaucer bibliography.

gopher or telnet to
utsainfo.utsa.edu
path: library/
local
chau

Composition and Grammar

For questions about writing and grammar, see **REFERENCE—Grammar and Form.**

Leeds Database of Manuscript English Verse

"The Brotherton Collection of Manuscript Verse is a database of individual items of English poetry contained in the 17th and 18th century manuscripts belonging to the Brotherton Collection of Leeds University Library. It contains approximately 2550 poems, listed by up to seventeen fields, including first lines, last lines, attribution, author, title, date, length, verse-form, and content."

telnet to
bcmsv.leeds.ac.uk (129.11.128.108)
login: bcmsv
password: bcmsv

List of Lists

For a source of lists devoted to literature and writing,

WWW to
http://www.clark.net/pub/listserv/
listserv.html

See also **APPENDIX—Lists**

Literature and Psychology

The annual bibliography of the Institute for Psychological Study of the Arts at the University of Florida is published on line. Subscribe to the list PSYART (see **APPENDIX—Lists/English—General**). The latest issue contains a bibliography of about 1550 books and articles.

gopher to
gopher.ufl.edu

National Council of Teachers of English (NCTE)

The National Council of Teachers of English maintains a gopher at

ncte.clemson.edu

Postmodern Culture

A journal devoted to all aspects of postmodern culture; send an e-mail message to

listserv@listserv.ncsu.edu
message: subscribe pmc-list

SCHOLAR

SCHOLAR is an on-line listserver for text analysis and natural language applications. Monthly digests give information on book reviews, databases, hardware, jobs, news, software, etc., which can be retrieved with an e-mail message and a GET command.

e-mail:
listserv@cunyvm.cuny.edu
message: subscribe SCHOLAR
<your full name>

SCHOLAR has also been WAIS-indexed and is available at Johns Hopkins University. Supports Boolean searches.

gopher to
musicbox.mse.jhu.edu
path: Other gophers
JH Universe—The JH CWIS
This Way to JHUniverse
Miscellaneous
SCHOLAR

WWW to
http://jhuniverse.hcf.jhu.edu:10010

Shakespeare

The Shakespeare Database project at West-faelische Wilhelms-Universitaet Muenster, Germany, maintains a site for the project's news and information on publications.

WWW to
http://ves101.uni-muenster.de/

For a site that provides a search engine for Shakespeare's plays,

WWW to
http://www.gh.cs.su.oz.au/Virtual/
fsearch

The Shakespeare Globe Centre Germany provides information about the Globe The-atre reconstruction. It also provides links to other Shakespeare-related sites on the Internet.

WWW to
http://www.rrz.uni-koeln.de/
phil-fak/englisch/
SHAKESPEARE/

Shaw Festival WWW Site

The Shaw Festival, the second-largest the-atre company in North America and the only company that specializes in plays written during Bernard Shaw's lifetime, has a home page.

WWW to
http://www.cyberplex.com/
CyberPlex/Arts/Shaw/Shaw.html

Sites

A number of Internet sites are particularly strong in resources in English, holding extensive electronic texts, links to other literary gophers, tips for computing in English, reference tools, and many other resources.

gopher to
Carnegie Mellon U at
english-server.hss.cmu.edu
U. of Pennsylvania at
gopher.upenn.edu
Rice U. at
riceinfo.rice.edu
U. of Michigan at
una.hh.lib.umich.edu

WWW to the U. of Chicago at
http://tuna.uchicago.edu/
ENGLISH.html

See also **ARCHIVES AND LIBRARY RESOURCES** and **LANGUAGE AND LITERATURE.**

ENGLISH AS A SECOND LANGUAGE (ESL)

See **TEACHING ENGLISH AS A SECOND LANGUAGE.**

ERIC

See **EDUCATION** and **U. S. GOVERNMENT.**

FAXING

Guide

It is possible to send faxes through the Internet. To retrieve a file explaining how, e-mail to

fax-faq-request@northcoast.com
subject: archive
message: send fax-faq

Or obtain the file "fax-faq" by anonymous FTP from

rtfm.mit.edu
path: pub
    usenet-by-group
    news.answers
    internet-services
    fax-faq

gopher to
gopher.eff.org
path: Net_info
    Technical
    Net-fax-faq

Services

E-mail to either of the following for more information:

info@awa.com
message: Help

tpc-faq@town.hall.org
message: Help

or get file "faxgate.help" by anonymous FTP to

ftp.pandora.sf.ca.us
path: pub
    elvis

FILM

CineMedia Site

A resource site for cinema, broadcasting and media can be accessed by WWW at

http://www.gu.edu.au/gwis/
    cinemedia/CineMedia.
    HOME.HTML

Filmmaker

For a magazine that focuses on independent movie making,

WWW to
http://found.cs.nyu.edu/CAT/
    affiliates/filmmaker/
    filmmaker.html

Reviews

For a collection of movie reviews,

gopher to
ashpool.micro.umn.edu
path: Fun
    Movies

or

gopher to
english-server.hss.cmu.edu
path: Film & Television

University of Manchester UK Film Databases

The Film Database at the University of Manchester Computing Center contains information on over 6500 films released before 1986. Boolean searches are allowed. Extensive information is provided on titles, plot summaries, producers, directors, actors, release dates, length, reviews, and extensive commentaries.

gopher to
info.mcc.ac.uk
path: External Services
    WAIS Searches
    Actors/Actresses/Directors

Additional move databases can be reached via WWW at

http://www.cm.cf.ac.uk/Movies/
   moviequery.html

or

http://www.msstate.edu/Movies

Virtual Mirror

For a survey of film and cinema listservs,

WWW to
http://mirror.wwa.com/mirror/

See also **APPENDIX—Lists, AUDIO VISUAL,** and **THEATER.**

FINGER

Via Mail

e-mail to
jfesler@netcom.com
subject: #finger <user@site>

or

dlangley@netcom.com
subject: #help

Via Telnet

telnet <site> 79
Once connected, type <username>

FRENCH

American Association of Teachers of French

For the American Association of Teachers of French,

gopher to
utsainfo.utsa.edu 7070

Art Exhibit On-Line

The French Ministry of Culture has mounted an "imaginary exhibition" on the World Wide Web: "Le Siède des lumières dans la peinture des musées de France." The 100 artists represent a panorama of French painting during the eighteenth century.

WWW to
http://dmf.culture.fr

ARTFL

For a collection of French texts,

WWW to
http://tuna.uchicago.edu/
   ARTFL.html

gopher to
gopher.uchicago.edu
path: Scholarly and Research
   Resources
   ARTFL

France FYI

"France FYI" is a monthly electronic news-letter published by Jack Kessler.

gopher to
infolib.berkeley.edu 72
path: Electronic Journals (Library
Oriented)
FYIFrance

or

gopher.cis.yale.edu
path: BrowseYaleInfo
Miscellaneous Internet
Resources
France
Jack Kessler's Bulletin

telnet to
a.cni.org
login: brsuser
path: Search
Select a Database
DRCT

Frantext

A database of 3000+ works of French litera-ture, from the 16th century to the present.

gopher to
cmcL2.nyu.edu:70
path: Library Facilities
Bobst Library/
NYU Library Resources
Electronic Resources via Internet
ARTFL
ARTFL Bibliography

French Embassy Gopher

This gopher contains information on news from France, official French policy state-ments, a database of 3000+ listing of French cultural events in the United States, and many other aspects of Franco-American re-lations.

gopher to
iep.univ-lyon2.fr 70
path: amb-wash.fr

French Internet FAQ

gopher to
gopher.nbnet.nb.ca
path: NBNet/Internet Info
Frequently Asked Questions
Questions Postes Frequement

Frognet

Daily postings of news from France. E-mail a request for an application to

frog@guvax.georgetown.edu

Georgetown CPET

For a centralized index of literary e-texts,

telnet to
guvax3.acc.georgetown.edu
login: CPET

Gopher Littératures

gopher to
Université de Montréal (Québec,
Canada)
path: Gopher Littératures

Minitel

Free software for accessing Minitel, the French electronic network, is available by calling 914 399 0800.

News

To subscribe to the French news distribution newsgroup, send an e-mail to

listserver@grasp1.univ-lyon1.fr
message: sub fr-news-distribution
    <your first last name>

Oxford Text Archive

See **TEXTS—Electronic.**

Yale University

gopher to
path: Browse YaleInfo
        Miscellaneous Internet
            Resources
        France

See also **APPENDIX—Lists** and **LANGUAGE AND LITERATURE.**

FTP

FAQ

For the file "Anonymous FTP: Frequently Asked Questions List,"

anonymous FTP to
oak.oakland.edu
path: SimTel/msdos/info

For a list of anonymous FTP sites, anonymous FTP to

oak.oakland.edu
path: SimTel
        msdos
        info
        ftp-list.zip

GEOGRAPHY

See **MAPS.**

GERMAN

American Association of Teachers of German

For more information,

e-mail:
73740.3231@compuserve.com

Dictionaries

Get "German.english.tar.Z" by FTP from

ftp.uni-muenster.de
path: pub
        dict
        german

WWW to
http://www.willamette.edu/
    ~tjones/Language-Page.html

German Academic Exchange Service (DAAD)

e-mail:
daadny@acf2.nyu.edu

gopher to
jhuniverse.hcf.jhu.edu
path: Divisions, Centers
        Centers and Affiliates
        American Institute–
            German Studies
        DAAD

Institut für Deutsche Sprache

The Institut für Deutsche Sprache at Mannheim, Germany, maintains a 30-million-word collection of German corpora.

telnet to
warum.uni-mannheim.de
login: gopher
password: <enter>

Syllabi Database

For a collection of teaching materials for German Studies,

anonymous FTP to
ftp.cit.cornell.edu
path: pub
    special
      DAADsyllabi

Tutorial

German Plus (gplus30.zip) is a language tutorial with review and exercises of over 500 nouns, adjectives, and verbs conjugated in the four major tenses (shareware).

anonymous FTP to
oak.oakland.edu
path: SimTel
    msdos
      langtutr

See also **ARCHIVES AND LIBRARY RESOURCES**, **HISTORY**, and **LANGUAGE AND LITERATURE.**

GOPHER

Information

gopher to
cwis.usc.edu 70
path: Other Gophers and
    Information Resources
    Gophers by Subject
    Gopher Jewels
    Gopher Jewels Information
      and Help

anonymous FTP to
ftp.einet.net
path: pub
    Gopherjewels-Tips

Publicly Accessible Sites

For publicly accessible gopher sites,

telnet to

consultant.micro.umn.edu
login: gopher

infoslug.ucsc.edu
login: infoslug

infopath.ucsd.edu
login: infopath

panda.uiowa.edu
login: panda

gopher to

english-server.hss.cmu.edu

gopher.uiuc.edu
path: Other Gopher and
    Information Servers
    All the Gopher Servers in the
      World

GRAMMAR REFERENCE

See **REFERENCE BOOKS.**

GRANTS INFORMATION

GrantSource

The Office of Research Services at the University of North Carolina-Chapel Hill has information available for nearly 10,000 documents available from major funding sources (full-text search capability).

gopher to
gibbs.oit.unc.edu
path: research
    grants

HELLENIC STUDIES

See **CLASSICAL STUDIES.**

HIGHER EDUCATION

American Association of University Professors (AAUP)

To contact the American Association of University Professors, send an e-mail message to

aaup@igc.apc.org

HISTORY

British Archives

Britain's National Register of Archives, set up in 1945, "collects information from record repositories throughout the UK on manuscript sources for British history outside of the public records. It consists of more than 38,000 unpublished lists and catalogues of manuscript collections, including those held privately by individuals, firms and institutions, with details, where available, on access to these records and repository addresses."

Limited and specific inquiries will be answered by e-mail at

sargent@rs1-hr.sas.ac.uk

Census Bureau Data

See **U. S. GOVERNMENT.**

Center for the Study of Southern Culture

Listings of regional special events, catalogue of videos, sound recordings, periodicals, and other items, the Blues Directory, and other resources.

WWW to
http://imp.cssc.olemiss.edu/

Questions or comments can be directed by e-mail to

tracy@imp.cssc.olemiss.edu

Civil War

A collection of Civil War letters from an Iowa soldier to his family can be found on the WWW.

WWW to
http://www.ucsc.edu/
    civil-war-letters/home.html

Guide to German History Resources

The "Internet Resources on German History" is an invaluable compilation. It is part of the Internet Resource Discovery Project.

gopher to
una.hh.lib.umich.edu
path: Humanities
        History
        German History

Historical Text Archive

For a wide selection of historical documents,

anonymous FTP to
ftp.msstate.edu
path: docs/history

WWW to
http://www.msstate.edu/Archives/
    History

History Index Information Server

For an index of history resources available on the Internet,

telnet to
ukanaix.cc.ukans.edu
login: history

Holocaust Archives Gopher

gopher to
jerusalem1.datasrv.co.il 70
path: Electronic Jewish Library
        hol

Holocaust FAQ

This is a rebuttal to the "Leuchter Report," which is a "revisionist" study of the holocaust. The FAQ authors, Ken McVay and Danny Keren, give point-by-point examination of the evidence and provide a very useful bibliography. The FAQ appears regularly on **alt.revisionism** and **soc.history** and can be obtained by

anonymous FTP to
rtfm.mit.edu
path: pub
        usenet
        news.answers
        holocaust

Job Guide

For a job guide for college and university teaching positions, send an e-mail to

listserv@uicvm.uic.edu
subject line: <leave blank>
Message: get h-net jobguide h-post

Journal

For the Online Modern History Review, a journal devoted to all historical subjects,

telnet to
freenet.victoria.bc.ca
login: guest

List of Lists

For a source of lists devoted to history

WWW to
http://www.clark.net/pub/listserv/
listserv.html

See also **APPENDIX--Lists.**

Marshall University Historical Archive

Material on diplomatic history, ethnic history, history as a discipline, teaching history (exams, syllabi), naval history, women's history, and many other topics.

anonymous FTP to
byrd.mu.wvnet.edu
path: pub/
    history

Or connect through the History Index Information Server discussed previously in this section.

The MetaNetwork

For an extensive collection of historical documents, gopher to the MetaNetwork at

tmn.com
path: Humanities
    Historical Documents

North Carolina State University

For material for the study of history, electronic texts, and links to other history sites

gopher to
dewey.lib.ncsu.edu 70
path: NCSU's "Library without Walls"
    Study Carrels (Organized by
        Subject)
    History

Queens Public Library

For a good historical documents collection, gopher to the Queens Public Library. The site includes the Declaration of Independence, the Emancipation Proclamation, the First Thanksgiving Proclamation, Gettysburg Address, Jefferson's First Inaugural Address, Lincoln's Second Inaugural Address, the Magna Carta, King's "I Have a Dream" speech, the Mayflower Compact, the Monroe Doctrine, Nelson Mandela's Inauguration Speech, The United States Constitution, and Washington's Farewell Address.

gopher to
vax.queens.lib.ny.us 70
path: Social Science
    History
    Historical Docs

Russian and East European Studies (WWW)

A hypertext guide for the interdisciplinary study of Russia and Eastern Europe.

WWW to
http://www.pitt.edu/~cjp/rees.html

Sixteenth-Century Journal

For a journal devoted to the culture and literature of the sixteenth century,

anonymous FTP to
escj%nemostate@academic.
    nemomus.edu

Texas A&M University

For the Dead Sea Scrolls Exhibit, historical documents, recent events archives, Vietnam era documents and archives, and links to many other history sites,

gopher to
gopher.tamu.edu
path: Browse Information by
    Subject
      History

United States Civil Rights Legislation

The Legal Information Institute at the Cornell Law School maintains an HTML version of the Civil Rights Code of the United States (Title 42, Section 21).

WWW to
http://www.law.cornell.edu/usc/
    42/21/overview.html

University of Kansas

For one of the largest on-line collections of historical documents,

telnet to
ukanaix.cc.ukans.edu
login: history

WWW at
http://history.cc.ukans.edu/history/
    WWW_history_main.html

University of Michigan

This site has the Bryn Mawr Classical Review, historical documents and treatises, history journals, exhibits, archives.

gopher to
una.hh.lib.umich.edu 70
path: socsci/
    history

Washington and Lee University

This site maintains many links to other history sources.

gopher to
liberty.uc.wlu.edu
path: Libraries and Information Access
    History

See also **ARCHIVES AND LIBRARY RESOURCES.**

HUMANITIES

Centre for Humanities Computing

The Centre for Humanities Computing at Oxford University hosts a WWW at

http://www.ox.ac.uk/depts/
    humanities/

Humanities Bulletin Board

Oxford University Press maintains a bulletin board for the humanities.

telnet to
sun.nsf.ac.uk
login: janet
password: uk.ac.humbul

Institute for Advanced Technology in the Humanities

The Institute for Advanced Technology in the Humanities offers an extensive collection of material on technological applications in the humanities.

 WWW to
http://jefferson.village.virginia.edu/home.html

Nobel Prize Web Site

This site maintains information on the Nobel Prize for literature: prize citations, press releases, announcements of winners, and a list of winners for each year from 1901 to the present.

 WWW to
http://logos.svenska.gu.se/academy.html

Scholarly Societies

The University of Waterloo Library maintains and updates links to servers of scholarly societies (such as the American Philosophical Association).

 gopher to
uwinfo.uwaterloo.ca

 telnet to
uwinfo.uwaterloo.ca
login: uwinfo
path: Electronic Resources Around the World
Campus and other information systems
Gophers of Scholarly Societies

 WWW to
http://www.lib.uwaterloo.ca/society/overview.html

Scholia

Scholia provides critical reviews of publications in the fields of ancient Greek and Roman art, archaeology, history, literature, and philosophy. Archives reviews can be retrieved by gopher or anonymous FTP.

To receive electronic reviews from Scholia, send an e-mail request to

 scholia@owl.und.ac.za

Archived reviews can be found at the ccat gopher at the University of Pennsylvania.

 anonymous FTP to
ccat.sas.upenn.edu
path: pub
scholia

Tennessee Technological University

This gopher site includes not only information about the history program at Tennessee Tech, but it also has links to numerous other gopher sites (electronic documents in history, archives, general resources, etc.).

 gopher to
gopher.tntech.edu
path: TTU Campus Information
Departments
History

University of Bergen, Norway

 gopher to
nora.hd.uib.no 70
path: Humanistisk Datasenter

University of California, Santa Barbara

gopher to
ucsbuxa.ucsb.edu 3001
path: The Subject Collections
Humanities

University of California, Santa Cruz

gopher to
scilibx.ucsc.edu 70
path: The Researcher
Arts and Humanities

University of Michigan

gopher to
una.hh.lib.umich.edu 70
path: Humanities
Arts and Music

University of Toronto

Dr. Willard McCarty
Assistant Director
Centre for Computing in the Humanities
University of Toronto

e-mail:
mccarty@epas.utoronto.ca

gopher to
gopher.epas.utoronto.ca
path: Centre for Computing in the
Humanities

WWW to
http://www.cch.epas.utoronto.ca:
8080/cch/cch.html

Washington and Lee University

gopher to
liberty.uc.wlu.edu 70
path: Libraries and Information Servers
Humanities

HUMAN RIGHTS

Amnesty International

FTP to
ftp.io.org
path: Pub
Human-Rights

IDLE PLEASURES

3-D Images

WWW to
http://fmechds01.tu-graz.ac.at/
heidrun/heidrun.html

Ballroom Dancing

WWW to
http://phenom.physics.wisc.edu/
~fosdal/UWMBDA

Catalogues

Choose from more than 10,000 catalogs in over 800 categories at the Catalog Mart. An electronic order form will allow you to order on -line.

gopher to
savvy1.savvy.com

Chocolate

Ann Hemyng Candy, Inc. has a home page devoted to chocolate. You can order chocolate online.

WWW to
http://mmink.cts.com/mmink/
dossiers/choco.html

Coffee

This WWW site offers coffee-related information (coffee terminology, mail-order vendors, links to other coffee resources on the net, file archives, trade publications, recipes, etc.).

WWW to
http://www.infonet.net/showcase/
coffee

Food

Virginia Diner

For gift catalogues, menus, recipes, try the Virginia Diner, in Wakefield, Virginia.

WWW to
http://www.infi.net/vadiner/
vadiner.html

Hot Sauce Shop

Appealing to chile-heads, the Hot Sauce Shop features hot sauces from around the world.

WWW to
http://www.hot.presence.com/hot

Foodwine

Try Foodwine, a discussion list for. . . food and wine. E-mail your request to

listserv@cmuvm.csv.cmich.edu
message: subscribe foodwine
<First name> <Last name>

Gardening

To enjoy the Virtual Garden (brought to you by *Time* magazine)

WWW to
http://www.timeinc.com/VG/

Or telnet to CATALPA, the on-line catalog of the Library of The New York Botanical Garden, Bronx, New York.

librisc.nybg.org
login: library

Golf

Subscribe to the ATP Tour Electronic Newsletter. E-mail your request to

rvach@jax.jaxnet.com

Nutrition and Health

Try Veggies Unite! This site has over 800 recipes (with a searchable index), plus storage tips, info on vitamins, and links to other health and nutrition sites around the world.

WWW to
http://www-sc.ucssc.indiana.edu/
goodies.html/

Serendipity

Connect here for a random link to a WWW site.

http://kuhttp.cc.ukans.edu/cwis/
organizations/kucia/uroulette/
uroulette.html

Shopping

For a copy of Dave Taylor's The Internet Mall, a guide to shopping on the net, send an e-mail message to

taylor@netcom.com
message: send mall

To subscribe to the regular updates to this guide, send an e-mail message to

listserv@netcom.com
subscribe imall-L
   <your e-mail address>

Sports

The WWW Sports Information Server has scores, schedules, and stats.

WWW to
http://www.netgen.com/sis/
   sports.html

Stargazing

For an other worldly experience, visit the Jet Propulsion Laborator's WWW for a collection of the best images from NASA's planetary exploration program.

WWW to
http://stardust.jpl.nasa.gov/planets/

Television

For a daily summary of the day's best TV, subscribe to the TV2Nite mailing list. Send an e-mail message to

tv2nite@metaverse.com
subscribe TV2NITE
   <your e-mail address>

The Top Ten List

The Top Ten List from The David Letterman Show is brought to you each weekday by listserv. To subscribe, send an e-mail request to

Listserv@listserv.clark.net
message: subscribetopten

or e-mail on individual days to
infobot@infomania.com
subject: topten

or subscribe to the newsgroup

alt.fan.letterman.top-ten

or
alt.fan.letterman

Wine

Visit the Wine Enthusiasts Web Site for an archive of tasting notes, a Washington Wine Tour, a FAQ on wine, as well as links to other wine-related web resources.

WWW to
http://augustus.csscr.
   washington.edu/personal/
   bigstar-mosaic/wine.html

INDEXING SERVICE

DataSmiths

DataSmiths Information Services provides indexes for books, journals, technical manuals, and textbooks. Specialties include library and information science; management, human resources, and other business areas; art and art history; computer science, applications, and technical documentation; how-to and self-help topics; and women's studies.

e-mail:
njsmith@bga.com

INTERNET ACCESS

See **ACCESS—Internet.**

INTERNET INFORMATION

Archie

See the Archie section for more information.

Books

For a comprehensive bibliography (title, author, publisher, ISBN, price, pages, publication date, and other information) of Internet-related books,

anonymous FTP to
rtfm.mit.edu
path: pub
    usenet
    news.answers
    internet-services
    book-list

This can also be retrieved by e-mail by sending a message to

mail-server@rtfm.mit.edu
subject line: <blank>
message: send usenet/news.answers/
    internet-services/book-list

Brandon University

Numerous links to Internet resources are available at the Brandon University site.

WWW to
http://www.brandonu.ca/~ennsnr/
    Resources/

December's Internet Guides

John December maintains a listing of information resources and documentation about retrieval tools and CMC forums (Internet Tools file) and information about sources related to the Internet and Computer-Mediated Communication (Internet-CMC file) at

http://www.rpi.edu/Internet/
    Guides/decemj/internet-cmc.html
http://www.rpi.edu/Internet/
    Guides/decemj/
    internet-tools.html

These are also available by anonymous FTP from

ftp.rpi.edu
path/file: pub/communications/
    internet-cmc.readme
pub/communications/
    internet-tools.readme

FAQ

For a general understanding of the Internet a valuable FAQ is available by anonymous FTP from

rtfm.mit.edu
path: pub/
    usenet/
    news.answers/
    internet-services

Gopherjewels Project

gopher to
cwis.usc.edu
path: Other Gophers and
      Information Resources
    Gophers by Subject
‘   Gopher Jewels

Harvest

Developed by the researchers at the University of Colorado–Boulder, Harvest (like Archie, Veronica, and Jughead) is a tool for gathering information from across the Internet. Harvest can be accessed by WWW at

http://harvest.cs.colorado.edu

Hobbes' Internet Timeline

For a chronicle of the development of the Internet, including yearly growth statistics, send an e-mail request to

timeline@hobbes.mitre.org

Internet by e-mail

For a useful document for exploiting the power of the Internet by e-mail, send an e-mail message to

listserv@ubvm.cc.buffalo.edu
subject: [blank]
message: GET INTERNET BY
    –EMAILNETTRAIN F=MAIL

Internet History

For a copy of Vinton Cerf's history of the Internet Activities Board (rfc1120.txt)

anonymous FTP to
ftp.merit.edu
path: documents
    rfc

Internet Timeline

Find out what happen when—

gopher to
lib-gopher.lib.indiana.edu 70
path: Useful Research Aids
    The Internet-Room
    Internet for Beginners
    History of the Internet
    Timeline

Internet Tools

For a site that provides convenient access to many Internet Tools (Archie, Veronica, Jughead, WAIS, WWW, Finger, Hytelnet, Search Gopher Servers by Name), gopher to the Ontario Institute for Studies in Education gopher at

gopher.oise.on.ca
path: tools

Internet Resources

For a collection of Internet resources

WWW to
http://www.hip.com/fanklin/
franklin.html

InterNIC InfoGuide

The on-line InterNIC Infoguide provides comprehensive information about the Internet and about on-line Internet resources.

WWW to
http://www.internic.net/info
guide.html

gopher to
gopher.internic.net

Jughead

See the chapter "Archie, Veronica, and Jughead" for more information.

Mark Lottor's Global Internet Statistics

For information regarding international statistics on connectivity (such things as the number of Internet hosts per country),

WWW to
http://www.nw.com

University of Michigan Guides to the Internet

An essential source of information is the extensive selection of Internet guides available from the University of Michigan.

gopher to
una.hh.lib.umich.edu
path: inetdirs

Yaleinfo

For a comprehensive collection of documents (from beginner level to advanced), gopher to Yale University at

yaleinfo.yale.edu
path: Browse YaleInfo
About the Internet

Here, you will find FAQs, the Internet Hunt, books (*Zen and the Art of the Internet* and *The Hitchhiker's Guide to the Internet*), network etiquette, information on getting connected, Scout Reports, resources, etc.

For more information on Internet resources, see the chapter "Keeping Current."

ITALIAN LANGUAGE AND LITERATURE

Dante

The Dante Society of America can be reached at

lansing@binah.cc.brandeis.edu

Italia

A site devoted to Italian language and literature, Italia can be reached by gopher.

gopher to
italia.hum.utah.edu 70

For more information, contact Maurizio Oliva at

maurizio.oliva@m.cc.utah.edu

WWW to
http://italia.hum.utah.edu/
italia.hum

Language Lessons

Beginning Italian lessons, written by Lucio Chiappetti, are available on the WWW at

http://www.willamette.edu/
~tjones/Language-Page.html/

University of Toronto

gopher to the University of Toronto

gopher.epas.utoronto.ca
path: Other Information Providers at
U of T
EPAS
Centre for Computing in the
Humanities
Other Academic Resources by
Discipline
Italian Studies

WWW to
http://www.crs4.it/HTML/
homecrs4.html

See also **LANGUAGE AND LITERA-TURE** and **NEWS.**

JOURNALS, MAGAZINES, AND NEWSPAPERS

Note: In some cases, only selected parts of these publications are on-line.

Cyberzine

Covers such topics as Beginners Luck, Toolbox Internet tools, the Web, Arts, Commerce, E-text, Home Stuff, Multimedia, Sports, Travel, Recreation, and more.

WWW to
http://cyberzine.org

e-mail
tomh@cyberzine.org

Directory of Electronic Journals

The Association of Research Libraries maintains a list of over 400 electronic journals and newsletters.

gopher to
arl.cni.org 70
path: Scholarly Communication
Directory of Electronic
Journals

Electronic Journal on Virtual Culture

gopher to
gopher.cic.net 70
path: Electronic Serials
CICNet E-Serials
Alphabetic List
e
Electronic Journal on Virtual
Culture

anonymous FTP to
byrd.mu.wvnet.edu
cd /pub/ejvc
get EJVC.INDEX.FTP
get <filename> [where file-name is
exact name of file in INDEX]
quit

The Electronic Newsstand

 gopher to
gopher.internet.com 70

 send an e-mail message to
gophermail@enews.com
subject line: <blank>
message: help

GNN: Global News Network

 WWW to
http://nearnet.gnn.com/news/
home/news.html

Internet Wiretap

 gopher to
wiretap.spies.com

Kibble

The Cyberpoet's Guide to Virtual Culture Journal. Available by anonymous FTP from

 ftp.etext.org
path: pub
Zines
Cyberpoet

Mother Jones

The Mother Jones web site is structured around important issues (such as health care, education, environment, U.S. government, etc.). It includes not only articles from *Mother Jones*, but also resources from around the Internet and Information kiosks for non-profit organizations.

 WWW to
http://www.mojones.com/mother-jones.html

The New Republic

 gopher to
gopher.internet.com 70
path: Electronic Newsstand
Magazines

Time

For full-text articles from *Time* magazine

 WWW to
http://www.timeinc.com

The Wilson Library Bulletin

 gopher to
gopher.hwwilson.com

Wired

 WWW to
http://www.wired.com

LANGUAGES AND LITERATURE

Human Languages Page

A collection of human-language resources on the Internet, from tutorials to dictionaries to software and literature. There are currently links for over 40 languages.

 WWW to
http://www.willamette.edu/
~tjones/Language-Page.html

Modern Language Association (MLA)

Modern Language Association
10 Astor Place
New York, NY 10003-6981

e-mail:
mlaod@cuvmb.cc.columbia.edu

Northeast Modern Language Association (NEMLA)

To contact the Northeast Modern Language Association, send an e-mail message to

skandele@snypotvx.bitnet

Southern Conference on Language Teaching (SCOLT)

To subscribe to the SCOLT list (Southern Conference on Language Teaching), send an e-mail message to

listserv@catfish.valdosta.
peachnet.edu

Wiretap

For a site dealing with various languages (e.g., Esperanto-English dictionary, Vietnamese computer terms, Hindu names, Japanese Grammar, Latin study guide, etc.),

gopher to
wiretap.spies.com
path: Wiretap Online
Library
Articles
Language

See also **ENGLISH, FRENCH, GERMAN, ITALIAN, RUSSIAN, SPANISH,** and the subject of "languages" in **APPENDIX—Lists**.

LIBRARIES

Billy Barron's Guide

Billy Barron has compiled and maintains an extensive guide to libraries around the world with telnet connections. The files can be retrieved in numerous formats: ASCII (with or without formatting), Postscript (compressed or not), WordPerfect, and by numeric address.

anonymous FTP to
ftp.unt.edu
path: pub
library

The files are

LIBRARIES.TXT—ASCII version
(with formatting)
LIBRARIES.TX2 —ASCII version
(without formatting)
LIBRARIES.PS —Postscript version
LIBRARIES.PS.Z—Postscript version
(Unix compress format)
LIBRARIES.WP5—WordPerfect 5.1
source (transfer in binary)
LIBRARIES.CON—WordPerfect 5.1
concordance file (binary)
LIBRARIES.ADR—Numeric IP addresses
of Internet libraries
LIBRARIES.CONTACTS—Contacts for
some of the Internet libraries

British

For a gopher menu based on the list maintained by the United Kingdom Office for Library and Information Networking,

gopher to.
ukoln.bath.ac.uk
path: UK-Library Gopher Servers

Special Collections

Various libraries have special collections in art (e.g., Marsden Hartley), drama, film, history, literature (e.g., Conrad Aiken, Louise Bogan, Harte Crane, D. H. Lawrence, G. B. Shaw, Mark Twain, H. G. Wells), music, poetry, popular culture, women's studies. For a comprehensive guide, compiled by Dana Noonan, send an e-mail message to

listserv@vm1.nodak.edu
path: nnews
message: send libcat.nnews
      send libcat-A.nnews
      send libcat-B.nnews
      send libcat-C.nnews

FTP to
vm1.nodak.edu
path: nnews

See also **ARCHIVES AND LIBRARY RESOURCES.**

LINGUISTICS

The Universal Survey of Languages is a WWW site containing audio files of spoken language and descriptions of morphology and phonology of the world's languages. It also contains a hypertext introduction to linguistics, the International Phonetic Alpha-bet, a linguistic dictionary, and information on language families.

WWW to
http://www.teleport.com/
   ~napoleon

LISTS

Bitnet Listserv Lists

For a comprehensive file (over 500K) of all bitnet listserv lists (about 6000 names), send an e-mail message to

listserv@bitnic.educom.edu
subject line: <blank>
message: list global

Kovacs' Directory of Scholarly Electronic Conferences

An essential source, Diane Kovacs' *Directory of Scholarly Electronic Conferences*, is a compilation of lists for (among many other topics) art, communications, dance, education, film, history, humanistic studies, languages, Latin American studies, linguistics, literature, music, philosophy, text analysis, theater, women's studies, and writing.

For more information on Kovacs' directory, send an e-mail message to

listserv@kentvm.kent.edu
subject line: <blank>
message: get acadlist readme f=mail

LISTSERVS

LISTSERV Guide

For documents which explain many of the LISTSERV commands in detail, send any or all of the following e-mail messages to a listserv address (e.g., listserv@brownvm.brown.edu):

get listserv memo
get listkeyw memo
get listserv refcard

Comprehensive Guide

A useful document on the various commands of each of the five listservers has been assembled by James Milles of Saint Louis University Law Library. For a copy, send an e-mail message to

listserv@UBVM.cc.Buffalo.edu
message: GET MAILSER CMD
NETTRAIN F=MAIL

LITERARY MAGAZINES

Archives for literary magazines can be found by

gopher to
wings.buffalo.edu
path: Libraries & library resources
Electronic journals
E-journals

Individual Titles

Angst

A literary magazine, available by gopher from

ftp.etext.org
path: Zines

ASH

ASH (Arts Sciences Humanities) is an interdisciplinary journal of creative writing and ideas. It invites submissions of innovative poetry, short fiction, essays, photography, or mixed/experimental media/genres. The editors are especially interested in essays which promote the increasing dispersal of debilitating institutional boundaries.
Send submission to

3amk6@qucdn.queensu.ca

Atmospherics

Quarterly journal of poetry and short stories.

Send submissions (in plain ASCII) to Susan Keeping at

keeping@vax.library.utoronto.ca

Include a short biography with your submission.

Back issues are available through anonymous FTP from

ftp.etext.org
path: Zines

gopher to
ftp.etext.org
path: Zines

Beatrice WWW

Beatrice WWW includes poetry, short fiction, articles, and reviews of music and literature.

WWW to
http://www.primenet.com/~grifter/

Core

Publishes fiction, poetry, and essays. For a subscription, e-mail to

rita@etext.org

For archives

anonymous FTP to
ftp.etext.org
path: pub
     Zines
       CORE_Zine

gopher to
ftp.etext.org

Cyberkind

A World Wide Web magazine of net-related fiction, nonfiction, poetry, and art.

WWW to
http://sunsite.unc.edu/ckind/
    title.html

For more information, contact Shannon Turlington at

shannon@sunsite.unc.edu

Dogwood Blossoms

Emphasis on haiku. For subscription, e-mail to

glwarner@samford.bitnet

WWW to
http://glwarner.
   samford.edu/haiku.htm

FICTION-ONLINE

A free bimonthly literary magazine, FICTION-ONLINE publishes a mixture of poetry, short-shorts, short stories, serialized novels, and short plays in the mainstream or in various genres. Subscriptions and submissions should be directed by e-mail to the editor, William Ramsay, at

ngwazi@clark.net

Back issues may be obtained by anonymous FTP at

ftp.etext.org

gopher to
gopher.cic.net

To subscribe, e-mail:

    ngwazi@clark.net

Gonzo

Georgetown Gonzo is a hypertext literary magazine devoted to satire, humor, and culture.

WWW to
http://sunsite.unc.edu/martin/
   gonzo.html

Grist On-Line

A journal of electronic network poetry, art, and culture.

To subscribe, e-mail to

    fowler@phantom.com

Also available by anonymous FTP at

ftp.etext.org
path: /pub/Poetry/Grist

INTER\FACE

A forum for the publication and distribution of creative work.

For information, e-mail

    interfac@cnsunik.albany.edu

WWW to
http://cscmosaic.albany.edu/
  ~interfac

InterText

A free, on-line bimonthly fiction magazine, InterText publishes mainstream fiction, as well as fantasy, horror, science fiction, and humor. It is in its fourth year of publication and is published in both ASCII and Post-Script formats. Stories should be under 15,000 words. Before submitting work request writers' guidelines from

    intertext@etext.org

Editor: Jason Snell
Assistant Editor: Geoff Duncan

For current or back issues

anonymous FTP to
ftp.etext.org
path: Zines
   InterText

or

    network.ucsd.edu
    path: intertext

gopher to
ftp.etext.org
path: Zines
   InterText

WWW to
http://www.etext.org/Zines/
  InterText/intertext.html

On Compuserve:
    GO EFFSIG
    path: Library 4: Zines from the Net

On America Online:
    keyword: PDA

NWHQ

A hypermedia literary/art journal, the first issue of NWHQ features writing by Alan Sondheim, Frank Stevenson, Tim McLaughlin, Bill New, Elizabeth Fischer, Jeff Keller, Irene Sosniak, and Attila Balogh.

WWW to
http://www.wimsey.com/~jmax/
    Knossopolis/

Quanta

A magazine of science fiction and fantasy. Published in both ASCII and PostScript. Request either version by sending a message to one of the following:

quanta+request-postscript
    @andrew.cmu.edu

or

quanta+request-ascii@
    andrew.cmu.edu

Send submissions to

quanta@andrew.cmu.edu

For back issues

anonymous FTP to
export.acs.cmu.edu
path: pub/
    quanta

RIF/T: An Electronic Space for New Poetry, Prose, and Poetics

"RIF/T provides a forum for poets who are conversant with the medium of electronic communication and wish to explore the full potential of a true electronic journal. Poetry, fiction, and criticism.

To subscribe, send a request to

e-poetry@ubvm.cc.buffalo.edu
message: sub e-poetry <your name>

or write to the editors, Kenneth Sherwood and Loss Pequeño Glazier, at

e-poetry@ubvm.cc.buffalo.edu

Archives of issues and hypermedia extensions can be found at the Electronic Poetry Center (Buffalo).

gopher to
wings.buffalo.edu

Search local menus for "rift."

rpoetik

Seeks new, lively, witty, and exciting writing in vernacular English.

e-mail:
listserv@wln.com
message: subscribe rpoetik
    <your name>

Sarko

A journal of fictional works-in-progress published bimonthly in ACSII format by D. I. H. Press.

anonymous FTP to
ftp.etext.org
path: pub
    Zines
    Sarko

Or send message to

sarko-request@mach.hk.super.net
Subject: <one of the following>:
Sarko-Announce <to be added
to announcement list>
Sarko-Distribution <to receive
each issue by e-mail>
Sarko-Request X.X <to request
a specific issue>

Spectra

The editors describe Spectra as an on-line journal of ideas, expression, and evolution. They seek personal essays, anecdotes, short fiction, parody, satire, and poetry. Subscribers receive monthly invitations to respond to various topics. Willing to consider all formats and styles and just about any topic.

WWW to
http://www.mother.com/

For a free subscription, send a request to

skeevers@netcom.com

or

phandaal@well.com

or

chimera@mother.com

For subscriptions, send the following message:

subscribe SPECTRA

TRee

A e-version of TapRoot, TRee is a quarterly review of micropress poetry and experimental language art. For a subscription, send an e-mail message to

au462@cleveland.freenet.edu

For archives

gopher to
wings.buffalo.edu

Trincoll Journal

The Trincoll Journal was the first weekly Internet publication to appear on the WWW—November 1993. It is a weekly multimedia magazine produced by students at Trinity College in Hartford, Connecticut, as well as by students and Internet users from around the world. The journal is located at

http://www.trincoll.edu/tj/trincoll
journal.html

If you would like to be included on the mailing list, which announces to readers when new issues are posted on the web, send an e-mail message to

journal@mail.trincoll.edu
subject: subscribe journal

TwentyNothing

WWW to
http://web.mit.edu/afs/
athena.mit.edu/user/t/h/tho-
masc/Public/twenty/intro.html

Twilight World

For a fiction magazine (with emphasis on science fiction)

anonymous FTP to
ftp.etext.org
path: pub
Zines

Undiscovered Country

The Undiscovered Country is an e-zine dedicated to "the sometimes lost art of creative writing," focusing on poetry, prose, short stories, free-form, philosophy, music, art, and life.

To subscribe, send an e-mail message to

 cblanc@pomona.claremont.edu

or

rm09216@academia.swt.edu

 anonymous FTP to
ftp.etext.org
path: pub
    Zines

We Magazine/ Descriptions of an Imaginary University

A free regular and sporadic electronic journal related to postmodern poetry and poetics, *We* is available by e-mail from

cf2785@albnyvms.bitnet

 gopher to
wings.buffalo.edu
path: Libraries & Library Research
    Electronic Journals
    Resources Produced Here at UB
    The Electronic Poetry Center

Webster's Weekly

A magazine containing reviews, poetry, photos, and cartoons.

 WWW to
http://www.awa.com/w2/

Contact the editor by e-mail at

 w2@casagato.edu

For more information, e-mail Brian Knatz at knatz@casagato.org

Whirlwind

A magazine devoted to literary fiction, poetry, essays.

 anonymous FTP to
ftp.etext.org
path: pub
    Zines
    Whirlwind

LODGINGS

See **TRAVEL—Lodgings.**

MAGAZINES

See also **JOURNALS AND MAGAZINES,** and **LITERARY MAGAZINES, SCHOLARLY JOURNALS,** and **SCHOLARLY ARTICLES.**

> Note: In this directory, long addresses, paths, and messages are carried over to successive lines. However, these should be read as single-line entities and commands.

MAIL

Accessing the Internet By E-Mail

To obtain a copy of this useful file, send an e-mail message to

listserv@ubvm.cc.buffalo.edu
subject: <blank>
message: GET INTERNET
    BY-EMAIL NETTRAIN F=MAIL

Yanoff's List

Scott Yanoff maintains an "Internet Services List," which contains many resources obtainable by mail (including finger, FTP, etc.). For information on how to obtain this file

e-mail (or finger):
yanoff@alpha2.csd.uwm.edu.

See also **ADDRESSES—Electronic**

MAPS

Atlas Information Service

For maps and geographic information, the Canadian National Atlas Information Service can be reached by

WWW at
http://www-nais.ccm.emr.ca

CIA Maps

CIA maps of many nations are available through WWW at

http://rowan.lib.utexas.edu/
path: Maps

Education

gopher to
unix5.nysed.gov

MEDIA ADDRESSES

Fox TV
    foxnet@delphi.com
Mother Jones
    x@mojones.com
NBC News
    nightly@nbc.ge.com
NBC Dateline
    dateline@nbc.ge.com
The New Republic
    editors@tnr.com
NPR ("Fresh Air")
    freshair@hslc.org
All Things Considered
    atc@npr.org
Weekend All Things Considered
    watc@npr.org
Sunday Morning Weekend Edition
    wesun@npr.org
Today Show
    today@news.nbc.com

MEDIEVAL STUDIES

See **ARCHIVES AND LIBRARY RE-SOURCES**, **HISTORY**, and **TEXTS**.

MOVIES

See **AUDIO VISUAL** and **FILM**.

MUSEUMS

See **ART HISTORY--Museums.**

MUSIC

The Beethoven Bibliography Database

This is a project of the Ira F. Brilliant Center for Beethoven Studies at San Jose State University. It indexes books and articles about Ludwig von Beethoven.

To connect to the database,

telnet to
sjsulib1.sjsu.edu (130.65.100.1)
login: lib
Select: D Connect to Another
   Database
Select: Beethoven Bibliography
   Database

Cantus

Cantus is a database for Gregorian Chants for the Divine Office. Contains both ASCII and binary files and has a search engine for locating specific chants. Also contains the catalogue of the Dom Mocquereau Microfilm

Collection, containing over 400 microfilms of medieval music manuscripts, including those indexed by CANTUS files.

gopher to
vmsgopher.cua.edu 70
path: Libraries
   Music Resources from CUA

CDNow!: The Internet Music Store

To shop for rock, pop, jazz, country, or classical music,

telnet to
cdnow.com

WWW to
http://cdnow.com

To subscribe to CDnow! Magazines, send an e-mail to

magazine@cdnow.com
subject: [blank]
message: subscribe pop
   <your e-mail address>
or
   subscribe classical
   <your e-mail address>

Gladis Catalog (Berkeley Library Catalogue)

The holdings are from 1977+. Can be searched by music number or music publisher.

telnet to
gopac.berkeley.edu (128.32.159.19)

Indiana University

This gopher is maintained by the School of Music and Music Library at Indiana University. It has a nice collection of music finding aids.

WWW to
http://www.music.indiana.edu/

Lists

See **APPENDIX—Lists: Music.**

MuSICA Database

This site is devoted to the scientific investigation of music, but many items in the database are useful for the music theorist.

gopher to
mbic.cwis.uci.edu:7046

telnet to
mila.ps.uci.edu
login: mbi
password: nammbi

Music Database for Music Research Literature

This is a database for music education, music medicine, music psychology, and music therapy. Searchable by keywords.

telnet to
utsaibm.utsa.edu (129.115.50.1)
type [case sensitive]: LIBRARY
LOCAL

Noteworthy Music on the Internet

Netmarket has established a World Wide Web for Noteworthy Music on the Internet. This company has a large inventory of discounted CDs available for sale, and they ship to over 70 foreign countries.

WWW to
http://www.netmarket.com/

telnet to
netmarket.com

Rice University

This is one of the most extensive music gophers on the net: archives, catalogues, discographies, guides, lyrics, jokes, music-related photographs, reference guides, scores, etc.

gopher to
riceinfo.rice.edu 70
path: Information by Subject Area
    Music

Russian

See **HISTORY: Russian and East European Studies.**

Texas A&M University

This site has resources and links to all things musical: barbershop quartet gopher, archives, lyrics search, software, scores, etc.

gopher to
gopher.tamu.edu
path: Browse by Subject
    Music

WWW Virtual Library: Music

Here you will find music catalogues, FTP archives, home pages of individual artists and groups, and much more.

WWW to
http://www.oulu.fi/music.html

University of California, Berkeley

WWW to
http://t-bone.hip.berkeley.edu

University of California, Santa Barbara

gopher to
ucsbuxa.ucsb.edu
path: UCSB Gopher Central
Infosurf
The Subject Collections
Arts Collection
Music

University of Michigan

For music journals and links to other music-related sources

gopher to
una.hh.lib.umich.edu
path: Humanities/
Arts and Music

University of Utah

gopher to
aserver.finearts.utah.edu 70
path: Music Dept

Wiretap

gopher to
wiretap.spies.com
path: Wiretap Online Library
Music

NEWS and NEWSLETTERS

Aftonbladet

A monthly Swedish newspaper devoted to literature, art, film, music, comics, debate, and Cyberspace. For a copy

WWW to
http://www.jmk.su.se/

The Chronicle of Higher Education

gopher to
chronicle.merit.edu

College Newspapers

A site that maintains links to campus newspapers on the Internet can be found by

WWW at
http://beacon-www.asa.utk.edu/
resources/papers.html

Der Spiegel

For news with illustrated features

WWW to
http://spiegel.nda.net/nda/spiegel

EDUPAGE

Published by EDUCOM, EDUPAGE is a thrice-weekly electronic newsletter which covers news about EDUCOM, its member institutions, its corporate affiliates, and other organizations that share EDUCOM's goals for transforming education through information technology. Send information and subscription requests to

info@educom.edu

Greek News Services

gopher to
alpha.servicenet.ariadne-t.gr

Newspapers—Various

gopher to
burrow.cl.msu.edu 70
path: News and Weather
      Electronic Newspapers

e-mail to
majordomo@marketplace.com
message: get online-news
      online-newspapers.list

WWW to
http://marketplace.com/
    e-papers.list.www/
    e-papers.home.page.html

For a site that carries international newspapers (Brazil, Canada, Denmark, France, Greece, Holland, etc.),

gopher to
gopher.nstn.ca
path: Cybrary
    News
    News

TV Evening News

gopher to
tvnews.vanderbilt.edu
path: Network Television
    News Abstracts

United Nations

Daily news reports from agencies at the UN.

gopher to
gopher.undp.org
path: U. N. Current Information/
    Daily Highlights

Voice of America

gopher to
gopher.voa.gov
path: voa news

White House

WWW to
http://www.whitehouse.gov

See also **USENET NEWS.**

NEWSGROUPS

See **USENET NEWS.**

PALEOGRAPHY

Scripta Project

This site is devoted to the history of handwriting, from the second century B.C. to the fifteenth century A.D.

WWW to
http://www.univ.trieste.it/scripta/
    scripta.html

PEDAGOGICAL AIDS

Lists

See **APPENDIX—Lists** for information on subscribing to discussion lists, many of which (such as TAMLIT-L) focus on pedagogical issues.

The New Yorker Education Program

For information about using *The New Yorker* in the classroom, send an e-mail message to

 tnyeduc@aol.com

Syllabi

The Centre for Computing in the Humanities, University of Toronto, maintains an extensive archive of material (syllabi, course materials, etc.) on humanities computing. Submissions to the archive are welcomed. Contact Willard McCarty at

 mccarty@epas.utoronto.ca

To access the archive

 gopher to
gopher.epas.utoronto.ca
select: Centre for Computing in the Humanities/
Humanities Computing Resources/
Courses/

See also **EDUCATION.**

PHILOSOPHY

American Philosophical Association

For information about the American Philosophical Association, contact

 Janet Sample, Membership Coordinator
jsample@brahms.udel.edu

Eric Hoffman, Executive Director
ehoff@brahms.udel.edu

Saul Traiger, E-mail Bulletin Board
traiger@oxy.edu

For archives and files

 gopher to
gate.oxy.edu 70

Electronic Journal of Analytic Philosophy

Articles and reviews devoted to analytic philosophy.

To subscribe, send an e-mail to

 listserv@iubvm.ucs.indiana.edu
message: subscribe ejap <first name> <last name>

 gopher to
tarski.phil.indiana.edu

 WWW to
http://phil.indiana.edu
path: Local Features

International Philosophical Preprint Exchange (American Philosophical Association)

Provides on-line abstracts and tables of contents to journals and book series in philosophy.

gopher to
apa.oxy.edu

WWW to
http://kasey.umkc.edu
path: Science studies

anonymous FTP to
Phil-Preprints.L.Chiba-U.ac.jp
path: Pub
      Preprints

e-mail:
phil-preprints-service@cogsci.L.
      Chiba-U.ac.jp

If you have questions, send e-mail to Carolyn L Burke

cburke@nexus.yorku.ca

List of Lists

For a source of lists devoted to philosophy

WWW to
http://www.clark.net/pub/listserv/
      listserv.html

See also **APPENDIX—Lists.**

Metaphysical Society of America

To contact the Metaphysical Society of America, send an e-mail message to

martineb@email.uah.edu

Objectivism

WWW to
http://www.vix.com/pub/
      objectivism

Peirce Edition Project

Contact Beth Eccles at

cpeirce@indycms.iupui.edu

Principia Cybernetica

WWW to
http://pespmc1.vub.ac.be/
      default.html

Rice University

gopher to
riceinfo.rice.edu 70
path: Subject
      Religion and Philosophy

University of Chicago Philosophy Project

 WWW to
http://csmaclab-www.uchicago.edu/
PhilosophyProject/philos.html

Wittgenstein

 gopher to
nora.hd.uib.no
path: humanistisk Datasenter

POETRY

B.A.W.P.

The Best-quality Audio Web Poems presents a collection of recordings, in MPEG2 audio format, of poetry readings and live spoken word performances.

 WWW to
http://www.cs.brown.edu/fun/
bawp

Carnegie-Mellon University

 gopher to
english-server.hss.cmu.edu 70
path: Poetry

Internet Poetry Archive

"The University of North Carolina Press joins the University of North Carolina Office for Information Technology's Sunsite Project in publishing the Internet Poetry Archive. The Archive will make available over the Internet selected poems from a number of contemporary poets in several languages. For each poet you will find: the texts of the poems, a picture of the poet, the voice of the poet reading the poems, a select, but fairly complete, bibliography, and a brief biographical note. The initial unit under construction features Seamus Heaney and the Nobel Prize winner in poetry, Czeslaw Milosz." [netnews announcement]

For Seamus Heaney,

 WWW to
http://sunsite.unc.edu/dykki/
poetry/heaney/heaney-cov.html

For Czeslaw Milosz,

 WWW to
http://sunsite.unc.edu/dykki/
poetry/milosz/milcov.html

Poetry Magazine

An index of the last six years of *Poetry Magazine* (founded in 1912 by Harriet Monroe) is located at the University of North Carolina.

 WWW to
http://sunsite.unc.edu

Poetry Shell

The Poetry Shell is a tool for producing hypermedia poetry editions. A hypertext of a poem will create links to a glossary or dictionary, associated text documents, and images.

A hypertext "Dream of the Rood" is a sample poem that has been produced by the Hypermedia in Language and Literature Subjects, Centre for Humanities Computing, Oxford University. This hypertext contains a full glossary and notes, an Old English grammar, translations, analogue material, background introductory essays, color photographic images, and a full bibliography.

For information on price and minimum system requirements for the Poetry Shell or on the sample poem, contact

 j.burgan@sheffield.ac.uk

Sunsite

 gopher to
calypso.oit.unc.edu
path: Worlds of Sunsite—By Subject
     poetry

University of Kansas

 telnet to
ukanaix.cc.ukans.edu
login: www

See also **TEXTS—Electronic.**

POSTAL CODES

United States

 gopher to
veronica.scs.unr.edu 70
path: Internet Jewels
     Desk Reference Tools
     City Zip Code Lookup

The geographic name server at Brandeis University is searchable by zip code or by city name. It returns information on city, state, country, latitude, longitude, population, elevation, and zip code.

 gopher to
pluto.cc.brandeis.edu 4320

PUBLISHERS—Commercial

Albion Books

 e-mail:
seth@albion.com

E. J. Brill

E. J. Brill
P.O. Box 9000
2300 PA Leiden
Netherlands
Phone: 31 71 312624
FAX: 31 71 317532

U.S. Address:
24 Hudson Street
Kinderhook, NY 12106
Phone: 518 758 1411, ext. 11
Book orders: 800 962 4406, ext. 11
FAX: 518 738 1959

 e-mail:
ejborders@ejbrill.com (book orders)

 gopher to
ejbrill.infor.com 4900

Other: Accepts Visa, MC, Amex, Eurocard

Subjects: Scholarly publishers in Ancient Judaism and Christian Origins; Ancient Near East and Egypt; Biblical Studies; Central and S. E. Asia; Christianity; Classical Studies; History; Islamic Studies and Middle East;

Literature and Linguistics; Philosophy; Religious Studies.

McGraw-Hill

e-mail:
primis@mgh.com
Subject line: info-request
Message: help

Online BookStore (OBS)

Laura Fillmore
Online BookStore (OBS)
Whistlestop Mall
Rockport, MA 01966
Phone: 508 546 7346
FAX: 508 546 9807

e-mail:
obs@marketplace.com

The Online BookStore specializes in full-text on-line publishing, translating two-dimensional books and publications into multidimensional Internet publications. The OBS offers fiction and nonfiction in a variety of electronic formats, free and for a fee, with immediate on-line verification of Visa and MasterCard. Established in 1992, OBS is the oldest full-text on-line bookstore on the Net.

Prentice Hall

e-mail:
books@prenhall.com

WWW to
http://www.prenhall.com

PUBLISHERS—University Presses

Note: A combined catalog for all university press books is running on both Web and Gopher at
http://aaup.pupress.
princeton.edu

aaup.pupress.
princeton.edu

Cambridge University Press

WWW to
http://www.cup.cam.ac.uk/

telnet to
ftp.cup.cam.ac.uk
login: cc
password: cup

The Catholic University of America Press

The Catholic University of America Press
620 Michigan Avenue, N.E.
Washington, DC 20064
Phone: 202 319 5052
FAX 202 319 5802
David J. McGonagle, Director

e-mail:
mcgonagle@cua.edu

Subjects: History, literature, philosophy, political theory, and theology.

Book Orders:
P.O. Box 4852
Hampden Station
Baltimore, MD 21211
Phone: 410 516 6953
FAX: 410 516 6998

 gopher to
gopher.cua.edu
path: The Catholic Univ. of America
        Gopher
        Special Resources
        CUA Press

Cornell University Press

Cornell University Press
John G. Ackerman, Director
750 Cascadilla Street
P.O. Box 250
Ithaca, NY 14852-0250
Phone: 607 277 2969
        800 666 2211
FAX: 607 277 6292

 e-mail:
cupress@cornell.edu

Book Orders: Same as above.

Duke University Press

Duke University Press—Books
Box 90660
Durham, NC 27708
Phone: 919 688 5134
FAX: 919 688 4574

 e-mail:
tfdpress@acpub.duke.edu
    (orders and requests)

Other: Payment by check or money order in U.S. funds; Visa, MasterCard, American Express.

Duke University Press—
        Journals Department
Box 90660
Durham, NC 27708
Phone: 919 687 3613 or 919 687 3600
FAX: 919 688 3524

 e-mail:
tfdpress@acpub.duke.edu

 gopher to
publications.math.duke.edu 70
path: duke-press

Harvard University Press

 gopher to
gopher.harvard.edu 23
path: Harvard Publications
        Harvard University Press

Book Orders:
Harvard University Press
79 Garden Street
Cambridge, MA 02138
Phone: 617 495 2480
[Monday–Friday, 9–4:30]

Indiana University Press

Indiana University Press
601 N. Morton Street
Bloomington, IN 47404-3797
Phone: 812 855 6804 or 800 842 6796
FAX: 812 855 7931

Includes information on editorial policy, review copy procedures, personnel, journals, special sales, and book series. Users may browse the entire IU Press trade list by author and title or search by keyword. Seasonal catalogues may also be accessed by subject area or keyword search. Also provides information on books IU Press distributes for British Film Institute and Indiana Historical Society. News releases and the Press's newsletter, METAMORPHOSES, are posted periodically.

gopher to
gopher.iupress.indiana.edu 7000

WWW to
http://www.iupress.indiana.edu

Also available through the Indiana University (Bloomington) Main Gopher server:
gopher.indiana.edu 70
path: IUB Library Gopher Server
Other IU Campus
Gopher servers
Indiana University Press
Gopher

Information:

Sales: iupsales@indiana.edu
Book orders: iuporder@ucs.indiana.edu
Queries: iupress@indiana.edu
Journals: journals@indiana.edu

The press also runs a special list devoted to its news and publications—**iupressl**. The press expects the list to generate about 3–4 messages a week (distribution only, no postings). To subscribe, send an e-mail message to

listserv@iubvm.ucs.indiana.edu
message: subscribe iupressl
<firstname lastname>

John Gallman, Director
jgallman@indiana.edu

Acquisition Editors:
Joan Catapano, Women's Studies, Black Studies, Film,
Literary Theory
jcatapan@indiana.edu

Robert Sloan, Religious Studies, Semiotics, History, Medical Ethics
rjsloan@indiana.edu

Johns Hopkins University Press

Johns Hopkins University Press
2715 N. Charles Street
Baltimore, MD 21218-4319
Phone: 410 516 6900
Fax: 410 516 6968

Catalogue: available by

anonymous FTP
jhunix.hcf.jhu.edu (128.220.2.5)
path: cd JHU_Press/.books-in-print
[case sensitive]

gopher to
jhunix.hcf.jhu.edu
path: JHUniverse

Journals:

anonymous ftp to
jhunix.hcf.jhu.edu (128.220.2.5)
path: cd JHU_Press/.journals

Subdirectories: contain files for journals in the classics (.class), history and culture (.hist), humanities (.hum), judaic studies (.jud), literary studies (.lit.), mathematics (.math), performing arts (.perf), and political science (.plsci).

Lehigh University Press

Lehigh University Press
302 Linderman Library
30 Library Drive
Bethlehem, PA 18015-3067
Phone: 610 758 3933
FAX: 610 974 2823
Director: Dr. Philip A. Metzger

e-mail:
inlup@lehigh.edu

Focus: "Special emphasis is given to areas of traditional strength at Lehigh: science, technology and society studies; economics and business studies; and 18th century studies. The press is also interested in attracting manuscripts that deal with eastern Pennsylvania and New Jersey" [from on-line file "LUP Information"].
Book Orders:
Associated University Presses
440 Forsgate Drive
Cranbury, NJ 08512
Phone: 609 544 4770
FAX: 609 655 8366

gopher to
gopher.cc.lehigh.edu
path: LUNA DEPARTMENTS
LUPRESS

MIT Press

The MIT Press
55 Hayward Street
Cambridge, MA 02142-1399
Phone: 617 253 5646
FAX: 617 258 6779

Book Orders

email:
mitpress-orders@mit.edu

Phone: 800 356 0343
FAX: 617 625 6660

Customer Service:
mitpress-order-inq@mit.edu
MIT Press Bookstore:
books@mit.edu
Catalog requests:
mitpress-catalogs@mit.edu

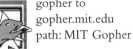
gopher to
gopher.mit.edu
path: MIT Gopher

WWW to
http://www-mitpress.mit.edu/

telnet to
techinfo.mit.edu
path: Around MIT—Offices &
Services
MIT Press

Other:
MIT Press Bookstore
292 Main Street
Cambridge, MA 02142-1399

e-mail:
books@mit.edu

Note: In this directory, long addresses, paths, and messages are carried over to successive lines. However, these should be read as single-line entities and commands.

Princeton University Press

Princeton University Press
41 William Street
Princeton, NJ 08540
Phone: 609 258 4900
FAX: 609 258 6305

Book Orders:
c/o California/Princeton Fulfillment
    Services, Inc.
1445 Lower Ferry Road
Ewing, NJ 08618
Phone: 609 883 1759 or 800 777 4726
FAX: 609 883 7413 or 800 999 1958

Subject Areas: Math, physics, biology, earth sciences, ornithology, astronomy, computer science, cognitive science, neuroscience, complexity, archaeology, political science, law, economics, history of science, classics, history, religion, political theory, philosophy, anthropology, sociology, film studies, literature, cultural studies, art history, music, gender studies.

 e-mail:
<firstname_lastname>@
    pupress.princeton.edu

Acquisitions Editors:

Malcolm DeBevoise: Political science, law, complexity, cognitive science, neuroscience.

Peter Dougherty: Economics, sociology.

Trevor Lipscombe: Math, physics, astronomy, computer science.

Mary Murrell: Anthropology, literature, film studies, gender studies, cultural studies.

Lauren Osborne: History, classics.

Elizabeth Powers: Art history, music.

Jack Repcheck: Economics, trade science.

Sara Van Rheenen: Earth sciences.

Ann Wald: Political theory, philosophy, religion.

Emily Wilkinson: Biology, life science, history of science archaeology, ornithology.

 gopher to
gopher.pupress.princeton.edu 70

 WWW to
http://aaup.pupress.princeton.edu

Rice University Press

Rice University Press
P.O. Box 1892
Houston, TX 77251
Phone: 713 527 6035
FAX: 713 285 5156

The Press publishes books in literary theory and criticism, photography, art and architecture, regional (Texas) studies, ethnic studies, Latin American studies, history, nature, and history of science.

Book Orders:
See **Texas A&M University Press Consortium.**

Rutgers University Press

Rutgers University Press
109 Church Street
New Brunswick, NJ 08901-1242
Phone: 908 932 7039

Books of general interest; American history; anthropology; art history and criticism; biography; black studies and literature; fiction; film; geography; history of science/technology; life and health sciences; literary criticism; regional interest; sociology; and women's studies.

 gopher to
info.rutgers.edu 70
path: Library
    Rutgers Publications
    Rutgers University Press

 WWW to
http://info.rutgers.edu

Southern Methodist University Press

Southern Methodist University Press
Box 415
Dallas, TX 75275-0415
Phone: 214 768 1430
FAX: 214 768 1428

 e-mail:
mpastine@sun.cis.smu.edu

SMU Press publishes in the fields of American studies, anthropology, archaeology, composition and rhetoric, ethics and human values, fiction, film and theater, regional studies, and religious studies. It does not invite submission of textbooks or poetry.

Book Orders:
See **Texas A&M University Press Consortium.**

SUNY Press

State University of New York Press
State University Plaza
Albany, NY 12246
Phone: 518 472 5000
FAX: 518 472 5038
Contact: Leslie Frank-Hass
Assistant to the Director
    and Rights Manager
 e-mail:
rlfh@snycenvm.bitnet

General scholarly publishing.

Book Orders:
c/o CUP Services
P.O. Box 6525
Ithaca, NY 14851
Phone: 800 666 2211

Book Orders
Phone:607 277 2211 or 800 666 2211
FAX: 800 688 2877

 gopher to
UACSC2.ALBANY.EDU 70
path: SUNYP

Temple University Press

Temple University Press
U. S. B. Rm. 305
Broad & Oxford Streets
Philadelphia, PA 19121
Phone: 215 204 8787 or 800 447 1656
(orders only)
FAX: 215 204 4719

e-mail:
tempress@astro.ocis.temple.edu

Subject Areas: Aesthetics, African American studies, American studies, anthropology, art and photography, Asian-American studies, community organizing, social science and religion, criminal justice, culture, music and dance, drugs, education ethics, ethnic studies, gay/lesbian, health care and disability, history, housing, human rights and peace, labor studies, law, literature, media studies, philosophy, philosophy of religion, political science and social theory, political science, psychology, regional studies, social science and social work, urban and regional development, women's studies/gender studies, and women and work.

Texas A&M University Press

Texas A&M University Press
Drawer C
College Station, TX 77843-4354
Phone: 800 826 8911
FAX: 409 847 8752

e-mail:
fdl@tampress.tamu.edu

Book Orders:
See **Texas A&M University Press Consortium.**

Subject Areas: Books dealing with Texas and the Southwest, American and western history, natural history, the environment, women's studies, military history, economics, business, architecture, art, veterinary medicine, nautical archaeology, Eastern European studies, and Borderlands studies. Submissions are not invited in poetry.

Special Series, Joint Imprints, and/or Co-publishing programs: Joe and Betty Moore Texas Art Series; Kenneth E. Montague Business and Oil History Series; Centennial Series of the Association of Former Students; Texas A&M Economics Series; W.L. Moody, Jr., Natural History Series; Louise Lindsey Merrick Texas Environment Series; Elma Dill Russell Spencer Foundation Series (essays on the history of the West); Environmental History Series; Nautical Archaeology Series; Wardlaw Books; Tarleton State University Southwestern Studies in the Humanities Series; Texas A&M Southwest Studies; Clayton Wheat Williams Texas Life Series; Texas A&M Military History Series; Charles and Elizabeth Prothro Texas Photography Series; Carolyn and Ernest Fay Series in Analytical Psychology; Studies in Architecture and Culture; and Sara and John H. Lindsey Series in the Arts and Humanities.

Texas A&M University Press Consortium

Made up of six presses: Texas A&M University Press, Rice University Press, Southern Methodist University Press, Texas Christian University Press, The Texas State Historical Association, and the University of North Texas Press.

Book Orders: 800 826 8911
Phone: 409 847 8752
FAX: 409 847 8752

gopher to
gopher.tamu.edu
path: Browse by Subject
        Publications
        Texas A&M Univ. Press
        Consortium

Texas Christian University Press

Texas Christian University Press
Box 30783
Fort Worth, TX 76129
Phone: 800 826 8911
FAX: 409 847 8752

Book Orders:
See **Texas A&M University Press Consortium.**

TCU Press publishes books in the humanities and social sciences with special emphasis on the history and literature of the American West; American studies; fiction and young adult fiction, with a special emphasis on Texas and the Southwest.

Acquisition Editor:
atrow@gamma.is.tcu.edu

Texas State Historical Association

Texas State Historical Association
2/306 Richardson Hall
University Station
Austin, TX 78712
Phone: 512 471 1525

The Association specializes in books of Texas history and Texana, both new titles and reprints of classics.

Book Orders:
See **Texas A&M University Press Consortium.**

Contact: George Ward
The Texas State History Association
2/306 Richardson Hall
University Station
Austin, TX 78712
Phone: 512 417 1525

University of Arizona

University of Arizona Press
1230 N. Park Avenue, Suite 102
Tucson, AZ 85719-4140
Phone: 602 621 1441
FAX: 602 621 8899

 e-mail:
uapress@ccit.arizona.edu

Book Orders:
Same address as above
Phone: 800 426 3797 or 602 882 3065
FAX: 602 621 8899

Subject Areas: American West, anthropology and archaeology, Chicano Studies, Native American Studies, environment, space sciences.

 WWW to
www.arizona.edu
path: Publications, Plans, Reports

University of Arkansas Press

The University of Arkansas Press
201 Ozark Ave
Fayetteville, AR 72701
Phone: 501 575 3246
FAX: 501 575 6044

 e-mail:
mwilliam@saturn.uark.edu

Book Order Address/phone/FAX/e-mail: Same as above.

Subject Areas: Black studies, women's studies, music history, history, biography, poetry and poetics.

The University of British Columbia Press

University of British Columbia Press
UBC Press
6344 Memorial Road
University of British Columbia
Vancouver, British Columbia
V6T 1Z2
Canada
Phone: 604 822 3259
FAX: 604 822 6083

 e-mail:
ubcpress@unixg.ubc.ca

Subject Areas: History, political science, anthropology, sociology, geography, art history, natural resources, the environment and sustainable development, native studies, Canada and the Canadian North, British Columbia, and the Pacific Rim. The Press also publishes the Canadian Yearbook of International Law.

 gopher to
gopher.ubc.ca 70
path: Libraries
Publications
UBC Press

Book Orders: orders@ubcpress.ubc.ca

 e-mail addresses:

R. Peter Milroy, Director
milroy@unixg.ubc.ca

Jean Wilson, Acquisitions Editor
wilson@ubcpress.ubc.ca

Laura Macleod, Acquisitions Editor,
lmacleo@unixg.ubc.ca

University of California Press

The University of California Press
Book Orders:
> contact Mike Kiley at
> 714 725 2430

gopher to
gopher.cwis.uci.edu 70
path: Entertainment, Events, Food,
> Shopping
> UCI Bookstore
> Publishers Catalogues
> U. of Cal. Press

The University of Chicago Press

The University of Chicago Press
Order Department
11030 South Langley Avenue
Chicago, IL 60628
Phone: 312 568 1550 (book orders)
FAX: 312 702 9756 (book orders)

e-mail:
marketing@press.uchicago.edu
> (queries)
> (The Press discourages orders
> by e-mail.)

gopher to
press-gopher.uchicago.edu

WWW to
http://press.gopher.uchicago.edu

University Press of Florida

gopher to
gopher.ufl.edu
path: University_Press

University of Illinois Press

University of Illinois Press
1325 S. Oak Street
Champaign, IL 61820
Phone: 217 333 0950
FAX: 217 244 8082

e-mail contact:
rwentwor@uiuc.edu
Richard L. Wentworth, Director and
> Editor-in-Chief

Book Orders:
University of Illinois Press
P.O. Box 4856
Hampden P.O.
Baltimore, MD 21211-4856
Phone: 800 545 5703
FAX: 410 516 6969

Scholarly books and serious nonfiction, with special interests in American history and literature and music, African-American history and literature, religious studies, women's studies, and sport history.

Book orders not accepted via e-mail.

Journal Orders:
Journals
University of Illinois Press
1325 S. Oak Street
Champaign, IL 61820-6903
Phone: 217 244 0626
FAX: 217 244 8082

e-mail:
Managing Editor: Theresa Sears
e-mail: t-sears@uiuc.edu

Journals Manager: Ann Lowry
Phone: 217 244 6856

e-mail:
alowry@uiuc.edu

Acquisition Editors:

Richard L. Wentworth, Editor-in-Chief (American history, African-American studies, regional books, communications, sport history)
e-mail:
j-roney@uiuc.edu

Ann Lowry (literature)
Phone 217 244 6856
e-mail:
alowry@uiuc.edu

Judith M. McCulloh
(music, folklore, Appalachian studies, popular culture)
Phone: 217 244 4681
e-mail:
jmccull@uiuc.edu

Richard J. Martin (political science, sociology, law, philosophy, architecture
Phone 217 244 8065
e-mail:
r-martin@uiuc.edu

Karen M. Hewitt (African-American literature, film, women's studies, environmental studies, popular culture)
Phone: 217 244 5687
e-mail:
k-hewitt@uiuc.edu

gopher to
gopher.cso.uiuc.edu 70
path: Libraries and Reference
Information
University of Illinois Press

University of Iowa Press

University of Iowa Press
1129 West Park Road
100 Kuhl House
Iowa City, IA 52242-1000
Phone: 319 335 2000
FAX: 319 335 2055

e-mail:
paul-zimmer@uiowa.edu
holly-carver@uiowa.edu
karen-copp@uiowa.edu

Subjects: Literary criticism, archaeology/anthropology, history of photography, regional studies, natural sciences, jazz, women's studies.

Acquisitions Editors:
Paul Zimmer, Director:
paul-zimmer@uiowa.edu
Holly Carver, Managing Editor:
holly-carver@uiowa.edu

Book Orders:
Publications Order Dept.
100 Oakdale Campus, M105 OH
Iowa City, IA 52242-5000
Phone: 319 335 4645 or 800 235 2665
FAX: 319 335 4039

University of Michigan Press

University of Michigan Press
P.O. Box 1104
839 Green Street
Ann Arbor, MI 48106-1104
Phone: 313 764 4393
FAX: 313 936 0456

e-mail:
um.press@umich.edu

Book Orders and Customer Service:
e-mail: umpress-orders@umich.edu
Phone: 800 764 4392
FAX: 800 876 1922

Subject Areas: Anthropology, Classical Studies, Economics, English as a Second Language (ESL), German Studies, Great Lakes Regional, Law Studies, Medieval and Renaissance History, Literary Theory and Criticism, Poetry Criticism, Political Science, Theater and Performance Studies, and Women's Studies.

Acquisition Editors:
Mary Erwin:
    merwin@umich.edu
LeAnn Fields:
    lfields@umich.edu
Ellen Bauerle:
    bauerle@umich.edu
Malcolm Litchfield:
    mlitchfi@umich.edu
Susan Whitlock:
    whitlock@umich.edu
Colin Day:
    colinday@umich.edu
WWW to
http://maniac.deathstar.org/

University of Minnesota Press

University of Minnesota Press
Book Orders:
Phone: 800 388 3863
       612 624 0005
FAX: 612 626 7313

Orders accompanied by a purchase order number or inquiries can be made by electronic mail

e-mail:
ump@maroon.tc.umn.edu

gopher to
joeboy.micro.umn.edu 70
path: providers
    upress

University of Nebraska Press

University of Nebraska Press
312 North 14th Street
Lincoln, NE 68588-0484
Phone: 402 472 3581
FAX: 402 472 6214

e-mail:
Michael Jensen, Electronic Media Manager
jensen@unlinfo.unl.edu

Book Orders:
Same address as above
Phone: 800 755 1105
FAX: 800 526 2617 (orders only)

e-mail:
kcard@unlinfo.unl.edu

Other: For free shipping offer, check on-line information.

Subject Areas: History of the American West, American Indians, psychology, human rights, musicology, Latin America, alternative agriculture, 20th century literature in translation, American literature, sociology sports history (especially baseball).

Acquisition Editors:

Dan J. J. Ross, editor-in-chief (history, anthropology, Latin America, sports history)
   dross@unlinfo.unl.edu

Nancy Rosen, science editor (psychology, political science, sociology, alternative agriculture, human rights)
   nrosen@unlinfo.unl.edu

Doug Clayton (literature, culture criticism)
   dclayton@unlinfo.unl.edu

Willis Regier (music, American Indian studies, Nebraskana)
   wregier@unlinfo.unl.edu

telnet to
crcvms.unl.edu (129.93.1.2)
login: info

gopher to
gopher.unl.edu

WWW to
http://www.unl.edu

University of New Mexico Press

University of New Mexico Press
1720 Lomas NE
Albuquerque, NM 87131-1591
Phone: 505 277 2346
FAX: 505 277 9270

e-mail:
unmpress@carina.unm.edu

Book Orders:
Same as above
Phone: 800 249 7737

FAX: 800 622 8667

Subject Areas: Scholarly books and serious nonfiction, with special interest in social and cultural anthropology; ethnic studies; archaeology; American frontier history; Western American literature; Latin American history; history of photography; art and photography; books that deal with important aspects of the Southwest or the Rocky Mountain states, including natural history and land grant studies.

University of North Carolina Press

The University of North Carolina Press
116 South Boundary Street
Chapel Hill, NC 27514
Phone: 919 966 3561
FAX: 919 966 3829

e-mail:
uncpress@unc.edu

Book Orders:
Attn: Customer Service
P.O. Box 2288
Chapel Hill, NC 27515-2288
Phone: 800 848 6224
FAX: 800 272 2817

Note: Please do not send orders by e-mail. The Internet is not secure, and your credit card could become public.

Subject Areas: African American Studies, American and European history; American and English literature; American studies; Civil War history; Southern studies; political science; sociology; folklore; religious studies; legal history; classics; women's studies; media studies; music; rural studies; urban studies; public policy; Latin American studies; anthropology; business and economic history; health care; regional trade; North Carolinians; and the following journals: Social Forces; The High School Journal; Studies in Philology; Early American Literature; Southern Literary Journal; and Journal for the Education of the Gifted. Submissions are not invited in fiction, poetry, or drama.

 gopher to
sunsite.unc.edu
path: UNC-Gopherspace
UNC Press On-line

 WWW to
http://sunsite.unc.edu/uncpress/

University of North Texas Press

University of North Texas Press
P.O. Box 13856
Denton, TX 76203-3856
Phone: 817 565 2142
FAX: 817 565 4590

UNT Press is presently producing approximately 14–18 new books annually, in the fields of Texana, book trade references, contemporary and social issues, general-interest nonfiction, guides, history, military studies, poetry, women's issues, writing and publishing, and critical biography.

Book Orders:
See **Texas A&M University Press Consortium.**

University of Pennsylvania Press

University of Pennsylvania Press
418 Service Drive
Philadelphia, PA 19104
Phone: 215 898 6261
FAX: 215 898 0404

 e-mail:
clancy@pobox.upenn.edu

Book Orders:
P.O. Box 4836
Hampden Station
Baltimore, MD 21211
Phone: 410 516 6948
        800 445 9880
FAX: 410 516 6998

Subject Areas: American history, medieval history, European history, literature, folklore, anthropology, art, art history, business, medicine, nursing, women's studies, linguistics, archaeology, human rights, history of science.

 Pat Smith:
        smithpr@pobox.upenn.edu
Jerome Singerman:
        singerma@pobox.upenn.edu
Tim Clancy:
        clancy@pobox.upenn.edu

Note: In this directory, long addresses, paths, and messages are carried over to successive lines. However, these should be read as single-line entities and commands.

University of South Carolina Press

University of South Carolina
Columbia, SC 29208
Phone: 803 777 5243
FAX: 803 777 0160

e-mail:
<firstname>@uscpress.scarolina.edu

Book Orders:
USC Press Distribution Center
205 Pickens Street
Columbia, SC 29208
Phone: 800 768 2500
FAX: 800 868 0740

Subject Areas: Southern history and culture; business, military history, maritime history, women's history, contemporary literature, natural history, international studies, industrial relations, health, marine science, religious studies, rhetorical studies, social work.

gopher to
gopher.press.scarolina.edu

WWW to
http://gopher.press.scarolina.edu

University of Tennessee Press

University of Tennessee Press
293 Communications Building
Knoxville, TN 37996-0325
Phone: 615 974 3321
FAX: 615 974 3724

e-mail:
UTPress2@utkvx.utk.edu

Book Orders:
University of Tennessee Press
Chicago Distribution Center
11030 S. Langley
Chicago, IL 60628
Phone: 800 621 2736
FAX: 800 621 8476

Subject Areas: African-American Studies, Native American Studies, American Religion, Anthropology/Archaeology/Sociology, Appalachian Studies, Caribbean Studies, Communications/Film Studies/ Art/Music, Environment and Nature Studies, Folklore/ Folklife/Material Culture/Vernacular Architecture, History, History of Medicine and Health Sciences, Literature, Political Science, Tennessee Studies, Women's Studies.

gopher to
gopher.lib.utk.edu 70
path: Other UTK Information
UTKPRESS

WWW to
http://gopher.lib.utk.edu:70/1/
UTKgophers/UT-PRESS

University of Texas Press

The University of Texas Press
P.O. Box 7819
Austin, TX 78713-7819
Phone: 512 471 7233
FAX: 512 320 0668

Book Orders:
P.O. Box 7819
Austin, TX 78713-7819
Phone: 512 471 4043 or 800 252 3206
FAX: 512 320 0668

Subject Areas: Latin American studies, Middle Eastern studies, Texana, natural sciences, environmental studies, social sciences, humanities, art and architecture, film and media studies.

Acquisition Editors:

social sciences, art, Texana:
theresa@utpress.ppb.utexas.edu
natural sciences, environmental studies:
shannon@utpress.ppb.utexas.edu
Middle East studies, film and media studies, humanities:
Ali@utpress.utexas.edu

gopher to
gopher.utexas.edu 70

WWW to
http://www.utexas.edu/
path: Academics

University Press of Virginia

*Subject Area*s: Series published by the press include Caribbean and African Literature, Feminist Issues, Victorian Literature and Culture; Studies in Religion and Culture; Knowledge: Disciplinarity and Beyond; Carter G. Woodson Institute Series in Black Studies; History of Early Modern Germany; Minds of the New South; A Nation Divided: New Studies in Civil War History; Southern Texts Society Series; Constitutionalism and Democracy; Recreating South African History; Race and Ethnicity in Urban Politics; and New World Studies.

gopher to
gopher.virginia.edu
path: Organizations and Publications

WWW to
http://www.virginia.edu
path: Organizations and Publications

University of Wisconsin Press

University of Wisconsin Press
114 N. Murray Street
Madison, WI 53715
Phone: 608 262 4928
FAX: 608 262 7560

Book Orders:
114 N. Murray Street
Madison, WI 53715
Phone: 608 262 8782
FAX: 608 262 7560

Subject Areas: Social sciences, anthropology, women's studies, African-American studies, environmental studies; classics, humanities, cinema studies, criminology.

e-mail:
Rosalie Robertson, Senior Editor
rmrobert@tacstaff.wisc.edu

Vanderbilt University Press

Vanderbilt University Press
Box 1813
Station B
Nashville, TN 37235
Phone: 615 322 3585
FAX: 615 343 8823

e-mail:
vupress@uansv3.vanderbilt.edu

Book Orders:
Vanderbilt University Press
c/o Publisher Resources, Inc.
P.O. Box 7018
La Vergne, TN 37086-7018
Phone: 800 937 5557
FAX: 615 793 3915

e-mail:
vupress@uansv3.vanderbilt.edu

Subject Areas: Philosophy, religion, anthropology, history, literary criticism, natural history, and titles of regional interest.
Acquisitions Editor:

Charles Backus, Director
backus@uansv3.vanderbilt.edu

For catalogue

gopher to
vuinfo.vanderbilt.edu 70
path: Publications at Vanderbilt
Vanderbilt University Press

QUOTATIONS

See **REFERENCE WORKS—
Quotations.**

REFERENCE WORKS

Acronyms

To obtain an expansion of an acronym, send an e-mail (with no message in the body) to

wsmith@wordsmith.org
subject: acronym <word>

To obtain additional information on this subject, send an e-mail to the same address with the following subject line:

info Acronym/by/Mail

Anagrams

To find the anagrams for a given word, send an e-mail (with no message in the body) to

wsmith@wordsmith.org
subject: anagram <word>

To obtain additional information on this service, send an e-mail to the same address with the following subject line:

info Anagram/by/Mail

Dictionaries

To obtain a quick definition of a word, send an e-mail (with no message in the body) to

wsmith@wordsmith.org
subject: define <word>

For more information on this dictionary service, send an e-mail to the same address with the following subject line:

info Dictionary/by/Mail

> Note: The info file for Dictionary/
> by/Mail has useful instructions for
> creating a file on the Unix operat-
> ing system to make retrieval of
> definitions easier.

gopher to
una.hh.lib.umich.edu
path: Gophers
    University of Michigan
    University Library
    General Reference Resources

e-mail to
jfesler@netcom.com
subject: #webster <word>

WWW to
http://crl.nmsu.edu/
    Dictionaries.html

http://math-www.uni-paderborn.de/
    HTML/Dictionaries.html

Grammar and Form

The Online Writing Laboratory (OWL) will answer questions about resumes, business memos, research papers, sexist language, English usage, and other topics. This site has numerous documents online. Responses are generally given within 48 hours.

e-mail:
owl@sage.cc.purdue.edu
subject: owl-request

WWW to
http://owl.trc.purdue.edu/

gopher to
owl.trc.purdue.edu

ftp to
owl.trc.purdue.edu

Miscellaneous

For information on various aspects of language (slang, mnemonics, palindromes, spoonerisms, malapropisms),

gopher to
wiretap.spies.com
path: Library
    Articles
    Language

Quotations

Archives of quotations and links to popular and interesting quotations sites across the Internet.

WWW to
http://pubweb.ucdavis.edu/
    Documents/Quotations/
    homepage.html

Another quotations archive, from the literary to the humorous, can be accessed by

WWW
http://pubweb.ucdavis.edu/
    Documents/Quotations/
    homepage.html

Thesaurus

To find synonyms for a word, send an e-mail (with no message in the body) to

wsmith@wordsmith.org
subject: synonym <word>

For more information on this service

e-mail:
wsmith@wordsmith.org
subject line: info Thesaurus/by/Mail

Writer's Handbook

Information on APA, MLA, and old-MLA bibliographic formats can be obtained by gopher from

gopher.cso.uiuc.edu
path: Libraries
        Writer's Workshop

This site is currently under expansion and eventually intends to include information about punctuation, mechanics, grammar, and style.

RELIGION

List of Lists

For a source of lists devoted to religion,

WWW to
http://www.clark.net/pub/listserv/
    listserv.html

RUSSIAN

E-Texts

Literary and nonliterary Russian texts are available by

anonymous FTP from
infomeister.osc.edu
path: pub
        central_eastern_europe
        russian
        corpora

e-mail:
mailserv@osc.edu
message:
    select russian
    size 1 MB
    limit 60KB
    cd corpora
    get asja.txt
    quit

WWW to
http://www.osc.edu/welcome.html
path: The OSC Gopher Server
        Other OSC Gophers
        OSC Central and Eastern
            European Gopher

See also **HISTORY— Russian and East European Studies.**

SCHOLARLY ARTICLES—Searching, Ordering, and Delivery

The Genuine Article

For information, send an e-mail message to
tga@isinet.com

UMI Article Clearinghouse

This service covers more than 12,500 titles—scholarly, technical, popular magazines, conference proceedings and transactions, newspapers, and government documents. UMI pays copyrights.

Standard service: 2 working days (pre-1988: 4 days).

Delivery: Rush First Class, Rush Overnight, FAX. Same day processing and shipment of orders placed before 1:30 P.M. EST.

Account Purchases: $8.50 (1000+ articles/ year)

$10.50 (1–999 articles/year)

Nonaccount Purchases: $12.50
Orders:

orders@infostore.com

User support on Internet ordering:
800 521 0600
(ext. 2524 or 2530).

The UnCover Company

The UnCover Company maintains an extensive library (over 16,000 multidisciplinary journals) of scholarly articles and book reviews from 1988 to the present. The search service is free. Over 3000 new article citations are added daily to the database, which is updated within 24 hours. Full texts of articles can be faxed within 24 hours. Visa, MasterCard, or American Express are accepted. Deposit account available for individuals or libraries.

The UnCover Company also provides a service of automatically mailing table of contents of various journals.

telnet to
database.carl.org
choose: vt100
path: Public Access Catalog
(PAC)
terminal: vt100
exit: //exit

UnCover can also be accessed directly at 303 758 1551 (8 data/No parity/1 Stop bit)

For questions about searching the database, placing orders, or the status of an order

e-mail:
uncover@carl.org

For questions about high volume discounts, purchasing an access password, or setting up a gateway

e-mail Brenda Bailey at
bbailey@carl.org
phone: 303 758 3030

As of October 1, 1994, UnCover S.O.S. (Single Order Source) came online. This service allows anyone to order articles from UnCover's database by either FAX, phone, electronic mail, or post. For more information, contact Donna Snyman at

sos@carl.org

SCHOLARLY JOURNALS—ONLINE

Configurations

WWW to
http://muse.mse.jhu.edu
path: Browse JHU Press Journals

Early Modern Literary Studies

Published by the University of British Columbia's English Department, *Early Modern Literary Studies: A Journal of Sixteenth- and Seventeenth-Century English Literature* is available free online both by WWW and by Gopher.

WWW to
http://unixg.ubc.ca:7001/0/
        e-sources/emls/emlshome.html

gopher to
edziza.arts.ubc.ca
path: English
        EMLS

ELH (English Literary History)

WWW to
http://muse.mse.jhu.edu
path: Browse JHU Press Journals

Indiana University Press Journals

gopher to
gopher.iupress.indiana.edu
path: IU Campus Gophers
        IU Press Gopher
        IU Press Journals
        IU Press Journals—Contents of
            Current Issues

MLN (Modern Language Notes)

WWW to
http://muse.mse.jhu.edu
path: Browse JHU Press Journals

Nineteenth-Century Literature— Electronic Edition

The electronic edition of Nineteenth-Century Literature includes the full texts of recent volumes of the journal, including tables of contents, articles, book review, notes, and descriptive lists of contributors.

gopher to
infolib.lib.berkeley.edu
path: Electronic Journals, Books,
        Indexes and Other Sources
        Electronic Journals
        Nineteenth-Century Literature

PROJECT MUSE

WWW to
http://muse.mse.jhu.edu

Comments to:
ejournal@jhunix.hcf.jhu.edu

Publishers' Catalogs

For access to over 50 publishers who have made their catalogs available, WWW to Peter Scott's Publishers' Catalogs Home Page at

http://www.usask.ca/~scottp/
        publish.html

SGML

Texts

University of Virginia Library (Middle English texts, the King James and Revised Standard Versions of the Bible, and the Michigan Early Modern English Materials).

For information

anonymous FTP to
etext.virginia.edu
path: pub

WWW to
http://etext.virginia.edu/

See also **TEI**.

SHOPPING

eMall

The eMall, a shopping and information center, offers a book and gift shop as well as an info-center for New York City.

WWW to
http://eMall.com/

The Internet Mall

To receive the list of commercial services available on the Internet, send an e-mail request to

taylor@netcom.com
subject: send mall

The Internet Shopkeeper

WWW to
http://www.ip.net/shops.html

Spencer Gifts

With over 30 years, experience in retailing, Spencer Gifts has now opened a Web site at

http://www.btg.com/spencer

SITES

Because of the sheer volume of the resources available, a number of sites are worthy of a summer vacation to explore fully. Here are a few of them.

Carnegie Mellon University

WWW to
http://www.cmu.edu
path: The English Server

Rice University

gopher to
riceinfo.rice.edu

University of California, Santa Barbara

gopher to
ucsbuxa.ucsb.edu

University of North Carolina Sunsite

gopher to
sunsite.unc.edu

University of Pennsylvania

gopher to
gopher.upenn.edu

Washington & Lee University

gopher to
liberty.uc.wlu.edu

SOFTWARE—DOS

FTP Site

For an extensive collection of freeware and shareware

anonymous FTP to
oak.oakland.edu
path: pub
      msdos

or

wuarchive.wustl.edu
path: /systems/ibmpc/msdos

Compression/Uncompression

PKZIP is a useful DOS compression/uncompression software program. It can be downloaded by anonymous FTP from

oak.oakland.edu
path: /pub/msdos/zip

or anonymous FTP to

garbo.uwasa.fi
path: /pc/arcers

Info-Zip is another such program which also works in UNIX and VAX environments. Download by anonymous FTP from

quest.jpl.nasa.gov (128.129.75.43)
path: pub

SOFTWARE—UNIX

Compression/Uncompression Software

See **SOFTWARE—DOS—Compression/Uncompression** (Info-Zip) above.

WDIFF

GNU WDIFF compares two texts for differences and produces a word-for-word comparison.

anonymous FTP to
src.doc.ic.ac.uk
path: gnu/wdiff-0.04.tar.gz

SOFTWARE—Windows

Hypertext

ANT_HTML.DOT is a template designed to work within Word for Windows 6.0 to facilitate the creation of hypertext documents.

For a copy of ANT_HTML.ZIP,

 anonymous FTP to
ftp.einet.net
path: einet
    pc

e-mail comments or questions to the author, Jill Swift, at

 jswift@freenet.fsu.edu

Mosaic

The NCSA Mosaic for Microsoft Windows (Version 2.0alpha5) is available by

 WWW from
http://www.ncsa.uiuc.edu/SDG/
    Software/WinMosaic/
      HomePage.html

 anonymous FTP from
ftp.ncsa.uiuc.edu
path: PC
    Mosaic

Software Site

 anonymous FTP to
ftp.cica.indiana.edu
path: /pub/pc/win3

WinNews

Microsoft's WinNews is an electronic newsletter created by Microsoft's Personal Operating Division.

To subscribe to WinNews, send e-mail to

 enews@microsoft.nwnet.com
message: subscribe WinNews
    <your e-mail address>

SPANISH

Comedia Electronic Bulletin Board

The Electronic Communication Committee of the Association for Hispanic Classical Theater (AHCT), in cooperation with the University of Arizona Computer Center, maintains an electronic bulletin board. To use the Bulletin Board, you must first subscribe to the Comedia list.

 e-mail:
listserv@arizvm1.ccit.arizona.edu
subject: <blank>
message: subscribe comedia
    <your name>

One of the benefits of the Bulletin Board is access to the videotape archive, which rents at modest cost videos for teaching and research. For more information on this service, e-mail

 kgregg@ccit.arizona.edu

Another service is a listing of comedia texts and translations that can be provided to AHCT members on floppy disks. Currently, there are over sixty texts available. For more information, contact Vern Williamsen at

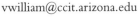 vwilliam@ccit.arizona.edu

Latin America Studies

For an on-line collection devoted to Latin America

WWW to
http://edb518ea.edb.utexas.edu/

Another site at the Universidade Federal de Rio Grande de Sul in Brazil can by accessed by

gopher to
asterix.ufrgs.br

Sor Juana Ines de la Cruz

The prose of Sor Juana Ines de la Cruz is available at Dartmouth College. For more information, contact

luis.villar@dartmouth.edu

See also **APPENDIX—Lists** and **LANGUAGE AND LITERATURE**

SPECIAL COLLECTIONS—Libraries

See **ARCHIVES AND LIBRARY RESOURCES** and **LIBRARIES—Special Collections.**

SPECIAL EDUCATION

Information Technology and Disabilities Journal

For a subscription to the Information Technology and Disabilities Journal,

e-mail:
listserv@sjuvm.stjohns.edu
subject line: <blank>
message: sub itd-jnl <your name>

One can also subscribe only to the table of contents of this journal by substituting the following message:

sub itd-toc <your name>

The full journal is also available by gopher to St. Johns University.

SPED ON-LINE

SPED ON-LINE, hosted by the University of Kansas, offers information about special education resources at the university. It also provides links to a comprehensive directory of Internet resources relating to disabilities.

WWW to
http://www.sped.ukans.edu/
spedadmin/welcome.html

STATE GOVERNMENT SITES

Metronet WWW

For a site that has links to state government information servers and that includes information on archives, education, cultural affairs, recreation, libraries, etc.

WWW to
http://garnet.msen.com:70 /
    Oh/vendor/maven/inet1/
    nnews/states.html

TEACHING ENGLISH AS A SECOND LANGUAGE (TESL)

CELIA

Archives of the CELIA (Computer Enhanced Language Instruction Archive) project can be accessed by

gopher to
gopher.archive.merit.edu
path: Merit Software Archive
    CELIA Archive

TESL-EJ

For Teaching English as a Second or Foreign Language: An Electronic Journal

e-mail:
listserv@cmsa.berkeley.edu
message: sub teslej-l
    <firstname lastname>

TELEPHONE SERVICES

1-800 Service

AT&T has developed a WWW 800 number directory that can be browsed by name or category.

WWW to
http://att.net/dir800

Area Codes (Worldwide)

gopher to
Veronica.scs.unr.edu
path: Internet Jewels
    Desk Reference Tools
    Area Code Lookup

Telephone Service (Discount)

For information

e-mail to
info@americom.com

Note: In this directory, long address, paths, and messages are carried over to successive lines. However, these should be read as single-line entities and commands.

TEXT ENCODING INITIATIVE (TEI)

TEI Guidelines

The Text Encoding Initiative (TEI) Guidelines (P3) were released in 1994. They can be obtained from the following location.

WWW to
http://www.oulu.fi/TEI.html

anonymous FTP to
sgml1.ex.ac.uk
path: pub
    SGML
      twi

ftp.ifi.uio.no
path: pub
    SGML
      TEI

by e-mail from

listserv@uicvm.uic.edu
message: get teip3 package
    [for sgml-tagged version]

or one of the following:
get p3ascii package [formatted, untagged
    ASCII only version]
get p3dtds package [TEI PC DTD files]
get p3all package [all three packages SGML,
    ASCII, and DTD]

TEI-L

The list for discussions of TEI is TEI-L

listserv@uicvm.uic.edu

Subscribers to TEI-L can obtain an introductory package of files pertaining to TEI by sending a message to the Listserver:

listserv@uicvm.uic.edu
message: Get TEIIntro Package

TEXTS—Electronic

General

Book Excerpt: For a general overview of issues concerning electronic texts, consult Richard Lanham's *The Electronic Word*, University of Chicago Press. An excerpt from this book is available by way of ftp or gopher.

anonymous FTP
press-gopher.uchicago.edu
dir: pub
    Excerpts
    Lanham.txt

gopher to
press-gopher.uchicago.edu 70
path: New Books from Chicago

For one of the largest collections of e-texts at a gopher site,

gopher to
gopher.psu.edu
path: Information Servers at Penn
    State
      University Libraries Gopher
      The Electronic Bookshelf
      Electronic Books and Texts

ALEX: A Catalogue of Electronic Texts on the Internet

ALEX indexes many books at various depositories (Project Gutenberg, Wiretap, the On-Line Book Initiative, ERIS, and OTA). New publications are added regularly.

gopher to
gopher.lib.ncsu.edu//11/library/
    stacks/Alex

WWW to
http://www.lib.ncsu.edu/stacks/
    alex-index.html

Questions and comments can be addressed to

alex@rsl.ox.ac.uk

ARTFL

WWW to
http://tuna.uchicago.edu/
    ARTFL.html

Authors

There are currently thousands of e-texts available on the Internet at anonymous FTP sites such as the following:

Finish University and Research
    Network (FUNET)
ftp.funet.fi
path: /pub/doc/literary/etext

Oakland University (OAK)
oak.oakland.edu
path: /pub/misc/books

On-Line Book Initiative (OBI)
ftp.std.com

Oxford Text Archive (OTA)
ota.ox.ac.uk

Project Gutenberg (PG)
mrcnext.cso.uiuc.edu

Wiretap (W)
wiretap.spies.com

Penn State Gopher (PSU)
psulias.psu.edu

Samizdat (S)
samizdat@world.std.com

The following list of authors/titles/sites is not meant to be exhaustive, merely illustrative.

Selected list of authors/titles and sites:

    Abbott, E. (FUNET) (OBI) (PG) (PSU)
        (W)
    Aeschylus (OTA)
    Aesop (FUNET) (OAK) (OBI) (OTA)
        (PG) (PSU) (S) (W)
    Agee, P. (OBI)
    Alcott, L. M. (PG) (S) (W)
    Alger, H. (OBI) (PSU) (S) (W)
    Anglo Saxon poetry (OTA)
    Ariosto, L. (OTA)
    Aristophanes (OTA)
    Aristotle (OTA)
    Augustine (OTA) (S) (U. of Notre Dame)
        (W)
    Austen, Jane (OBI) (OTA) (PG) (PSU) (S)
        (W)
    Bacon, F. (OBI) (PSU) (S) (W)
    Balzac, H. (OTA)
    Barrie, J. M. (FUNET) (OBI) (PG) (PSU)
        (W)
    Baum, L. F. (FUNET) (OAK) (PG) (S) (W)
    Beaumont, Francis (OTA)
    Beckett, S. (OTA)

Bede (OTA)

Beethoven (PG)

Behn, A. (OTA)

Beowulf (OTA) (S) (W)

Berryman, John (OTA)

Bible—Concordance
    (U. North Carolina, Sunsite)

Bible—KJV (OAK) (OTA) (PG) (S)

Bible—RSV (OTA)

Bierce, A. (FUNET) (OBI) (S) (W)

Bill of Rights (PG)

Blake, William (OBI) (OTA) (PSU)

Boccaccio, Giovanni (OTA)

Boethius (OTA)

Book of Mormon (PG)

Bronte, E. (FUNET) (OBI) (OTA) (PSU)
    (S) (W)

Browning, R. (OTA) (W)

Bunyan, J. (PG) (S)

Burnett, F. H. (OTA) (W)

Burns, Robert (OTA)

Burroughs. E. R. (FUNET) (OBI) (PG)
    (PSU) (S) (W)

Byron, G., Lord (OTA)

Caesar (U. of Washington)

Calvino, I. (OTA)

Carlyle, T. (OTA)

Carroll, Lewis (FUNET) (OAK) (OBI)
    (OTA) (PG) (PSU) (S) (W)

Castiglione, B. (OTA)

Cather, Willa (FUNET) (OTA) (PG) (S)
    (W)

Cato (OTA)

Catullus (OTA) (U. of Washington)

Chapman, G. (OTA)

Chaucer (OBI) (OTA) (PSU) (S) (W)
    (U. of Texas–San Antonio)

Chesterton, G. K. (PG) (W)

Chopin, K. (PG)

Cicero (OTA) (S) (U. of Washington)

Cleland, J. (FUNET) (OBI) (OTA) (PSU)
    (W)

Clemens, S. L. (See Twain, M.)

Clinton, W. (PG)

Coleridge, S. T. (OTA) (PG) (W)

Collins, Wilkie (OTA) (PG) (S)

Conrad, Joseph (FUNET) (OBI) (OTA) (S)
    (W)

Constitution of the United States (OTA)
    (PG)

Coombs, N. (PG)

Cooper, J. F. (S)

Cowper, W. (OTA)

Crane, S. (PG) (S) (W)

Dante (Dartmouth) (OTA)

Darwin, Charles (OBI) (OTA) (PSU) (S)
    (W)

Declaration of Independence (OTA) (PG)
    (W)

Defoe, Daniel (OTA)

Dekker, T. (OTA)

Demosthenes (OTA)

Descartes (FUNET) (OAK) (PG) (S) (W)

Dickens, C. (FUNET) (OBI) (OTA) (PG)
    (PSU) (S) (W)

Disraeli, B. (OTA)

Dostoevski, F. (OTA)

Donne, J. (OBI) (OTA) (PSU)

Douglas, F. (FUNET) (OAK) (OTA) (PG)
    (W)

Doyle, A. C. (FUNET) (OTA) (PG) (PSU)
    (S) (W)

Dryden, J. (OTA) (S)

Eliot, G. (OTA) (PG) (S) (W)

Eliot, T. S. (OTA)

Emerson, R. W. (OTA)

Engels, F. (OTA) (W)

Erasmus (OTA)

Eschenback, W. von (OTA)

Euclid (OTA)

Euripides (OTA)

Everyman (OTA)

Faulkner, William (OTA)

Federalist Papers (OTA) (W)

Fielding, Henry (OTA)

Fitzgerald, F. Scott (OTA)

Fletcher, John (OTA)

Ford, J. (OTA)

Franklin, Benjamin (OTA) (PG)
    (U. of Penn.) (W)

Frederic, H. (PG) (S) (W)

Frost, Robert (OTA)

Fry, C. (OTA)
Frye, Northop (OTA)
Gaskell, E. (OTA) (S)
Gay, J. (S) (W)
Gide, A. (OTA)
Gilman, C. P. (FUNET) (OTA) (PG) (S)
  (W)
Goethe, W. von (OTA)
Gower (OTA)
Graves, R. (OTA)
Greene, G. (OTA)
Grimm, Jakob and Wilhelm (OBI) (OTA)
  (PSU)
Hardy, Thomas (FUNET) (OAK) (OTA)
  (PG) (S) (W)
Hawthorne, N. (FUNET) (OAK) (OBI)
  (OTA) (PG) (PSU) (S) (W)
Hearst, Patti (OTA)
Henry, P. (PG)
Herodotus (OTA)
Herrick, R. (OBI) (PSU)
Hesiod (OTA)
Hesse, H. (OTA)
Heywood, J. (OTA)
Hippocrates (OBI) (OTA) (W)
Homer (OTA)
Hope, A. (PG) (S) (W)
Hopkins, G. M. (OTA)
Horace (OTA)
Houseman, A. E. (OBI) (OTA) (PSU)
Howells, W. D. (PG)
Hugo, V. (OTA) (PG) (S) (W)
Hume, D. (OBI) (PSU) (S) (W)
Irving, W. (FUNET) (OAK) (PG) (W)
James, H. (OTA) (PG) (S)
James, W. (FUNET) (OBI) (PSU) (S) (W)
Jefferson, T. (OTA) (PG)
Johnson, S. (OTA)
Jonson, B. (OTA) (S)
Joyce, J. (OTA)
Juvenal (OTA)
Kafka, F. (OTA)
Kant, I. (OTA)
Keats, J. (OBI) (OTA) (PSU)
Kennedy, J. F. (PG)
Kierkegaard, S. (OTA)

King, M. L. (OBI) (OTA) (PSU)
Kipling, R. (OBI) (PSU)
Kirkland, W. (S)
Kyd, T. (OTA)
Lamb, C. (OTA)
Lang, A. (PG)
Langland, W. (OTA)
Latin-English Dictionary
  (U. of Washington)
Latin Texts (OTA) (W)
Lawrence, D. H. (OTA)
Lessing, D. (OTA)
Lewis, S. (OBI) (PSU) (S) (W)
Lincoln, A. (PG)
Livy (OTA)
Locke, J. (OTA) (W)
London, J. (FUNET) (OTA) (S) (W)
Longfellow, H. W. (FUNET) (OTA) (W)
Lowell, R. (OTA)
Machiavelli, N. (OTA)
Malamud, B. (OTA)
Malraux, A. (OTA)
Mann, T. (OTA)
Mansfield, K. (FUNET) (OBI) (OTA)
  (PSU)
Marlowe, C. (OTA)
Marx, K. (FUNET) (OTA) (PG)
Marston, J. (OTA)
Martial (OTA)
Marvell, A. (OBI) (OTA) (PSU) (S)
Marx, K. (OBI) (OTA) (PSU) (W)
Massinger, P. (OTA)
Maugham, W. S. (S) (W)
Maupassant, Guy de (OTA)
Mayflower Compact (PG)
Melville, H. (FUNET) (OAK) (OBI)
  (OTA) (PG) (PSU) (S) (W)
Michelangelo (OTA)
Middleton, T. (OTA)
Mill, J. S. (OBI) (PSU) (S) (W)
Millay, E. St. V. (PG) (S) (W)
Milton, John (FUNET) (OAK) (OBI)
  (OTA) (PG) (PSU) (S) (W)
Monroe Doctrine (PG)
Montaigne, Michel (OTA)
More, T., Sir (OBI) (OTA)

Morley, C. (OBI) (PSU) (S) (W)
Morris, W. (S)
Morte Arthure (OTA)
More, T. (PSU) (S) (W)
Murdoch, I. (OTA)
Nashe, T. (OTA)
New Latin
Newman, J. H. (OBI) (PSU)
Norris, F. (PG) (S) (W)
O'Casey, S. (OTA)
O. Henry (FUNET) (W)
Orwell, G. (OTA)
Orczy, E. (PG) (S) (W)
Osborne, J. (OTA)
Ovid (OTA)
Owen, W. (OBI) (PSU)
Paine, T. (OBI) (OTA) (PG) (PSU) (W)
Pearl (OTA)
Petrarch (OTA)
Phillips, D. G. (S)
Pindar (OTA)
Pinter, H. (OTA)
Plath, Sylvia (OTA)
Plato (OBI) (OTA) (PG) (PSU) (W)
Plotinus (U. of Notre Dame)
Plutarch (OTA)
Poe, E. A. (FUNET) (OBI) (OTA) (PSU)
    (S) (W)
Pope, Alexander (OTA)
Porter, G. S. (PG) (W)
Pound, E. (OBI) (OTA) (PSU)
Powell, A. (OTA)
Proust, Marcel (OTA)
Racine, Jean (OTA)
Rimbaud, A. (OTA)
Robbe-Grillet, A. (OTA)
Roosevelt, F. D. (PG)
Rosetti, D. G. (OTA)
Saki (FUNET) (OBI) (W)
Sandberg, C. (S) (W)
Sartre, Jean-Paul (OTA)
Scott, Sir W. (FUNET) (OBI) (PG) (PSU)
    (S) (W)
Service, R. (W)
Shakespeare (FUNET) (OBI) (OTA) (PG)
    (PSU) (S) (U. of Pennsylvania)

Shelley, M. W. (OBI) (PG) (PSU) (S) (W)
Shelley, P. B. (OBI) (OTA) (PSU)
Shikibu, M. (OTA)
Sidney, P. Sir (OTA)
Sinclair, U. (PG) (S)
Sir Gawayne and the Grene Knyght (OTA)
Sophocles (FUNET) (OAK) (OTA) (PG)
    (S) (W)
Spender, S. (OTA)
Spenser, E. (OTA) (W)
Stendhal (OTA)
Sterne, L. (OTA)
Stevenson, R. L. (FUNET) (OAK) (PG) (S)
    (W)
Stoker, B. (FUNET) (OBI) (PSU) (S) (W)
Stoppard, T. (OTA)
Swift, Jonathan (OTA)
Swinburne, A. C. (OBI) (OTA)
Tacitus (OTA)
Tasso (OTA)
Taylor, A. J. P. (OTA)
Tenniel, J. (PG)
Tennyson, Alfred (OBI) (OTA) (PSU)
Theocritus (OTA)
Thomas, D. (OTA)
Thoreau, Henry David (FUNET) (OBI)
    (OTA) (PG) (PSU) (W)
Thucydides (OTA)
Thurber, J. (OTA)
Trollope, Anthony (FUNET) (OTA) (S)
Tzu, Sun (PG) (W)
Twain, Mark (FUNET) (OBI) (OTA) (PG)
    (PSU) (S) (W)
Verne, J. (PG) (S) (W)
Virgil (FUNET) (OBI) (OTA) (PSU) (S)
    (U. of Washington) (W)
Washington, B. T. (OBI) (PSU) (W)
Waugh, E. (OTA)
Webster, J. (OTA)
Wells, H. G. (FUNET) (OAK) (OTA) (PG)
    (S) (W)
Wharton, E. (PG)
Whitman, Walt (OBI) (OTA) (PSU)
Whittier, J. G. (PSU)
Wilde, O. (OBI) (OTA) (PSU)
Williams, T. (OTA)

Wittgenstein, L. (OTA)
Wollstonecraft, M. (PG) (S) (W)
Woolf, V. (OTA) (PG) (W)
Wordsworth, W. (OBI) (OTA) (PSU)
Wyatt, T. (OTA)
Wycherley (OTA)
Xenophon (OTA)
Yeats, W. B. (FUNET) (OBI) (OTA) (PSU)

CABAL

WWW to
http://tuna.uchicago.edu/
ENGLISH.html

Catalogue of Projects in Electronic Text (CPET)

The CPET includes texts in literature and philosophy (see also **Labyrinth**).

gopher to
gopher.georgetown.edu
path: Computing
    Humanities Resources
    The Catalogue of Projects in
      Electr. Text
    Digests Organized by
      Discipline
    Literature

WWW to
http://www.georgetown.edu/
guhome.html

Center for Electronic Texts in the Humanities—CETH (Rutgers University)

WWW to
http://www.rutgers.edu

Dartmouth College Electronic Text Center

gopher to
gopher.dartmouth.edu

WWW to
http://www.dartmouth.edu

Directory

For a directory of worldwide electronic text centers

e-mail:
etextctr@phoenix.princeton.edu

WWW to
http://cethmac.princeton.edu/
CETH/elcenter.html

Educational Technology Services of the University of Pennsylvania

gopher to
ccat.sas.upenn.edu

WWW to
http://ccat.sas.upenn.edu

Electronic Beowulf Project

Test images from the Beowulf manuscript (British Library, Cotton MS. Vitellius A.XV) are available by

anonymous FTP from
beowulf.engl.uky.edu
    (University of Kentucky)
path: ftp
    pub
    beowulf

or

    othello.bl.uk (British Library)
    path: mss
        beowulf

For an illustrated copy of Kevin Kiernan's paper "Digital Preservation, Restoration, and Dissemination of Medieval Manuscripts,"

WWW to
http://www.uky.edu/ArtsSciences/
    English/Beowulf

Electronic Text Center of New York University

gopher to
cmcl2.nyu.edu
path: Libraries
        Bobst_Library

WWW to
http://www.nyu.edu
path: Information Severs at NYU
        University Libraries
        Bobst Library/NYU Library
            Resources
        Electronic Resources at Bobst
            Library
        Electronic Text Center

Electronic Text Center of North Carolina State University

gopher to
dewey.lib.ncsu.edu

WWW to
http://dewey.lib.ncsu.edu

Electronic Text Center of the University of Virginia

The Electronic Text Center at Alderman Library, University of Virginia. For information, e-mail a request to

        etext@virginia.edu

gopher to
gopher.virginia.edu

WWW to
http://www.lib.virginia.edu/etext/
    ETC.html

Electronic Text Center of Yale University

gopher to
yaleinfo.yale.edu

Go-MLink (University of Michigan)

For a repository of electronic texts and links to other sites

gopher to
mlink.hh.lib.umich.edu

Information Arcade of Iowa University

gopher to
gopher.arcade.uiowa.edu

WWW to
http://www.arcade.uiowa.edu

Library Electronic Text Resource Service of Indiana University

gopher to
gopher.indiana.edu
path: Library and Research Services
    LETRS

Labyrinth (medieval studies)

WWW to
http://www.georgetown.edu/
    labyrinth/labyrinth-home.html

Online Book Initiative

gopher to
world.std.com
path: OBI
    The Online Books

Oxford Text Archives (OTA)

anonymous FTP to
ftp.ox.ac.uk
path: pub
    ota

To receive a copy of the archive directory file, type

get textarchive.list

Another useful file to receive:

get textarchive.info

In order to obtain specific texts from OTA, one must first complete the User Declaration, which is included in the file textarchive.info, and return it in hard copy (by mail or fax) to OTA.

Project Gutenberg

anonymous FTP to
mrcnext.cso.uiuc.edu

cd etext/etext91 [for 1991 releases]

cd etext/etext92 [for 1992 releases]

Project Gutenberg e-texts are also available by anonymous FTP from other sites:

U.S.
    text.archive.umich.edu (Michigan)
    ftp.etext.org
    ftp.cdrom.com (California)
    freebsd.cdrom.com
    oak.oakland.edu ((Michigan)
    nptn.org
    ftp.uu.net
    sunsite.unc.edu (N. Carolina)
    inform.umd.edu (Maryland)
    calypso-2.oit.unc.edu (N. Carolina)

England
    src.doc.ic.ac.uk

France
ftp.cnam.fr
Germany
alice.fmi.uni-passau.de

Japan
news3.yasuda-u.ac.jp

Sweden
ftp.sunet.se

Taiwan
ftp.edu.tw

Project Libellus (Classical Latin texts)

anonymous FTP to
ftp.u.washington.edu
cd: pub
user-supported
libellus

Scholarly Communications Project (Virginia Polytechnic Institute and State University)

gopher to
scholar.lib.vt.edu

WWW to
http://scholar.lib.vt.edu

Spectrum Press

Electronic texts on disk for PC and MAC on the following topics: modern fiction, poetry, drama, criticism; lesbian/feminist fiction and nonfiction; gay fiction and nonfiction; classics; nonfiction and reference.

e-mail
contact: Karen Olsen
73774.2733@compuserve.com

University of Kansas

For an extensive collection of electronic texts

telnet to
ukanaix.cc.ukans.edu
log-on: www
path: Inter-Links
Library Resources

This site has searchable on-line texts as well as links to Eris Project, OBI, UMN, and Wiretap.

University of Virginia SGML Textual Analysis Resources

The University of Virginia Library has Internet accessible text collections. Users must access by way of client software developed by the University of Virginia.

anonymous FTP to
etext.virginia.edu
path: pub

Vatican Exhibit

The 1993 traveling exhibit from the Vatican Library is available from the Library of Congress.

anonymous FTP to
seq1.loc.gov
cd pub
vatican.exhibit
exhibit

The following directories are available: a-vatican-library, b-archeology, c-humanism, d-mathematics, e-music, f-medicine-bio, g-nature, h-orient-to-rome, and i-rome-to-china.

Get files as appropriate (suggested: FILELIST, Master-list, and README). If you do not already have a gif viewer, you will also need to cd to viewers and GET files as appropriate.

Wiretap

anonymous FTP to
wiretap.spies.com
path: Library
Classic

Women Writers Project

The Women Writers Project at Brown University provides texts for British, Irish, Scottish, and Welsh women writers before 1830. For additional information, subscribe to WWP-L (**See APPENDIX—Lists**).

THEATER

Cornell University Gopher

gopher to
gopher.cornell.edu

Guide to Theater Resources on the Internet

gopher to the University of
Michigan
una.hh.lib.umich.edu
path: Clearinghouse of
Subject-Oriented Res. Guides
All Guides
Theater

by anonymous FTP to
una.hh.lib.umich.edu
path: inetdirsstacks/
theater:torresmjvk

Heathcote Video Archive

See the International Centre for Studies in Drama in Education.

International Centre for Studies in Drama in Education

For information, contact David Davis at

deba3603G@university-central-
england.ac.uk

At this address, information is also available about the Heathcote Video Archive, a repository of films concerning the teaching of drama.

Playwrights' and Screenwriters' Home Page

This site contains a directory of theater professionals, newsgroups, active theatre groups, a Shakespeare play archive, and more.

WWW to
http://www.mit.edu:8001/

Reviews

To read Diana Cantu on theater,

WWW to
http://www.thegroup.net

Screenwriters' and Playwrights' Home Page

For a great deal of information about theater-related items

WWW to
http://www.teleport.com/
~cdeemer/scrwriter.html

Texts

Carnegie Mellon University has an excellent selection of theater texts.

gopher to
english-server.hss.cmu.edu 70
path: Drama

TDR

TDR: The Journal of Performance Studies examines performance in the context of theater, music, dance, entertainment, media, sports, politics, aesthetics of everyday life, games, plays, and ritual.

Editor: Richard Schechner (NYU)
Publisher: MIT Press

gopher to
gopher.internet.com

gopher to
gopher.mit.edu
path: Interesting Sites to Explore
    Electronic Newsstand
    Magazines, Periodicals and
    Journals (all titles)
      All titles Listed Alphabetically
      S–Z

To order

e-mail:
journals-orders@mit.edu

University of Manchester UK

See **FILM**.

Theater

See also **ARCHIVES AND LIBRARY RESOURCES** and **FILM**.

THESAURUS

See **REFERENCE BOOKS—Thesaurus.**

TRANSLATIONS

The Eurodictautom database translates words or abbreviations from a number of languages (Danish, Dutch, English, French, German, Italian, Spanish, and Portuguese) into target languages.

WWW to
http://www.uni-frankfurt.de/~felix/
    eurodictautom.html

TRAVEL

Airline Telephone Numbers

For toll-free telephone numbers

gopher to
cs4sun.cs.ttu.edu
path: Reference Shelf
    Airlines Toll-free Numbers

or to the University of Nebraska-Omaha, where you will also find the 3-letter codes for airport designations and other information:

gopher-library.unomaha.edu
path: Find Information by Subject
    Aviation

Airline Tickets

A no-fee airline reservation and ticketing service, PCTravel is available by

telnet at
pctravel.com

WWW to
http://www.nando.net/pctravel.html

Amtrak Schedules

gopher to
gwis.circ.gwu.edu
path: General Information
        Train Schedules

Australian Railway Timetables

WWW to
http://brother.cc.monash.edu.au/
        ccstaff2/che/bromage/WWW/
        tt/
Books

Cambridge-London British Rail Timetables

gopher to
gopher.cam.ac.uk
path: Miscellaneous
        British Railway

Moon Travel Handbooks

gopher to
gopher.moon.com: 7000

WWW to
http://www.moon.com: 7000/

e-mail
travel@moon.com

City and Geographical Information

CityLink
Access to information on many U. S. cities

WWW to
http://www.NeoSoft.com/citylink/
        default.html

Here are some web sites devoted to particular cities and areas:

Edinburgh,
WWW to
http://www.efr.hw.ac.uk/EDC/
        Edinburgh.html

Hawaii
WWW to
http://www.hawaii.net/

Napa Valley, California:
WWW to
http://www.freerun.com/

New York City
WWW to
http://www.mediabridge.com/

Triangle, North Carolina
WWW to
http://www.trinet.com/tgp/

Philadelphia,
telnet to
libertynet.org
login: liberty

Current Foreign Exchange Rates

WWW to
http://www.ora.com/cgi-bin/ora/
currency

German Railway Timetables

WWW to
http://www.rz.uni-karlsruhe.de/
~ule3/

Guides

For an extensive collection of travel guides,
anonymous FTP to

ftp.cc.umanitoba.ca
path: rec-travel

WWW to
http://www.city.net/

Lodgings

Hyatt Hotels maintains a WWW site at

http://www.travelweb.com/thisco/
common/tweb.html

Promus Hotels has on-line information on
Embassy Suites, Hampton Inn, and Homewood Suites: address, telephone number, directions, amenities, local points of interest,
visual images of the property, toll-free reservation telephone number, EASSY SABRE
booking reference, and e-mail address for
comments and suggestions

webmaster@promus.com

Access these electronic directories by
WWW to

http://www.promus.com/
embassy.html

http://www.promus.com/
hampton.html

http://www.promus.com/
homewood.html

Subway Navigator

The subway and metro systems of Vienna,
Paris, Munich, Athens, Hong Kong, Boston,
New York, and many other cities can be
traveled in virtual reality. Choose a starting
and stopping point in the city of your
choice, and the service will map out the
route and tell you how long the trip will
take.

gopher to
gopher.jussieu.fr
path: Subway Navigator

telnet to
metro.jussieu.fr10000
    (134.157.0.132 10000)

Times

To find local times throughout the world

WWW to
http://www.hilink.com.au/

Worldwide Guides

WWW to
http://wings.buffalo.edu/world

UNITED STATES GOVERNMENT

AskERIC

A project of the U.S. Department of Education, AskERIC provides a variety of information on education.

WWW to
http://ericir.syr.edu

telnet to
ericir.syr.edu
login: gopher

Census

anonymous FTP to
ftp.census.gov
path: pub

gopher to
gopher.census.gov

WWW to
http://www.census.gov

Problems or questions should be directed to

gatekeeper@census.gov

Consumer Information Center (CIC)

gopher to
gopher.gsa.gov

anonymous FTP to
www.gsa.gov
path: Pub
      CIC

telnet to
sbaonline.sba.gov
path: Outside Resources
      Gateways to Other Online
         Services
      Federal: Public Access (no Fee)
      General Services Admin.—CIC

telnet to
fedworld.gov

Department of Justice

gopher to
gopher.usdoj.gov

EDGAR

Information on corporate reports and other documents filed with the Securities and Exchange Commission.

WWW to
http://town.hall.org/cgi-bin/
      srch-edgar

anonymous FTP to
town.hall.org

ERIC

The U.S. Department of Education maintains an on-line library, which includes the full text of the GOALS 2000: Educate America Act, the Prisoners of Time report, press releases, grant announcements, and much more. In addition, the complete collection of electronic ERIC Digests is now available as a WAIS searchable database at the ED/OERI Gopher Server. The database supports searches which include Boolean and multiword expressions. This collection includes 143 new ERIC Digests. These provide brief overviews of research on topics in education.

gopher to
gopher.ed.gov
path: CERI
      ERIC

WWW to
http://www.ed.gov/
path: U.S. Dept. of Education Main
      Gopher Server
      Other Educational Resources
      U.S. Educational Resources
        Information Center

anonymous FTP to
ftp.ed.gov
path: eric
      cooked

Federal Communications Commission

gopher to
fcc.gov

WWW to
http://www.fcc.gov

anonymous FTP to
ftp.fcc.gov
path: pub

FedWorld Gateway

For government databases, libraries, etc.,

telnet to
fedworld.doc.gov

Government Printing Office

For access to the Federal Register and Congressional Bills,

gopher to
pula.financenet.gov
path: Documents, Publications and
      Standards
      Central Agencies, Councils and
      Task Forces
      Government Printing Office
      Document Access

House of Representatives

Bills
The House of Representatives House Information Services (HIS) has placed the full text of all house bills on a WAIS server.

gopher to
gopher.house.gov
path: Legislative Resources

Also available through WAIS servers at sites such as Washington & Lee University, Rice University, etc.

Mail

e-mail to
congress@hr.house.gov

Library of Congress

See **ARCHIVES AND LIBRARY RE-SOURCES.**

National Archives and Records

See **ARCHIVES AND LIBRARY RE-SOURCES.**

Senate

gopher to
gopher.senate.gov

anonymous FTP to
ftp.senate.gov

White House

WWW to
http://www.whitehouse.gov

ing to any number of the larger sites (such as the University of Michigan, Stanford University, Sunsite, etc.).

Active Newsgroups

A complete list of newsgroups is regularly posted to **news.lists, news.groups, news.announce.newgroups,** and **news.answers**.

anonymous FTP to
ftp.uu.net
path: /usenet/news.lists

Posting news via e-mail

To post messages to usenet news by way of e-mail, send message to one of the following:

<news-group-name>@paris.ics.uci.edu
<news-group-name>@cs.utexas.edu
<news-group-name>@news.demon.co.uk
<news-groupname>.usenet@decwrl.dec.com

See the chapter "Usenet News."

> Note: In this directory, long addresses, paths, and messages are carried over to successive lines. However, these should be read as single-line entities and commands.

USENET NEWS

Many installations have news readers on their computer systems. These are usually invoked by typing "nn," "rn," "tin," or "trn" at the system prompt. If these do not work, consult with your system administrator.

If your system does not support a news reader, you can still consult the news by gopher-

VERONICA

FAQ

A Veronica FAQ is available by

gopher from
veronica.scs.unr.edu
path: Internet Jewels
    Gopher Jewels
    Library Reference and News
    General Reference Resources
    General Reference Collections
    On-line Ready Reference
    Virtual Reference Desk
    Additional Virtual Reference
      Disk
    Internet Assistance

gopher to
veronica.scs.unr.edu:70/00/
    veronica/
    how-to-query-veronica

WAIS

The Wide Area Information Service (WAIS) allows the user to do keyword searches. If your site does not support WAIS, telnet to one of the following publicly accessible sites:

California
    swais.cwis.uci.edu
    login: swais

North Carolina:
    sunsite.unc.edu
    login: swais

WEATHER

For the latest weather reports for various cities,

gopher to
wx.atmos.uiuc.edu
path: [state of your choice]

or

gopher to
riceinfo.rice.edu
path: Weather
    Weather Forecasts

WOMEN'S STUDIES

Brown Women Writers Project

The Brown Women Writers Project
Box 1841
Brown University
Providence, RI 02912
Phone: 401 863 3619

e-mail:
wwp@brownvm.brown.edu

WWW to
http://twine.stg.brown.edu/
    projects/wwp/
    wwp_home.html

Cairns Collection, University of Wisconsin

The Cairns Collection, a rare book collection of early American women's writing (pre-1914), is accessible via gopher at
silo.adp.wisc.edu

(See **ARCHIVES AND LIBRARIES—University of Wisconsin–Madison** for more information on access.)

Feminist Activist Resources

This is a web page for activist feminists and includes such topics as Communicating with other Feminists, Current Feminist Issues, Women's Organizations, Feminist Resources, and General Resources for Political Activists.

WWW to
http://www.clark.net/pub/s-gray/
    feminist.html

National Women's Studies Association

Founded in 1977, the National Women's Studies Association is dedicated to furthering the development of women's studies throughout the world at every educational level.

e-mail to
nwsa@umail.umd.edu

The Peripatetic, Electric Gopher

gopher to
peg.cwis.uci.edu 7000
path: Women's Studies and
    Resources

Sunsite

For an extensive collection of women's studies resources,

WWW to
http://sunsite.unc.edu

Syllabi

For a collection of women's studies syllabi

e-mail:
listserv@umdd.umd.edu
message: index syllabi

See also APPENDIX—Lists and **TEXTS–Electronic.**

WORLD WIDE WEB (WWW)

Beginner's Index

For new users of WWW, this is an invaluable source of information.

anonymous FTP to
rtfm.mit.edu
path: pub
    usenet
    news.answers
    www
    faq

WWW to
http://sparky.cyberzine.org/html/
    wwwindex/

Cello Software

Cello software is a WWW browser available by

anonymous FTP from
ftp.law.cornell.edu
path: pub
    LII
    Cello

FAQ

WWW to
http://sunsite.unc.edu/boutell/faq/
www_faq.html

e-mail:
mail-server@rtfm.mit.edu
message: send usenet/news.answers/
finding-sources

Guides

For a beginner's guide to WWW

WWW to
http://www.ncsa.uiuc.edu/General/
Internet/WWW/
HTMLPrimer.html

or

http://www.eit.com/web/
www.guide/

anonymous FTP to
ftp.eit.com
path: pub
web.guide
directory

HTMLTOC

HTMLTOC is a Perl program to generate a Table of Contents for HTML documents. For more information

anonymous FTP to
ftp.uci.edu
path: pub
dtd2html

Index

To receive the WWW Index, a regularly appearing compilation of new WWW providers,

e-mail:
www-request@drasnia.it.com.au
message: <your name> <e-mail
address>

JPEG Viewer

A freeware JPEG viewer (lview31.zip) is available by

anonymous FTP from
ftp.msstate.edu
path: pub
docs
history
jpeg

List

To examine John Makulowich's "The Awesome List,"

WWW to
http://www.clark.net/pub/
journalism/awesome.html

Lycos-List

To subscribe, send an e-mail message to

majordomo@mail.msen.com
subscribe lycos-users

See also **Lycos Web Index** below.

Lycos Web Index

The Lycos Web Index is a search service which accesses more than of 600,000 documents on the WWW.

WWW to
http://lycos.cs.cmu.edu/

See also **Lycos-List** above.

Lynx

Lynx software can be obtained by

anonymous FTP from
ukanaix.cc.ukans.edu
path: pub
lynx

Mail

For information on WWW-by-mail,

e-mail:
listproc@info.cern.ch
subject: <blank>
message: HELP

To obtain a web page by e-mail

e-mail:
listproc@www0.cern.ch
message: <URL of web page you
want>

Mosaic Software

For a copy of Mosaic

anonymous FTP to
ftp.ncsa.uiuc.edu

Mosaic Guide

The guide "The World-Wide Web and
Mosaic: An Overview for Librarians" can be
retrieved by sending an e-mail message to

listserv@uhupvm1.uh.edu
message: get morgan prv5n6 f=mail

It is also available by

gopher at
info.lib.uh.edu
path: Looking for Articles
Electronic journals
E-journals collected by the
U. of Houston Library
The Public-Access Computer
Systems Review
V5
N6

Netscape

For information on Netscape

WWW to
www.mcom.com

e-mail:
info@netscape.com

Newsletters and Magazines

Sparky in CyberSpace

WWW to
http://cyberzine.org

Web Word

For a sample copy

e-mail:
innovation@euronet.nl
message: intro <your e-mail
address> <your name>

WWW to
http://www.euro.net/innovation/
Web_Word_Base/TWW1-
html/TWW1.html

WEBster

An electronic magazine covering the
WWW. For a free trial subscription to
WEBster, send a blank e-mail message to

4free@webster.tgc.com

Webster's Weekly

WWW to
http://www.awa.com/w2/

What's New with NCSA Mosaic

The "newspaper" of the Web.

WWW to
http://www.ncsa.uiuc.edu/SDG/
Software/Mosaic/Docs/
whats-new.html

Robot List

For a list of Web wanderers

WWW to
http://web.nexor.co.uk/mak/doc/
robots/active.html

Telnet Sites

Publicly accessible telnet sites:

wuacc.edu
login: aallnet

fatty.law.cornell.edu
login: www

gopher.msu.edu
login: www

telnet.w3.org

library.wustl.edu

marvel.loc.gov
login: gopher

sun.uakom.sk
login: www

sunsite.unc.edu
login: lynx

suntid.bnl.gov
login: brookhaven

ukanaix.cc.ukans.edu
login: www

vms.huji.ac.il
login: www

www.edu.tw
login: www

www.law.indiana.edu
login: www

www.njit.edu
login: www

www.twi.tudelft.nl
login: lynx

Virtual Library

The WWW Virtual Library can be accessed by

WWW to
http://info.cern.ch/hypertext/
DataSources/bySubject/
Overview.html

Another on WWW Development can be accessed at

http://www.charm.net/~web/
Vlib.html

WebCrawler

For a WWW search utility

WWW to
http://webcrawler.cs.
washington.edu/Web Crawler
WebQuery.html

Winsock Application FAQ

For a directory of Winsock applications that are available by FTP,

WWW to
http://www.lcs.com/

Worm

For a site that allows searches on the web

WWW to
http://www.cs.colorado.edu/home/
    mcbryan/WWWW.html

ZIP CODES

See **POSTAL CODES.**

PART 3

Keeping Current

56 Ways to Stay Current

The face of the Internet changes day by day. New resources and sites come on-line hourly. It might seem as if trying to stay abreast of the latest developments is a hopeless situation. But it is possible. You may want to investigate some of the meta-sources that are listed in this chapter. Obviously, the cumulative total of the information that is provided by all of these is itself overwhelming, but by trial and error, you will find the resources that will consistently provide you with the information you want.

1. alt.internet.services

This is a Usenet News group that announces information about new and existing Internet sources.

2. Archie

You have heard of a new freeware or shareware program that's out? The net holds many anonymous FTP sites, but changes take place at these sites everyday. Use Archie to track down the files you need. See the chapter, "Archie, Veronica, and Jughead."

3. Bits-N-Bytes

The sub title to this net-letter says it all: *The Electronic Newsletter for Information Hunter-Gatherers*. A recent issue included a "Flame Form Letter," "What Religion Is Your Operating System?," "Online Service Provider News Roundup," and "Censorship in Cyberspace." For a subscription, send an e-mail message to

    listserv@acad1.dana.edu
    subject: [blank]
    message: SUBSCRIBE bits-n-bytes

    gopher to
    gopher.dana.edu
    path: Electronic Journals

    anonymous FTP to
    ftp.dana.edu
    path: periodic

4. Boardwatch Magazine Online

Focusing on bulletin boards, "Boardwatch Online" contains, among other things, Alan's Internet Picks (interesting net sites) and Christopher Blaise's bulletin board home page.

    telnet to
    boardwatch.com

    anonymous FTP to
    boardwatch.com

    WWW to
    http://www.boardwatch.com

For a subscription, send an e-mail message to
subscriptions@boardwatch.com

5. BUBL (Bulletin Boards for Libraries)

Originally the **BU**lletin **B**oard for **L**ibraries (United Kingdom), BUBL has evolved into a general information service, with resources on electronic journals, recreation, reference works, publishers' catalogues, texts, directories of networked resources, and much more. BUBL's primary aim is to encourage, develop, coordinate, and support the emerging Library and Information Science networking community in the UK.

telnet to
BUBL.Bath.ac.uk (138.38.32.45)
login: bubl

gopher to
bubl.bath.ac.uk 7070

WWW to
http://www.bubl.bath.ac.uk/BUBL/home.html

6. comp.infosystems.gopher

A Usenet news group devoted to gopher.

7. comp.infosystems.www

A Usenet news group devoted to the World Wide Web.

8. comp.internet.library

A Usenet News group devoted to discussion of electronic libraries.

9. Computer Mediated Communication Magazine

The "CMC Magazine" is available on the WWW. A recent issue reported on a recent International WWW conference, on using the network as a place for social discourse, on a symposium on large-scale networking, and on using MOO WWW to

http://www.rpi.edu/~decemj/cmc/mag/current/toc.html

Back issues are available at

http://www.rpi.edu/~decemj/cmc/mag/archive.html

10. Computer Underground Digest

A weekly electronic newsletter, "Computer underground Digest" recently had articles about English on the Internet, an announcement of a new guide ("A Citizen's Guide to Internet Resources on the Rights of Americans"), an overview of the beta version of SlipKnot, and an announcement regarding an upcoming HoHoCon, a conference devoted to the computer underground. To subscribe, send an e-mail message to

listserv@vmd.cso.uiuc.edu

message: sub cudigest <your name>

11. connect!

connect! is an e-mail-based newsletter for people interested in keeping up with the computer industry. It is issued 48 times a year. For back issue and order form, send an e-mail to

info@pax.com

subject: CONNECT

connect! is edited and published by J.W. Smith (pax@pax.com).

12. Cool Site of the Day

As the title suggests, this site is dedicated to listing a new—and cool!—site every day. The home page also allows access to previous cool sites, so you shouldn't feel bad about missing a day every now and then. The list of past cool sites included "The Nine Planets," "Lurker's Guide to Babylon," "Find the Spam," "The White House," "Paris," "Juggling Information Service," "Speleology Server," and "The New York City Information Page."

WWW to
http://www.infi.net/cool.html

13. CyberNews

A monthly publication, CyberNews contains software reviews, interviews, and feature stories. To subscribe, send an e-mail message to

subscribe@supportu.com

WWW to
http://cyberwerks.com

14. EDUPAGE

"Edupage" contains timely news bits of interest to those in the educational community.

e-mail:
listproc@educom.edu
message: subscribe edupage <your name>

15. Effector

The Electronic Frontier Foundation (EFF) newsletter. The EFF works to ensure civil liberties in the electronic age. A recent issue had articles on encryption standards and on an FCC crackdown on Free Radio Berkeley.

For a subscription to the Effector, e-mail to

listserv@eff.org
message: subscribe effector-online

For a copy of the current issue, anonymous FTP to
ftp.eff.org
path: pub
    EFF
    Newsletters
    EFFector
For more information, contact
info@eff.org

16. Electronic Privacy Information Center (EPIC)

Part of the Computer Professionals for Social Responsibility (CPSR) Internet Library, The Electronic Privacy Information Center is a public interest research center established in 1994. It focuses on emerging privacy issues as regards the National Information Infrastructure (e.g., the Clipper Chip).

To subscribe to the EPIC Alert, send an e-mail message to
listserv@cpsr.org
message: subscribe cpsr-announce <firstname lastname>

Alert is also distributed to the USENET newsgroup
comp.org.cpsr.announce

Back issues are available via anonymous FTP, WAIS, and gopher at
cpsr.org

WWW at
http://cpsr.org
path: Computer Professionals for Social Responsibility
    Privacy
    Epic

17. Electronic Public Information Newsletter (EPIN)

The Electronic Public Information Newsletter is published 24 issues a year in paper format and also in electronic format on the Internet. Its purpose is to disseminate news about the policies and practices surrounding the transformation of public information to electronic form. A recent issue contained articles on "Free GPO Access to Online Services Faces Limitations," "GPO Access, White House WWW Are Big News in Seattle," "White House Proves to Be a Technological Leader," "IITF Sets Up Interagency Group to Deal with STI Dissemination."

For more information on the Electronic Public Information Newsletter, contact epin@access.digex.net

FAX: 301 365 3621

18. Everybody's Internet Update

This monthly newsletter is put out by the Electronic Frontier Foundation. To subscribe, send an e-mail message to

listserv@eff.org
subject: [blank]
message: subscribe <your e-mail address> net-guide-update

anonymous FTP to
ftp.eff.org
path: pub
     Net_info
     EFF_Net_Guide
     Updates

19. The Gopherjewels List

This list gives frequent updates of new and existing gopher sites. To subscribe, send an e-mail request to

listproc@texas=one.org
message: subscribe gopherjewels <name>

For information on how to retrieve archived files from the list, send an e-mail message to

ftpmail@tpis.cactus.org
subject: <leave blank>
message: get gj-index.txt

20. HOTT-LIST (Hot off the Tree)

The largest known list with over 38,000 subscribers, HOTT-LIST summarizes more than 100 printed publications dealing with computers and technology.

To subscribe, send an e-mail request to
listserv@ucsd.edu
subject: <blank>
message: subscribe HOTT-LIST

21. HotWired

HotWired is an on-line magazine devoted to reporting on the net. Check out its home page.

WWW to
http://www.hotwired.com/

For a subscription to the HotFlash mailing list (now with 17,000+ subscribers), e-mail a request to

info-rama@wired.com
subject: [blank]
message: subscribe hotflash

For a FAQ (which includes departmental e-mail addresses), send a message to info@wired.com

22. HUMANIST: Humanities Computing

HUMANIST is a listserver that posts general information, queries, answers, software announcements, news on electronic texts, and many other topics. This is a necessary list for anyone interested in computer use in the humanities.

For a subscription, send an e-mail message to
listserv@brownvm.brown.edu
message: subscribe HUMANIST <first name> <last name>

23. HUMBUL Gateway

Maintained at Oxford University Computing Center in England, HUMBUL is a gateway to accessing international resources in the humanities.
WWW to
http://www.ox.ac.uk/depts/humanities/

24. Internet Facts

For a collection of interesting facts about the Internet, send an e-mail message to

internet–index–request@openmarket.com
message: subscribe internet-index

This is also available on the WWW at
http://www.openmarket.com/info/internet-index/current.html

25. Internet Hunt

This monthly quiz tests the user's ability to navigate the net.
For more information,
e-mail:
rgates@locust.cic.net

gopher to
gopher.cic.net
path: The Internet Hunt

WWW to
http://www.hunt.org/

26. Internet Index

The Internet Index is a Web page that indexes and links information alphabetically and by subject.
WWW to
http://www.silverplatter.com

27. Internet Mall

For a subscription to the Internet Mall List, an electronic list of commercial shops on the net (with regular updates), send an e-mail request to

listserv@netcom.com

Message: subscribe imall-l

28. Internet Monthly Report

The *Internet Monthly Report* is published by the Internet Research Group with the intention of "recording the accomplishments, milestones. . . or problems discovered by the participating organizations." This report is on the high end of the techie-scale, so it is not light reading. But the newsletter provides important information and statistics on the state of the net: new domain registrations, monthly statistics on disconnect times, histograms of the number of nodes experiencing instability as evidenced by outages, lists sites with notable outages, and other information.

For a copy, send an e-mail request to

rfc-info@isi.edu

subject: [blank]

message: Retrieve: IMR

       Doc-ID: IMR<yearmonth>

For example, Doc ID: IMR9504 will return a copy of the April 1995 issue. Substitute year/month (e.g., imr9410) for other issues.

This site also has an extensive listing of Internet documents. For an informative message about how to retrieve various items, send an e-mail request with the following message:

rfc-info@isi.edu

help: help

29. The Internet Press

Subtitled *A Guide to Electronic Journals about the Internet*, *The Internet Press* is an annotated listing of electronic publications about the net.

To subscribe, send an e-mail message to

ipress-request@northcoast.com

subject: subscribe

To receive one issue of the Internet Press, send an e-mail to
ipress-request@northcoast.com
subject: Archive
message: send ipress

30. Jasbits

A newsletter. Articles in a recent issue include "Games and Things for Fun," "Things to Fear," "MUD/RPG Abuse Leads to Death," "Space and NASA," "Humor from the Net," "Net Resources: Things to Read, Grab, and Do," "Real Life Humor, and "Cool Signatures of the Week."

For a subscription, send an e-mail request to

jsquires@cerf.net
subject: [blank]
message: Subscribe <your name>

31. Learned NewsWire

This newsletter reports on various events and services on the net. A recent issue had articles on access tools, Europe's on-line market, new electronic library developments, social science and humanities news, and reviews. To access it,

WWW to
http://info.learned.co.uk

gopher to
info.learned.co.uk

32. MLink News

M-Link News is a weekly newsletter announcing new lists and miscellaneous information. To subscribe, send an e-mail message to

davidsen@umich.edu

33. NCSA What's New

NCSA regularly updates additions to the WWW. Connect at
WWW to
http://www.ncsa.uiuc.edu/SDG/Software/Mosaic/Docs/whats-new.html

34. Net-happenings

Frequent daily updates on Internet Resources (such as conference announcements, call for papers, publications, newsletters, network tools updates, and network resources). It is an "announcements only" mailing list. There are about 10–20 announcements a day.

e-mail to
majordomo@is.internic.net
subject line: blank
message: subscribe net-happenings

subscribe to the Usenet newsgroup
comp.internet.net-happenings

Net-happenings archives can be searched and retrieved on the CNI Search Server.

telnet or gopher to
gopher.cni.org
login: brsuser

A net-happenings WAIS-index is available by gophering to
gopher.internic.net
path: InterNic Information Services (General)
    WAIS

WWW to
http://www.internic.net/internic/

35. Net-Letter Guide

This is a self-described "newshound's guide to newsy periodicals available through the Internet." It is regularly updated.

    e-mail:
    listserv@netcom.com
    message: subscribe net-letter

36. Netnews

Whether your computer site supports a news reader or not, you can still garner the benefits of news by tracking discussions of selected topics through Netnews, a product of the Database Group at Stanford University. A subscription will give you reports on topics you request. For example, you might have a special interest in tracking discussions of the Holocaust. A subscription under that keyword will bring you daily digests of Usenet articles in which that word is mentioned. You can then order the specific news item.

    To receive a guide to using this service, send an e-mail message to
    netnews@db.stanford.edu
    message: help

37. Netsurfer Digest

This newsletter surveys the Internet scene, identifying new and noteworthy sites. For people who want to know about the latest general-interest news about the net, this is essential reading.

    Send an e-mail request to
    nsdigest-request@netsurf.com
    subject: [blank]
    message: subscribe nsdigest-text <first last name>

    or for hypertext format, send the following message:
    subscribe nsdigest-html

    The Netsurfer Digest Home Page can be found at WWW
    http://www.netsurf.com/nsd/index.html

anonymous FTP to
ftp://ftp.netsurf.com/pub/nsd/

Other addresses:
pressrm@netsurf.com	Submission of Newsworthy Items
editor@netsurf.com	Letters to the Editor
ad@netsurf.com	Advertiser and Sponsor Inquiries
info-request@netsurf.com	General Information
http://www.netsurf.com/	Netsurfer Communications

38. Nettrain

This is a list for network trainers and it often contains useful discussions about Internet resources.

listserv@ubvm.cc.buffalo.edu
message: subscribe NETTRAIN

39. Network News

To subscribe to Dana Noonan's Network-News, send an e-mail message to
listserv@vm1.nodak.edu
message: subscribe nnews

For copies of past issues,
anonymous FTP to
vm1.nodak.edu
path: nnews

40. The Network Observer

The Network Observer is distributed through the Red Rock Eater News Service. Articles from a recent issue included "The Internet Lingua Franca," "Users' Groups as Collective Action," "Gender and Social Networks," "A Bunch of New Network Resources." For a subscription, send an e-mail request to

rre-request@weber.ucsd.edu
subject: subscribe <firstname lastname>
message: [blank]

WWW to
http://communication.ucsd.edu/pagre/tno.html

For more information about the Red Rock Eater, send an e-mail message to the same address with the subject line:
    help

For back issues, use the subject line:
    archive send index

41. Networks and Community

For a subscription, send an e-mail request to
    cvington@netcom.com
    subject: [blank]
    message subscribe <your name>

gopher to
gopher.well.sf.ca.us
path: Community
        Civic Nets

42. Newbie Newz

The Newbie Newz will allow the neophyte Internet user to learn the basics of anonymous FTP, telnet, WWW, and other resources. For a subscription, send an e-mail request to

    newbienewz-request@io.com
    subject: [leave blank]
    message: subscribe newbienewz <your e-mail address>

For more information about Newbie Newz, send an e-mail request to

    majordomo@penta.goaio.com
    message: info newbienewz

A related item is the list NewbieNet, which is a forum for new net users to introduce themselves to other new users. To subscribe, send an e-mail request to

    newbienet-request@io.com
    message: subscribe Newbienet

43. news.announce.newusers

A Usenet News group that posts announcements for new users.

44. news.answers

A Usenet News group which posts periodic usenet articles.

45. NEWSLTR

A list devoted to disseminating electronic newsletters (ALAWON, EPIN, E-d-u-p-a-g-e, InfoCycle, etc.), NEWSLTR is distributed daily at midnight. To subscribe, send an e-mail message to

    listserv@vm1.nodak.edu
    message: subscribe Newsltr <yourfirstname yourlastname>

46. NSF Network News

Send an e-mail request to
newsletter-request@internic.net
subject: [blank]
message: subscribe nsf-network-news

WWW to
http://www.internic.net/newsletter/

gopher to
gopher.internic.net

Send an e-mail request to
mailserv@is.internic.net
message: get /about-internic/newsletter/nsfnews-aug94.txt

47. REACH

Research and Educational Applications of Computers in the Humanities (REACH) is a newsletter of the Humanities Computing Facility of the University of California at Santa Barbara. A recent issue had a notice of an upcoming conference on humanities computing, information about subscribing to the ACL-L, a listserver group run maintained by the Association for Computational Linguistics, and an update on the electronic address of the journal Postmodern Culture.

To subscribe to the REACH list, send an e-mail message to
listserv@ucsbuxa.ucsb.edu
subject: <blank>
message: subscribe REACH <your name>

48. SCHOLAR

This is a listserver for text analysis and natural language applications. A monthly digest alerts subscribers to articles on a wide range of topics, which can be retrieved by requests.

To subscribe, send an e-mail message to
listserv@cunyvm.cuny.edu
message: subscribe scholar <first name> <last name>

49. Scout Report

Distributed every week, the Scout Report is an essential publication that provides highlights of new resource announcements and other news about the Internet. Frequency: weekly.

e-mail:
majordomo@is.internic.net
message: subscribe scout-report <your e-mail address>

gopher to
is.internic.net

WWW to
http://www.internic.net/infoguide.html

50. Tradewinds

A monthly review of articles about the Internet in trade and industry magazines.
gopher to
gopher.std.com

anonymous FTP to
ftp.std.com
path: periodicals/TRADEWINDS

51. Veronica

Searching for information about the latest…anything…on the net? Do a Veronica search.

See the chapter "Archie, Veronica, and Jughead."

52. Views

An electronic newsletter devoted to exploring issues of community and the net.
Send an e-mail to
seeviews@telecomp.com
message: GET VIEWS NN

53. WEBster

This is a wide-ranging newsletter with well-written articles about the current state of the Internet.

For a free sample, send an e-mail request to
4free@webster.tgc.com

54. The Web Word

Devoted to news in the WWW community, The Web Word recently had articles on "This Month's Top Ten Sites," "Breaking News on the Web," "Interview: Quotecom," "Financial," "How to Use a Web Robot," and "Getting Plugged In: Your Guide to Software." It can be accessed by WWW at
http://www.euro.net/innovation/WelcomeHP.html

e-mail to
webinfo@euronet.nl

Subscription information
innovation@euronet.nl

55. World Wide Web Index

World Wide Web Index is published periodically on **alt.internet.services**. It categorizes Web sites under such headings as Information, Browsers, Magazines, Newspapers, Education, Public Libraries, Computers, Environment, Stock Market, Sports, etc. For more information,

e-mail
www-request@drasnia.it.com.au

WWW to
http://drasnia.it.com.au/wwwindex

56. Yanoff's Special Internet Connections

Scott Yanoff maintains a "Special Internet Connections" file. For a copy of the latest issue,

anonymous FTP to
ftp.csd.uwm.edu
path: pub
inet.services.txt

send an e-mail to
inetlist@aug3.augsburg.edu
subject: [blank]
message[blank]

To subscribe to the regular mailings, send an e-mail message to
listserv@csd.uwm.edu
message: subscribe inetlist <your full name>

See also **RESOURCES—Internet Information** for many documents relating to the Internet.

PART 4

Appendices

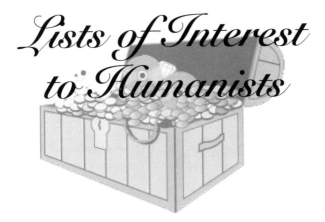

Lists of Interest to Humanists

GENERAL

Book Collecting/Rare Books

EXLIBRIS
listserv@rutvm1.rutgers.edu

Academic Departmental Chairs

CHAIRS-L
listserv@acc.fau.edu

E-Texts and Computing

AHC-L
[Association for History &
 Computing]
listproc@gwdg.de

CETH
[Center for Texts in the Humanities]
listserv@pucc.princeton.edu

CHUG-L
[Brown University Computing in the
 Humanities]
listserv@brownvm.brown.edu

ETEXTS-L
listserv@piranha.acns.nwu.edu

GUTENBERG
[Project Gutenberg]
listserv@vmd.cso.uiuc.edu

HUMANIST
listserv@brownvm.brown.edu

NOTABENE
[Word processor]
listserv@vm.tau.ac.il

RUSTEX-L
[Russian TeX and Cyrillic Text Processing List]
listserv@ubvm.cc.buffalo.edu

STLHE-L
[Society of Teaching and Learning in Higher Ed.]
listserv@unbvm1.csd.unb.ca

TEI-L
[Text Encoding Initiative]
listserv@uicvm.uic.edu

TEX-D-L
[German TeX Users Communication List]
listserv@vm.gmd.de

Honors

HONORS
listserv@gwuvm.gwu.edu

AFRO-AMERICAN

AFAM-L
listserv@mizzou1.missouri.edu

AFAS-L
listserv@kentvm.kent.edu

ART and ART HISTORY

AAMD-L
[Association of Art Museum Directors]
listserv@emuvm1.cc.emory.edu

AAT-L
[Art and Architecture Thesaurus Discussion]
listserv@uicvm.uic.edu

AIA
[Archaeological Institute of America]
listserv@brynmawr.edu

ARLIS-L
[Art Libraries Society]
listserv@ukcc.uky.edu

ARTCRIT
[Art criticism]
listserv@vm1.yorku.ca

ART DEADLINES
rgardner@charon.mit.edu
message: SUBSCRIBE DEADLINES
    <your e-mail address>

ARTIFACT
[Material culture]
listserv@umdd.umd.edu

ARTIST-L
listserv@uafsysb.uark.edu

ARTMGT-L
[Arts management]
listserv@bingvmb.cc.
    binghampton.edu

CAAH
[Consortium of Art and Architectural
    Historians]
listserv@pucc.princeton.edu

CLAYART
[Ceramic]
listserv@ukcc.uky.edu

DELPHI-L
[Arts policy]
listserv@vmd.cso.uiuc.edu

DESIGN-L
listserv@psuvm.psu.edu

FINE-ART
listserv@rutvm1.rutgers.edu

HERITAGE
[Historical Sites]
majordomo@massey.ac.nz

HISTARCH
[Historical archaeology]
listserv@asuvm.inre.asu.edu

MEDART-L
[Medieval]
listserv@vm.utcc.utoronto.edu

MUSEUM-L
[Museums]
listserv@unmvma.unm.edu

PUBLHIST
[Public history]
listserv@husc3.harvard.edu

CINEMA

CINEMA-L
listserv@auvm.american.edu

FILMMAKERS
majordomo@dhm.com

FILM-THEORY
majordomo@world.std.com
Message: subscribe film-theory
    <your e-mail address>

FILMUS-L
[Film music]
listserv@iubvm.ucs.indiana.edu

MOVIES-LIST
listserv@netcom.com

MUSIC-AND-MOVING-
    PICTURES
mailbase@mailbase.ac.uk

SCREEN-L
listserv@ua1vm.ua.edu

CLASSICS

BMCR-L
listserv@cc.brynmawr.edu

CLASSICS
[Ancient Greek and Latin]
listproc@u.washington.edu

NT-GREEK
[New Testament Greek]
nt-greek-request@virginia.edu

DANCE

BALLET-MODERN-DANCE
listserv@netcom.com

DANCE-L
listserv@hearn.nic.surfnet.nl

DISABILITIES

ABLE-JOB
[Jobs]
listserv@sjuvm.stjohns.edu

AXSLIB-L
[Library access]
listserv@sjuvm.stjohns.edu

EASI
[Computer access]
listserv@sjuvm.stjohns.edu

EDUCATION

ACSOFT-L
[Academic software discussion]
listserv@wuvmd.wustl.edu

AEDNET
[Adult education discussion]
listserv@alpha.acast.nova.edu

AERA
[American Educational Research
    Association]
listserv@asuvm.inre.asu.edu

AERA-A
[Educational Administration Forum]
listserv@asuvm.inre.asu.edu

AERA-B
[Curriculum Studies Forum]
listserv@asuvm.inre.asu.edu

AERA-C
[Learning and Instruction]
listserv@asuvm.inre.asu.edu

AERA-D
[Measurement and Research
    Methodology]
listserv@asuvm.inre.asu.edu

AERA-G
[Social Context of Education]
listserv@asuvm.inre.asu.edu

AERA-GSL
[Graduate studies]
listserv@asuvm.inre.asu.edu

AERA-H
[School Evaluation and Program
    Development]
listserv@asuvm.inre.asu.edu

AERA-I
[Education in the professions]
listserv@asuvm.inre.asu.edu

AERA-J
[Post-secondary education]
listserv@asuvm.inre.asu.edu

AERA-K
[Teaching and teacher education]
listserv@asuvm.inre.asu.edu

AI-ED
[Artificial intelligence in education]
ai-ed-request@sun.com

❋ Lists of Interest to Humanists

ALTLEARN
[Alternative approaches to education]
listserv@sjuvm.stjohns.edu

AMTEC
[Media and technology in education]
mailserv@camosun.bc.ca

BGEDU-L
[Educator's Forum on reform]
bgedu-l@ukcc.uky.edu

CNEDUC-L
[Computer networking in education]
listserv@tamvm1.tamu.edu

COMMCOLL
[Community College Discussion]
listserv@ukcc.uky.edu

CURRICUL
[Curriculum development]
listserv@saturn.rowan.edu

DEOS-L
[Study of distance education]
listserv@psuvm.psu.edu

DISTED
[Distance education]
listserv@alpha.acast.nova.edu

DTS-L
[Dead Teachers Society]
listserv@iubvm.ucs.indiana.edu

ECENET
[Early childhood education]
listserv@vmd.cso.uiuc.edu

EDNET
[Discussion of education and
    networking]
listserv@nic.umass.edu

EDPOL
[Education policy discussion]
listproc@wais.com

EDPOLYAN
[Education policy analysis]
listserv@asuvm.inre.asu.edu

EDRES-L
[Educational resources
    on the Internet]
listserv@unb.ca

EDSTYLE
[Discussion of educational styles]
listserv@sjuvm.stjohns.edu

EDTECH
[Education and technology]
listserv@msu.edu

EDUPAGE
[EDUCOM's News Update]
edupage@educom.edu

ELED-L
[Elementary education]
listserv@ksuvm.ksu.edu

EUITLIST
[Educational uses of information
    technology]
euitlist@bitnic.educom.edu

IECC [International E-mail
    Classroom Connection]
iecc-request@stolaf.edu

INCLASS
[Using the Internet in the classroom]
listproc@schoolnet.carleton.ca

INFED-L
[Computers in the classroom]
listserv@ccsun.unicamp.br

JEI-L
[Technology, esp. CD-ROM, in k-12]
listserv@umdd.umd.edu

KIDCAFE
listserv@vm1.nodak.edu

KIDINTRO
[Children's penpal]
listserv@sjuvm.stjohns.edu

KIDLINK
[KIDS-95]
listserv@vm1.nodak.edu

KIDS-ACT
[Activity projects]
listserv@vm1.nodak.edu

KIDSNET
[World-wide K-12 Network]
kidsnet-request@vms.cis.pitt.edu

KIDSPHERE
[KIDLINK discussion]
kidsphere@vms.cis.pitt.edu

K12ADMIN
[Educational administration]
listserv@suvm.syr.edu

LM_NET
[Library media specialist information
    exchange]
listserv@suvm.syr.edu

MEDIA-L
[Media in education]
listserv@bingvmb.cc.binghamton.edu

MULTI-L
[Multilingual education]
listserv@vm.biu.ac.il

MY-VIEW
[Global creative writing exchange
    for children]
listserv@sjuvm.stjohns.edu

NAEATASK
[NAEA Art Teacher Education Task
    Force]
listserv@arizvm1.ccit.arizona.edu

NEWEDU-L
[New patterns in education]
listserv@uhccvm.uhcc.hawaii.edu

SCHOOL-L
[Primary and secondary schools]
listserv@irlearn.ucd.ie

SIGTEL-L
[Telecommunications in education]
listserv@unmvma.unm.edu

STLHE-L
[Teaching and Learning in Higher
    Education]
listserv@unbvm1.csd.unb.ca

TEACHART
[NMAA Art Curriculum Teacher
    Conference]
listserv@sivm.si.edu

TEACHEFT
[Teaching effectiveness]
listserv@wcupa.edu

UKERA-L
[Education reform policy making]
listserv@ukcc.uky.edu

WALDORF
[Waldorf Education]
listserv@sjuvm.stjohns.edu

XTAR
[Teacher-researchers]
listserv@lester.appstate.edu

ENGLISH

General

ADS-L
[American Dialect Society]
listserv@uga.cc.uga.edu

BIBSOCAN
[Bibliographical Society of Canada]
listserv@vm.utcc.utoronto.ca

CHILDLIT
listserv@rutvm1.rutgers.edu

COPYEDITING-L
listproc@cornell.edu

DERRIDA
listserv@cfrvm.cfr.usf.edu

DOROTHYL
[Mystery literature]
listserv@kentvm.kent.edu

E-GRAD
[MLA graduate students conference]
listserv@rutvm1.rutgers.edu

ENGLISH
[English faculty and computing]
listserv@utarlvm1.uta.edu

ENGLISH-TEACHERS
majordomo@ux1.cso.uiuc.edu

KIDLIT-L
listserv@bingvmb.cc.
    binghampton.edu

LIT-19TH-CENTURY
majordomo@world.std.com

LIT-ABSURDIST
majordomo@world.std.com

LIT-ANCIENT
majordomo@world.std.com

LIT-BORGES
majordomo@world.std.com

LIT-DOSTOEVSKI
majordomo@world.std.com

LITERATURE
majordomo@world.std.com

LIT-EXISTENTIALIST
majordomo@world.std.com

LIT-GABRIEL-MARQUEZ
majordomo@world.std.com

LIT-GOETHE
majordomo@world.std.com

LIT-HERMAN-HESS [sic]
majordomo@world.std.com

LIT-HOMER
majordomo@world.std.com

LIT-KAFKA
majordomo@world.std.com

LIT-POSTCOLONIAL
majordomo@world.std.com

LIT-POSTMODERN
majordomo@world.std.com

LIT-PROUST
majordomo@world.std.com

LIT-RILKE
majordomo@world.std.com

LITSCI-L
[Society for Literature and Science]
listserv@vmd.cso.uiuc.edu

LIT-THOMAS-MANN
majordomo@world.std.com

LIT-TOLSTOY
majordomo@world.std.com

ORTRAD
[Oral tradition]
listserv@mizzou1.missouri.edu

PMC-LIST
listserv@listserv.ncsu.edu

PMC-TALK
listserv@listserv.ncsu.edu

PROSODY
listserv@msu.edu

PSYART
listserv@nervm.nerdc.ufl.edu

RHETORIC
listserv@vm.its.rpi.edu

SEDIT-L
listserv@umdd.umd.edu

SGML-L
listserv@vm.urz.uni–heidelberg.de

SHARP-L
listserv@iubvm.ucs.indiana.edu

TACT-L
[Discussion of Textual Analysis
    Computing Tools (TACT)]
listserv@vm.utcc.utoronto.ca

TEACHER
[Computing in the Humanities]
listserv@vmutcc.utoronto.edu

WORDS-L
listserv@uga.cc.uga.edu

American Literature

AMLIT-L
listserv@mizzou1.missouri.edu

CHICLE
[Chicano literature]
listserv@unmvma.unm.edu

ERNEST
[Hemingway]
listserv@cfrvm.cfr.usf.edu

ISHMAIL-L
[Melville]
ishmail-request@vaxc.hofstra.edu

JACK-LONDON
jack-london-request@sonoma.edu

JAMESF-L
listserv@wvnvm.wvnet.edu

LIT-EDGAR-ALLEN-POE
[sic]
majordomo@world.std.com

LIT-GERTRUDE-STEIN
majordomo@world.std.com

LIT-WILLIAM-BURROUGHS
majordomo@world.std.com

NABOKOV-L
listserv@ucsbvm.ucsb.edu

NATIVELIT-L
listserv@cornell.edu

PYNCHON-L
listserv@sfu.ca

T-AMLIT
listserv@bitnic.cren.net

TWAIN-L
listserv@vm1.yorku.ca

British and Irish Literature

ANSAX-L
listserv@wvnvm.wvnet.edu

AUSTEN-L
listserv@vm1.mcgill.ca

BRONTE
majordomo@world.std.com
    subscribe bronte
    [note: do not include your
        name in sub request]

CAMELOT
camelot-request@castle.ed.ac.uk

CHAUCER
listserv@unl.edu

DICKNS-L
listserv@ucsbvm.ucsb.edu

FWAKE-L
[Discussion of Joyce's *Wake*]
listserv@irlearn.ucd.ie

FWAKEN-L
[Notes on Joyce's *Wake*]
listserv@irlearn.ucd.ie

LIT-SAMUEL-BECKETT
majordomo@world.std.com

LIT-BLAKE
majordomo@world.std.com

LIT-CS-LEWIS
majordomo@world.std.com

LIT-JAMES-JOYCE
majordomo@world.std.com

LIT-SHAKESPEARE
majordomo@world.std.com

LIT-YEATS
majordomo@world.std.com

MEDEVLIT
[Medieval English literature]
listserv@siucvmb.bitnet

MEDTEXTL
listserv@vmd.cso.uiuc.edu

MILTON-L
milton-request@urvax.urich.edu

MODBRITS
listserv@kentvm.kent.edu

MODERN-BRITISH-FICTION
mailbase@mailbase.ac.uk

REED-L
[Records of Early English drama]
listserv@vm.utcc.utoronto.edu

SHAKSPER
listserv@vm.utcc.utoronto.edu

TROLLOPE
majordomo@world.std.com
  [no name in body of message]

VICTORIA
listserv@iubvm.ucs.indiana.edu

WWP-L
[Brown University Women Writer's
 Project]
listserv@brownvm.brown.edu

Composition

CCCC-L
listserv@ttuvm1.ttu.edu

CW-L
[Computers and writing]
listserv@ttuvm1.ttu.edu

WAC-L
[Writing across the curriculum]
listserv@vmd.cso.uiuc.edu

Linguistics

LINGUIST
listserv@tamvm1.tamu.edu

Writing

CREWRT-L
listserv@mizzou1.missouri.edu

E-POETRY
listserv@ubvm.cc.buffalo.edu

FICTION
listserv@psuvm.psu.edu

MBU-L
[Megabyte University/Writing
 instruction]
listserv@ttuvm1.ttu.edu

NOUS REFUSE
[Experimental poets]
e-mail contact:
  jamato@ux1.cso.uiuc.edu

RPOETIK
listserv@wln.com

SCRNWRIT
listserv@tamvm1.tamu.edu

WRITERS
listserv@vm1.nodak.edu

WWP-L
[Brown University Women Writer's
 Project]
listserv@brownvm.brown.edu

ENGLISH AS A SECOND LANGUAGE

CHAT-SL
[Low-level general discussion]
majordomo@latrobe.edu.au

DISCUSS-SL
[High-level general discussion]
majordomo@latrobe.edu.au

ENGL-SL
[Learning English discussion]
majordomo@latrobe.edu.au

❋ Lists of Interest to Humanists

EVENT-SL
[Current events discussion]
majordomo@latrobe.edu.au

MOVIE-SL
[Movies discussion]
majordomo@latrobe.edu.au

MUSIC-SL
[Music discussion]
majordomo@latrobe.edu.au

SPORT-SL
[Sports discussion]
majordomo@latrobe.edu.au

TESJB-L
[Jobs and employment]
listserv@cunyvm.cuny.edu

TESLCA-L
[Computer assisted language learning]
listserv@cunyvm.cuny.edu

TESLEJ-L
[ESL electronic journal]
listserv@cmsa.berkeley.edu

TESLFF-L
[Fluency First]
listserv@cunyvm.cuny.edu

TESLIE-L
[Intensive English]
listserv@cunyvm.cuny.edu

TESLIT-L
[Adult education and literacy]
listserv@cunyvm.cuny.edu

TESLK-12
[K–12]
listserv@cunyvm.cuny.edu

TESL-L
[Teachers of ESL]
listserv@cunyvm.cuny.edu

FILM

See **Cinema.**

FOLKLORE

FOLKLORE
listserv@tamvm1.tamu.edu

LORE
listserv@vm1.nodak.edu

FOREIGN LANGUAGES

General

FLAC-L
[Foreign language across the
    curriculum]
listserv@brownvm.brown.edu

Arabic

ARABIC-L
mailserv@yvax.byu.edu

ITISALAT
listserv@guvm.ccf.georgetown.edu

Armenian

AIEA
[Assoc. Internationale des Études
    Arméniennes]
listserv@gomidas.mi.org

HAYASTAN
hayastan-request@think.com

Australian-Indian

NAT-LANG
listserv@tamvm1.tamu.edu

Aztec

NAHUAT-L
nahuat-request@faucc.fau.edu

Berber

AMAZIGH-NET
amazigh-request@ensisun.imag.fr

Catalan

CATALA
listserv@puigmal.cesca.es

Celtic

CELTIC-L
listserv@irlearn.ucd.ie

CELTLING
acarnie@mit.edu

GAELIC-L
listserv@irlearn.ucd.ie

WELSH-L
listserv@irlearn.ucd.ie

Chinese

CCNET-L
listserv@uga.uga.edu

CHINESE
chinese-request@kenyon.edu

CHPOEM-L
listserv@ubvm.cc.buffalo.edu

Czech

MUTEX
listserv@vm.ics.muni.cz

Dutch

NEDER-L
listserv@nic.surfnet.nl

Esperanto

ESPERANTO
esperanto-request@rand.org

ESPER-L
listserv@vm3090.ege.edu.tr

Estonian

E-LIST
listserv@vilo.cs.helsinki.fi

French

AATFREN
listserv@bitnic.educom.edu

BALZAC-L
listserv@cc.umontreal.ca

BIBLIO-FR
biblio-request@univ.rennesl.fr

CAUSERIE
listserv@uquebec.ca

FRENCHTALK
listproc@yukon.cren.org

FROGTALK
listserv@bitnic.educom.edu

LANGUES
listserv@UQuebec.ca

Gaelic

GAELIC-L
listserv@irlearn.ucd.ie

German

AATG
listserv@indycms.iupui.edu

DEUTSCHE-LISTE
listserv@ccu.umanitoba.ca

GERLINGL
[German to about 1500]
listserv@vmd.cso.uiuc.edu

GERMNEWS
listserv@vm.gmd.de

GER-RUS
listserv@vm1.nodak.edu

GRAD-L
listserv@vm.ucs.ualberta.ca

GRMNHIST
listproc@gwdg.de

HESSE-L
listserv@ucsbvm.ucsb.edu

MENDELE
listserv@yalevm.cis.yale.edu

RIBO-L
listserv@uriacc.uri.edu

UKTEX-L
listserv@vm.urz.uni-heidelberg.de

WIG-L
listserv@cmsa.berkeley.edu

Greek, Modern

HELLAS
listserv@psuvm.psu.edu

ELLHNIKA
listserv@vm.urz.uni-heidelberg.de

Hebrew

E-HUG
[Hebrew Electronic Users]
listserv@dartcms1.dartmouth.edu

HEBLANG
listserv@nysernet.org

OT-HEBREW
[Old Testament]
ot-hebrew-request@virginia.edu

Hungarian

HUNGARY
listserv@gwuvm.gwu.edu

Iberian [Medieval Catalan, Spanish, Ladino, Galician]

MEDIBER
listserv@merle.acns.nwu.edu

Indonesian

IS-LAM
is-ad@macc.wisc.edu

Iroquoian

IROQUOIS
listserv@vm.utcc.utoronto.ca

Italian

LANGIT
listserv@icineca.cineca.it

Japanese

JTEM-L
listserv@uga.cc.uga.edu

JTIT-L
listserv@psuvm.psu.edu

Korean

HANGUL
hangul-request@cair.kaist.ac.kr

Ladino

SEFARAD
listserv@nysernet.org

Latin

CLASSICS
listproc@u.washington.edu

LATIN-L
[Modern Latin]
listserv@psuvm.psu.edu

Macedonian

MAK-NEWS
listserv@uts.edu.au

Polish

POLAND-L
listserv@ubvm.cc.buffalo.edu

Portuguese

LETRAS-L
mailserv@fpsp.fapesp.br

Romanian

Romanian
mihai@sep.stanford.edu

Sanskrit

INDOLOGY
listserv@liverpool.ac.uk

Scandinavian

DISC-NORDIC
disc-nordic-request
@mail.unet.umn.edu

Serbo-Croatian

VIZANTIJA
dimitrije@buenga.bu.edu

Sign language

SLLING-L
listserv@yalevm.cis.yale.edu

Slavic

SEELANGS
[Slavic and East European Languages]
listserv@cunyvm.cuny.edu

Slovak

SLOVAK-L
listserv@ubvm.cc.buffalo.edu

Slovenian

BOSNET
listserv@math.gmu.edu

OGLASNA-DESKA
oglasna-deska@uni.lj.si

PISMA-BRALCEV
pisma-bralcev@uni.lj.si

Spanish

COMEDIA
[Hispanic classic theater]
listserv@arizvm1.ccit.arizona.edu

ESPAN-L
listserv@vm.tau.ac.il

INFORM-L
[Cultural information]
listserv@vmtecslp.slp.itesm.mx

Tamil

TAMIL-L
listserv@vm.urz.uni-heidelberg.de

Telugu

TELUGU
telugu@vm1.nodak.edu

Tolkien

TOLKLANG
tolklang-request-server@dcs.ed.ac.uk

Turkish

BILDIL
listserv@vm.cc.metu.edu.tr

TURKCE-L
listserv@cc.itu.edu.tr

Vietnamese

VIETNET
listserv@vm.usc.edu

Welsh

WELSH-L
listserv@irlearn.ucd.ie

Yiddish

MAIL-YIDDISH
dave@lsuc.on.ca

MENDELE
listserv@yalevm.cis.yale.edu

HISTORY

General

AERA-F
[History and historiography]
listserv@asuvm.inre.asu.edu

AEROSP-L
{Aerospace history]
listserv@sivm.si.edu

C18-L
[18th century]
listserv@psuvm.psu.edu

COMMHIST
[History of human communication]
listserv@vm.its.rpi.edu

ECONHIST
[Economic history]
listserv@miamiu.acs.muohio.edu

EMHIST-L
[Early-modern history]
listserv@rutvm1.rutgers.edu

ETHNOHIS
[General ethnology and history]
listserv@nic.surfnet.nl

GLBL-H
[Global history]
listserv@ocmvm.cnyric.org

HASTRO-L
[History of astronomy]
listserv@wvnvm.wvnet.edu

H-BUSINESS
lists@cs.muohio.edu
Message: subscribe H-Business <First
    Last Name>, College

H-DEMOG
[Demography]
listserv@uicvm.uic.edu

H-DIPLO
[Diplomatic history]
listserv@uicvm.uic.edu

H-DURKHM
listserv@uicvm.uic.edu

H-ETHNIC
[Ethnic and immigration]
listserv@uicvm.uic.edu

H-FILM
listserv@uicvm.uic.edu

H-GRAD
listserv@uicvm.uic.edu

H-IDEAS
listserv@uicvm.uic.edu

HISLAW-L
[History of law]
listserv@ulkyvm.louisville.edu

HISTNEWS
listserv@ukanvm.cc.ukans.edu

HISTORY
listserv@earn.cvut.cz

HISTORY
listserv@irlearn.ucd.ie

HISTORY
listserv@vm1.mcgill.ca

HISTORY
listserv@psuvm.psu.edu

HISTORY
listserv@rutvm1.rutgers.edu

HISTORY
listserv@ubvm.cc.buffalo.edu

HISTORY
listserv@umrvmb.umr.edu

HISTORY-CURRICULUM
mailbase@mailbase.ac.uk

HISTORY-ECON
mailbase@mailbase.ac.uk

HISTORY-IHR
mailbase@mailbase.ac.uk

HISTORY-METHODS
mailbase@mailbase.ac.uk

HISTORY-NEWS
mailbase@mailbase.ac.uk

HISTORY-TEACHING
mailbase@mailbase.ac.uk

H-LABOR
listserv@uicvm.uic.edu

H-LAW
listserv@uicvm.uic.edu

H-MAC
[History and Macintosh Society]
listserv@msu.edu

HOLOCAUS
listserv@uicvm.uic.edu

HOPOS-L
[History of the philosophy of science]
listserv@ukcc.uky.edu

HOST
[History of science and technology]
jsmith@epas.utoronto.edu

H-PCAACA
[Popular Culture Association and
    American Culture]
listserv@uicvm.uic.edu

H-RHETOR
[History of rhetoric]
listserv@uicvm.uic.edu

H-RURAL
listserv@uicvm.uic.edu

H-TEACH
listserv@uicvm.uic.edu

HTECH-L
[History of Technology]
listserv@sivm.si.edu

H-URBAN
listserv@uicvm.uic.edu

H-W-CIV
[Teaching western civilization]
listserv@msu.edu

H-WOMEN
listserv@uicvm.uic.edu

H-WORLD
[World history and world survey texts]
listserv@msu.edu

MAPHIST
listserv@harvarda.harvard.edu

MEMOIR-L
[Diaries, expeditions, correspondence]
listserv@vm.cc.latech.edu

OHA-L
listserv@ukcc.uky.edu

PUBLHIST
mailserv@husc3.harvard.edu

ROOTS-L
listserv@ndsuvm1.ndsu.edu

SHOTHC-L
[History of computing issues]
listserv@sivm.si.edu

WORLD-L
listserv@ubvm.cc.buffalo.edu

American

AMERICAN-STUDIES
mailbase@mailbase.ac.uk

AMWEST-L
[American West]
listserv@dosuni1.rz.
    uni-osnabrueck.de

AMWEST-H
listserv@umrvmb.umr.edu

EARAM-L
[Society of Early Americanists]
listserv@kentvm.kent.edu

H-AMSTDY
listserv@uicvm.uic.edu

H-CIVWAR
listserv@uicvm.uic.edu

H-LOCAL
[State and local history, museum
    studies]
listserv@msu.edu

H-POL
listserv@uicvm.uic.edu

H-SHGAPE
[U.S. Gilded Age and Progressive Era]
listserv@uicvm.uic.edu

H-SOUTH
listserv@uicvm.uic.edu

H-STATE
[Welfare state]
listserv@uicvm.uic.edu

H-SURVEY
[Teaching U.S. survey]
listserv@msu.edu

H-WEST
[American West]
listserv@uicvm.uic.edu

IEAHCNET
[American colonial history]
listserv@uicvm.uic.edu

JSH
[Journal of Southern history]
listserv@ricevm1.rice.edu

KANSAS-L
listserv@ukanaix.cc.ukans.edu

PREZHIST
listserv@kasey.umkc.edu

STHCULT
listserv@unc.edu

WESTAM-L
[Western Americana]
listserv@yalevm.cis.yale.edu

Ancient

ANCIEN-L
[Ancient Mediterranean]
listserv@ulkyvm.louisville.edu

LT-ANTIQ
listserv@univscvm.csd.scarolina.edu

Asia

H-ASIA
listserv@uicvm.uic.edu

Australian

AUSTRALIA-NZ-HISTORY-L
majordomo@coombs.anu.edu.au

Austria

HABSBURG
[Austria since 1500]
listserv@vm.cc.purdue.edu

British

H-ALBION
listserv@uicvm.uic.edu

China

EMEDCH-L
[Medieval China]
listserv@vm.usc.edu

Feminist

See **Women's Studies.**

French

FRANCEHS
listserv@vm.cc.purdue.edu

H-FRANCE
listserv@uicvm.uic.edu

German

H-GERMAN
listserv@uicvm.uic.edu

Greek

PERSEUS
listserv@brownvm.brown.edu

India

INDOLOGY
listserv@liverpool.ac.uk

Islam

ISLAM-L
listserv@ulkyvm.louisville.edu

NAHIA-L
listserv@msu.edu

Italy

H-ITALY
listserv@uicvm.uic.edu

Judaism

H-ANTIS
[History of anti-Semitism]
listserv@uicvm.uic.edu

H-JUDAIC
listserv@uicvm.uic.edu

JEWSTUDIES
listserv@nysernet.org

PERSIA-L
[Jewish literature and history in the
    Persian period]
listserv@emuvm1.cc.emory.edu

Latin America

H-LATAM
listserv@uicvm.uic.edu

MCLR-L
[Latino]
listserv@msu.edu

Medieval

INTERSCRIPTA
listserv@morgan.ucs.mun.ca

MEDIEV-L
listserv@ukanvm.cc.ukans.edu

Military

MILHST-L
listserv@ukanvm.cc.ukans.edu

VWAR-L
[Vietnam]
listserv@ubvm.cc.buffalo.edu

WWI-L
listserv@ukanaix.ukans.edu

WWII-L
listserv@ubvm.cc.buffalo.edu

Portugal

HISTORY-VASCO
mailbase@mailbase.ac.uk

Renaissance

FICINO
listserv@vm.utcc.utoronto.edu

RENAIS-L
listserv@ulkyvm.louisville.edu

Russia/Soviet Union

H-RUSSIA
listserv@uicvm.uic.edu

RUSHIST
listserv@umr.vmb.umr.edu

RUSHIST
listserv@earn.cvut.cz

RUSSIAN-STUDIES
mailbase@mailbase.ac.uk

SOVHIST
listserv@earn.cvut.cz

Victorian

VICTORIA
listserv@iubvm.ucs.indiana.edu

Virginia

VA-HIST
listserver@leo.vsla.edu
[note: not listserv, listserver]

HUMANITIES

COMPARATIVE-LITERATURE
mailbase@mailbase.ac.uk

GOTHIC-LITERATURE
mailbase@mailbase.ac.uk

HUMANIST
listserv@brownvm.brown.edu

HUMGRAD
mailbase@mailbase.ac.uk

LITERARY
listserv@bitnic.cren.net

SCHOLAR
listserv@cunyvm.cuny.edu

TECHEVAL
[Evaluation of technological work in
the humanities]
listserv@miamiu.acs.muohio.edu

VOXHUM-L
listserv@emuvm1.cc.emory.edu

MUSIC

ALLMUSIC
listserv@auvm.american.edu

BGRASS-L
listserv@ukcc.uky.edu

BLUES-L
listserv@brownvm.brown.edu

CLASSM-L
listserv@brownvm.brown.edu

MODERATED CLASSICAL
   MUSIC LIST
lampson@crl.com

EARLYM-L
listserv@awiuni11.edvz.univie.ac.at

EMUSIC-L
[Electronic music]
listserv@auvm.american.edu

FOLKTALK
[Folk music]
listserv@leo.vsla.edu

IRTRAD-L
[Irish traditional]
listserv@irlearn.ucd.ie

LATAMMUS
[Latin American]
listserv@asuvm.inre.asu.edu

MILES
[Miles Davis]
listserv@nic.surfnet.nl

MLA-L
[Music Library Association]
listserv@iubvm.ucs.indiana.edu

MUSIC-ED
listserv@vm1.spcs.umn.edu

OPERA-L
listserv@fpsp.fapesp.br
opera-l-request@fpsp.fapesp.br

ROCK
listserv@cc.itu.edu.tr

SOCO-L
[Southern rock]
listserv@ubvm.cc.buffalo.edu

PHILOSOPHY

AQUINAS
majordomo@world.std.com

APHIL-L
[Australian Philosophy Forum]
majordomo@coombs.anu.edu.au

ARISTOTLE
majordomo@world.std.com

ARISTOTLE-ETHICS
majordomo@world.std.com

AYN-RAND
listserv@iubvm.ucs.indiana.edu

AYN-REVU
[Objectivist philosophy]
listserv@iubvm.ucs.indiana.edu

BERKELEY
majordomo@world.std.com

BERGSON
majordomo@world.std.com

BIOMED-L
listserv@vm1.nodak.edu

BRAIN-L
listserv@vm1.mcgill.ca

CAMUS
majordomo@world.std.com

CPAE
[Center for Professional and Applied
  Ethics]
listserv@catfish.valdosta.peachnet.edu

CYBERMIND
majordomo@world.std.com
Subject line: <blank>
Message: subscribe cybermind
  <your e-mail address>

DESCARTES
majordomo@world.std.com

DELEUZE-GUATTARI
majordomo@world.std.com
Subject line: <blank>
Message: subscribe deleuze-guattari
  <your e-mail address>

ETHICS
majordomo@world.std.com

EXISTENTIALISM
majordomo@world.std.com

FICINO
listserv@vm.utcc.utoronto.edu

FICTION-OF-PHILOSOPHY
majordomo@world.std.com
Subject line: <blank>
Message: subscribe fiction-of-
  philosophy <your e-mail address>

FNORD-L
[New Ways of Thinking]
listserv@ubvm.cc.buffalo.edu

FOUCAULT
majordomo@world.std.com
Subject Line: <blank>
Message: subscribe foucault
  <your e-mail address>

HEGEL
listserv@ibm.ucis.vill.edu

HEIDEGGER
majordomo@world.std.com

HINDU-PHILOSOPHY
majordomo@world.std.com

HPSST-L
[History and philosophy of science]
listserv@qucdn.queensu.ca

HUSSERL
majordomo@world.std.com

ISLAMIC-PHILOSOPHY
majordomo@world.std.com

KANT
majordomo@world.std.com

KANT-L
listserv@bucknell.edu

KIERKEGAARD
majordomo@world.std.com

LEIBNIZ
majordomo@world.std.com

MARXISM
majordomo@world.std.com
Subject line: <blank>
Message: subscribe marxism
  <your e-mail address>

✳ *Lists of Interest to Humanists*

NIETZSCH-L
listserv@dartmouth.edu

OBJECTIVISM-L
listproc@cornell.edu

PAGAN
pagan-request@
    drycas.club.cc.cmu.edu

PEIRCE-L
listserv@ttuvm1.ttu.edu

PHILCOMM
listserv@vm.its.rpi.edu

PHIL-LIT
[Philosophy and Literature]
listserv@tamvm1.tamu.edu

PHILOS-L
listserv@liverpool.ac.uk

PHILOSED
listserv@suvm.syr.ed

PHILOSOP
listserv@vm1.yorku.ca

PHILOSOPHY-L
listserv@netcom.com

PRAGMATISM
majordomo@world.std.com

PRESOCRATICS
majordomo@world.std.com

PROCESS PHILOSOPHY
[Process Thought Discussion]
mailbase@mailbase.ac.uk

SARTRE
majordomo@world.std.com

SOCETH-L
listserv@vm.usc.edu

SOCORG-K
listserv@vm.utcc.utoronto.edu

SOPHIA
listserv@liverpool.ac.uk

SPINOZA
majordomo@world.std.com

SWIP-L [Feminist]
listserv@cfrvm.cfr.usf.edu

THINK-L
[Critical Thinking]
listserv@umslvma.umsl.edu

RELIGION

General

AGNOSTICA
listserv@proof.ergo.cs.cmu.edu

BELIEF-L
listserv@brownvm.brown.edu

BIBLE-L
listserv@gitvm1.gatech.edu

BUBER
majordomo@world.std.com

BUDDHIST-PHILOSOPHY
majordomo@world.std.com

ECOTHEOL
mailbase@mailbase.ac.uk

LITURGY
mailbase@mailbase.ac.uk

POSTMODERN-CHRISTIAN
mailbase@mailbase.ac.uk

RELIGIOUS-STUDIES-UK
mailbase@mailbase.ac.uk

THEOLOGY
umnews@maine.bitnet
Message: "tell umnews at maine
   sendme umbb helpnet"
   [without quotation marks]

THEOLOGY
majordomo@world.std.com

Bible

NT-GREEK
listserv@virginia.edu

OT-HEBREW
listserv@virginia.edu

Catholicism

AMERCATH
listserv@ukcc.uky.edu

CATHOLIC
listserv@auvm.american.edu

ISLAMIAT
listserv@ulkyvm.louisville.edu

SISTER-L
[Catholic women]
listserv@suvm.syr.edu

VATICAN2
listserv@vm.temple.edu

Christianity

KOINONIA
[Christian ecumenical dialogue]
listserv@vm.utcc.utoronto.ca

ORTHODOX
listserv@iubvm.ucs.indiana.edu

Feminist

WMSPRT-L
[Women's spirituality and
   feminist-oriented religions]
listserv@ubvm.cc.buffalo.edu

Islam

ISLAM
majordomo@world.std.com

MSA-L
listserv@psuvm.psu.edu

MUSLIMS
listserv@asuvm.inre.asu.edu

Judaism

IOUDAIOS-L
listserv@lehigh.edu

NHILLEL
listserv@gwuvm.gwu.edu

Mormon

MORMON-L
listserv@byuvm.bitnet

Shaker

SHAKER
listserv@ukcc.uky.edu

Taoism

TAOISM
majordomo@world.std.com

TAOISM-STUDIES-L
majordomo@coombs.anu.edu.au

Zen

ZENBUDDHISM-L
majordomo@coombs.anu.edu.au

THEATER

ASTR-L
[American Society for Theatre
   Research]
listserv@vmd.cso.uiuc.edu

PERFORM
[Medieval performing arts]
listserv@iubvm.ucs.indiana.edu

STAGECRAFT
stagecraft-request@zinc.com

THEATRE
listserv@pucc.princeton.edu

THEATRE-THEORY
listserv@mit.edu

WOMEN'S STUDIES

ECOFEM
[Women and the environment]
listserv@csf.colorado.edu

EDUCOM-W
listserv@bitnic.cren.net

FEMAIL
femail-request@lucerne.eng.sun.com

FEMINISM.DIGEST
listserv@netcom.com

FEMISA
listserv@csf.colorado.edu

FEMINIST
listserv@mitvma.mit.edu

FEMINIST-THEOLOGY
mailbase@mailbase.ac.uk

FEMREL
listserv@mizzou1.missouri.edu

GENDER
listserv@vm.its.rpi.edu

H-WOMEN
listserv@uicvm.uic.edu

LIBWAT-L
[Library women and technology]
listserv@ubvm.cc.buffalo.edu

LIT-FEMINIST
majordomo@world.std.com

MEDFEM-L
[Medieval studies]
listproc@u.washington.edu

SAPPHO
sappho-request@mc.lcs.mit.edu

SASH
listserv@asuvm.inre.asu.edu

STOPRAPE
listserv@brownvm.brown.edu

WHIRL
[Women's History in Rhetoric and
    Language]
listserv@psuvm.psu.edu

WIG-L
[Feminist study of German literature,
    language, and culture]
listserv@cmsa.berkeley.edu

WIML-L
[Music librarianship]
listserv@iubvm.ucs.indiana.edu

WISP-L
[Women in scholarly publishing]
listserv@iubvm.ucs.indiana.edu

WMST-L
listserv@umdd.umd.edu

WOMENS-STUDIES
mailbase@mailbase.ac.uk

WWP-L
[Women's Writing Project]
listserv@brownvm.brown.edu

Glossary

Archie
A number of sites carry Archie servers, which allow for broad spectrum searches for specific software and files. See chapter on "Archie, Veronica, and Jughead."

BITNET (Because It's Time Network)
Managed by EDUCOM, BITNET has several thousand hosts, mainly at universities in Canada, Europe, and the United States.

BTW
An acronym for "by the way."

CFP
An acronym for "call for papers."

E-Mail
Electronic Mail

E-Text
Electronic Text

FAQ
Frequently Asked Questions

Flame
An uncivilized response to an error (usually minor) made in a public electronic forum (such as a posting to a list or to a newsgroup). Flaming is universally discouraged and generally practiced.

Freeware   Software available on the Internet that one can retrieve and use without cost.

FTP (File Transfer Protocol)
                            Used for transferring files from one computer to another.

Gateway   A computer that connects two or more networks.

Gopher   Named after the mascot of the University of Minnesota (where the software was developed), gopher provides menus and submenus with links to files, directories, and telnet sites around the Internet. See the chapter "Gopher."

HTTP   See URL below.

IMHO   Acronym for "in my humble opinion."

Jughead   A search engine often found on a gopher menu, Jughead allows keyword searches. Unlike Veronica searches, Jughead searches the links at a single site only.

LAN (Local Area Network)
                            Local interconnected computers, usually having the benefit of high-speed operation.

List   A narrowly defined interest group (such as the list Pynchon, devoted to discussion of Thomas Pynchon, author of *Gravity's Rainbow*), whose management operations (subscribing, unsubscribing, etc.) are mechanized by listserver software.

Listserver   This can refer both to the software that is used to run a list and to the site where a list is located. See the chapter "Lists."

PPP   Point-to-Point Protocol, one of the software programs for accessing the Internet.

RFC   An acronym for "Request for Comments," a position paper, often on some technical aspect of the Internet.

RTFM   An acronym for "Read the Fascinating Manual."

SGML   Standard Generalized Markup Language. A uniform encoding of texts (based on descriptive rather than prescriptive principles) that allows the same interpretation of a textual element (such as a title or an italicized word). Regardless of the software package used, SGML has become the standard markup language.

Shareware   Software that can be retrieved and used and which requires a payment to be made to the author—usually a modest fee.

SLIP (Serial Line Internet Protocol)

Used for serial connections running TCP/IP.

Smileys   Visual images made from keyboard characters, often used to indicate humor, sarcasm, etc., in order to forestall misunderstanding.

Snail Mail   A phrase used to describe traditional hard-copy mail, with an implied invidious comparison to the quickness of electronic mail (e-mail).

Spamming   The act of sending a message (usually self-serving and often involving profit) to a large number of USENET newsgroups or lists without regard to the appropriateness of the subject matter. A recent celebrated case involved two lawyers who indiscriminately advertised their services of obtaining green cards for immigrants by broadcasting their message to hundreds of newsgroups. Spamming is not only frowned upon, but actively discouraged by site administrators. It is likely to produce vituperative responses from users of the net.

TCP/IP (Transmission Control Protocol/Internet Protocol)

This is the software that allows the many different kinds of computers on the net to communicate with each other—despite the differences of their operating systems.

TEI   Text Encoding Initiative is an international research project to develop guidelines for the encoding of machine-readable texts. See also SGML.

Telnet   Protocol that permits a user to make a connection with a remote host. See the chapter "Telnet and FTP."

URL   Uniform Resource Locator. The prefix for an electronic address that identifies the protocol of the transmission. Some examples are

ftp://	File Transfer Protocol
gopher://	Gopher
http://	World-Wide Web
telnet://	Telnet

Usenet	Often referred to as "News," Usenet operates on the Internet, allowing for people with similar interests to share information in a public forum.
Veronica	A program found on many Gopher menus, Veronica allows for broad-spectrum keyword searches of over 10 million files on the Internet.
W3	See World Wide Web.
World Wide Web	Sometimes referred to as WWW or W3, World Wide Web provides hypertext (text, audio, video) links to sites on the Internet
WWW	See World Wide Web.

Index of Names

Franklin, Benjamin 127, 128, 226
FranText 165
Frederic, H. 226
French Embassy 165
French Ministry of Culture 164
French Monarchy Collection 116
Fresh Air 189
Friedman, Rodger 142
Frognet 165
Frost, Robert 226
Fry, C. 227
Frye, Northop 227

G

Garland, Hamlin 128
Gaskell, E. 227
Gass, William 114
Gay, J. 227
Geiger's Books 142
Genuine Article 217
Georgetown CPET 165
Gerber, Dan 116
German Academic Exchange Service (DAAD) 166
Germany 236
Gettysburg Address 170
Gide, A. 227
Gilman, C. P. 227
Gilman, Daniel Coit 114
Gilman, Elisabeth 114
Ginsberg, Allen 161
Gladis 190
Glass, Gene 155
Glassgow, Ellen 130
Glyn's Books 148
GNN: Global News Network 180
Goals 2000 157
Godine, David 148
Goethe, W. von 227
Go-MLink 231
Gonzo 185
Gopherjewels List 255
Gopherjewels Project 177
Gordimer, Nadine 114
Government Printing Office 238
Gower 227
Graham, Billy 133
Grange, Harold "Red" 132
GrantSource 168
Graves, R. 227

Gray, James, & Devon 142
Greece 193
Greene, G. 227
Greyhavens' Antiquarian Books 142
Grimm, Jakob, and Wilhelm 227
Grist On-Line 185
Guide to Theater Resources 233

H

Haley, Alex 129
Hampton Inn 236
Hardy, Thomas 227
Harlem Renaissance 129
Harris, William J. 124
Harrison, Jim 116
Harry Ransom Humanities Research Center 129, 154
Hartley, Marsden 182
Harvard U.
        Library 113
        Press 199
        Theatre Collection 113
Harvest 177
Hawaii 235
Hawthorne, N. 227
Heaney, Seamus 126, 196
Hearst, Patti 227
Heathcote Video Archive 233
Heldfond Book Gallery 143
Hemingway, Ernest 127, 129
Hemyng, Candy Ann 173
Henry, P. 227
Herodotus 227
Herrick, R. 227
Hesiod 227
Hesse, H. 227
Heywood, J. 227
Hill, Jonathan A. 143
Hill's Books 143
Hippocrates 227
History Book Club 148
Hitchhiker's Guide to the Internet 178
Hobbes Internet Timeline 177
Holocaust Archives 169
Homer 227
Homewood Suites 236
Hope, A. 227
Hopkins, Gerard Manley 129, 227
Horace 227

Murray, John 126
Musica Database 191
Music Database, 191
Musical Fund Society of Philadelphia 127

N

Naipaul, V. S. 130
Napa Valley, California 235
NASA K-12 Internet Project 158
Nashe, T. 228
Nathan, Adele Gutman 133
National Archives and Records Administration (NARA) 116
National Council of Teachers of English (NCTE) 161
National Public Radio 189
National Register of Archives 119, 168
National Women's Studies Association 241
NBC Dateline 189
NBC News 189
NCSA What's New 259
Netfind 111
Net-happenings 260
Net-Letter Guide 261
Netnews 261
Netscape 243
Netsurfer Digest 261
Nettrain 262
Network News 262
Network Observer 262
Networks and Community 263
Network USA 107
Newberry Library 117
Newbie Newz 263
New Latin 228
Newman, J. H. 228
New Republic 180, 189
NEWSLTR 264
New York Art Line 136
New York Botanical Garden 174
New York City 235
New York State Department of Education 136, 158
New York U.
    Electronic Text Center 230
    Library 117
New Yorker Education Program 194
Nineteenth-Century Literature 218
NixPub List 108

Nobel Prize 172
Norris, F. 228
North Carolina State U. 170
    Electronic Text Center 230
Northeast Modern Language Association (NEMLA) 181
Novae>>Group>> 159
NSF Network News 264
NWHQ 186
Nye, Russel B., Popular Culture Collection 116

O

O'Casey, S. 228
O. Henry 228
Objectivism 195
Ogham Books 144
Ohio State U.
    Bookstore 150
    Department of Art 136
Old England Bookshop 144
OmniMedia 150
O'Neal, Maston 124
Online Book Initiative 225, 231, 232
Online Bookstore 198
Online Educator 159
Online Modern History Review 169
Oral History Center (Louisville), 124
Oral History Program (New Mexico), 126
Orczy, E. 228
Oregon State U. Library 117
Orwell, G. 228
Osage Indians 130
Osborne, J. 228
OTIS 137
Overbury, Sir Thomas 114
Ovid 228
Owen, W. 228
OWL 215
Oxford Text Archive (OTA) 95, 225, 231
Oxford U. Press 148

P

Paine, T. 228
Papyrus Books 144
Parmer Books 144
Pauling, Ava Helen 118
Pauling, Linus 118
PDial List 108

Twain, Mark 127, 131, 140, 182, 228
TwentyNothing 187
Twice-Told Books 147
Twilight World 187
Tzu, Sun 228

U

UMI Article Clearinghouse 217
UnCover Company 217
Undiscovered County 188
United Nations 193
United States
 AskERIC 237
 Census Bureau 237
 Consumer Information Center (CIC) 237
 Department of Education 159, 238
 Department of Justice 237
 EDGAR 237
 ERIC 237
 Federal Communications Commission 238
 FedWorld Gateway 238
 Government Printing Office 238
 House of Representatives 238
 Library of Congress 115
 National Archives and Records Administration 116
 Senate 239
 White House 239
U. de Montréal 165
U. of Arizona 137, 206
U. of Arkansas Press 206
U. of Bergen 172
U. of British Columbia Press 206
U. of California—Berkeley 192
U. of California—Davis Library 122
U. of California-Irvine
 Bookstore 152
 Press 207
U. of California—Los Angeles Library 122
U. of California—San Diego 167
 Library 122
U. of California—Santa Barbara 137, 173, 192, 220
U. of Californi—Santa Cruz 167, 173
U. of Chicago 153, 162
 CABAL 229
 Library 123
 Philosophy Project 196
 Press 207

U. of Delaware Library 123
U. of Georgia Library 124
U. of Illinois—Chicago 137
U. of Illinois—Urbana-Champaign 137, 167
 Press 207
U. of Iowa 153, 167
 Library 124, 153
 Press 208
U. of Kansas 169, 171, 197, 232
U. of Louisville 138
 Library 124
U. of Manchester Film Database 164
U. of Massachusetts 159
U. of Memphis 138
U. of Michigan 162, 171, 173, 178, 192
 Press 208
U. of Minnesota 167, 209
 Film and Video 139
U. of Mississippi Library 125
U. of Missouri—St. Louis Library 125
U. of Nebraska
 Library 125
 Press 209
U. of New Mexico
 Library 126
 Press 210
U. of North Carolina at Chapel Hill 220
 Library 126
 Press 210
U. of North Carolina at Charlotte Library 127
University of North Texas Press 211
U. of Oklahoma 127
U. of Pennsylvania 162, 220
 Educational Technology Services 229
 Library 127
 Press 211
U. of South Carolina Press 212
U. of Southern California 167
 Library 128
U. of Tennessee at Knoxville
 Library 129
 Press 212
U. of Texas at Austin
 HRHRC 129
 Press 212
U. of Toronto 173, 179
U. of Tulsa Library 130
U. of Utah 192
U. of Virginia
 Electronic Text Center 230
 Library 130

Yanoff, Scott 189
Yanoff's Special Internet Connections 267
Yeats, William Butler 129, 229

Z

Zen and the Art of the Internet 178
Zigrosser, Carl 127
Zubal, John T. 148

Comments and suggestions should be sent to

clark@cs.widener.edu

For additons and updates to the directory, be sure to check out the home page for *Cultural Treasures* at

http://shirley.cs.widener.edu/clark/clark.html